A Question of Time

A Question of

The Kent State

University Press

Kent, Ohio, &

London, England

TIME

J. R. R. Tolkien's

Road to *Faërie*

Verlyn Flieger

© 1997 by The Kent State University Press, Kent, Ohio 44242

ALL RIGHTS RESERVED

Library of Congress Catalog Card Number 97-6777

ISBN 0-87338-574-8 (cloth)

ISBN 0-87338-699-X (paper)

First paper edition 2000

Manufactured in the United States of America

10 09 08 07 06 05 04   9 8 7 6 5 4 3

Library of Congress Cataloging-in-Publication Data

Flieger, Verlyn, 1933–

A question of time : J. R. R. Tolkien's road to *Faërie* / Verlyn Flieger

p.   cm.

Includes bibliographical references and index.

ISBN 0-87338-574-8 (cloth : alk. paper) ∞

ISBN 0-87338-699-X (paper : alk. paper) ∞

1. Tolkien, J. R. R. (John Ronald Reuel), 1892–1973—Criticism and interpretation. 2. Literature and history—England—History—20th century. 3. Fantastic literature, English—History and criticism. 4. Medievalism—England—History—20th century. 5. England—Intellectual life—20th century. 6. Middle Earth (Imaginary place) 7. Time travel in literature. 8. Middle Ages in literature. 9. Dreams in literature. 10. Time in literature. I. Title.

PR6039.O32Z646   1997

828'.91209—dc21   97-6777

British Library Cataloging-in-Publication data are available.

And see ye not yon bonny road
    That winds about yon fernie brae?
That is the road to fair Elfland,
     Where thou and I this night maun gae.
                       —"Thomas Rymer"

. . . certainly there was an Eden on this very unhappy earth. We all long for it, and we are constantly glimpsing it: our whole nature at its best and least corrupted, its gentlest and most humane, is still soaked with the sense of "exile."
                       —J. R. R. Tolkien

And as he were of faierie
He scheweth him tofore here yhe.
                —John Gower, *Confessio Amantis*

Contents

Acknowledgments

I am grateful to the Trustees of the Tolkien Trust as copyright owners for permission to quote from Tolkien's unpublished papers and to the Bodleian Library and the Archive of Marquette University for granting me access to the unpublished materials housed in their respective Tolkien collections.

Copyrighted material from Tolkien's published writings and from Humphrey Carpenter's *Tolkien: A Biography* and Professor T. A. Shippey's *The Road to Middle-Earth* is reprinted with the permission of HarperCollins Publishers. The William Morris Agency has granted permission to reprint selections from Leon Edel's *Henry James: A Life,* copyright 1985 by Harper & Row. The lines from "Burnt Norton" and "Little Gidding" from *Four Quartets,* copyright 1943 by T. S. Eliot and renewed in 1971 by Esme Valerie Eliot, are reprinted by permission of Harcourt Brace & Company.

Portions of chapter 4, "Over a Bridge of Time," appeared in a slightly different version in *Mythlore* 16 (Spring 1990). Portions of chapter 11, "Pitfalls in Faërie," appeared in slightly different form in *Mythos Journal* (Winter 1995) and were reprinted in *Saga* 1 (1996).

Thanks beyond measure go to Christopher Tolkien for his generosity in giving me access to unpublished materials in his possession and for his unstinting help, advice, and encouragement during the years of this book's composition. Thanks also to Baillie Tolkien for warm hospitality and good company over many visits. I am more than grateful to Priscilla Tolkien, who over many years of rewarding friendship has provided help and counsel and who first mentioned to me the name of J. W. Dunne. This would have been a lesser book without her.

Members of the Tolkien Symposium, forced year after year to listen to papers on Tolkien and J. W. Dunne, offered valuable criticism. I thank them all for their patience. Thanks go to Joe Christopher and Wayne Hammond, readers par excellence, for their editorial advice; to Doug Anderson for his critical reading; and to Carl Hostetter for his advice on philology, both Germanic and Tolkienian.

Thanks to Rose Solari for giving me a handrail.

I owe a great and largely unpayable debt to John Rateliff and the late and still-mourned Taum Santoski, who in 1984 first showed me Tolkien's comments on time in the manuscript drafts of *The Lord of the Rings*.

And finally, thanks to Vaughn Howland for endless patience in reading multiple drafts, and for love and encouragement over many years.

Introduction

He had dared to be of a time not his own.
—Robertson Davies

J. R. R. Tolkien's academic career spanned a period of nearly forty years, from his first appointment in 1920 as Reader in English Language at Leeds University until his 1959 retirement from the position of Merton Professor of English Language and Literature at Oxford. During these years he established a distinguished reputation as a scholar and teacher in the field of Middle and Old English[1] and produced a significant body of critical work. He collaborated with E. V. Gordon on a critical edition of *Sir Gawain and the Green Knight* that is still in use, as is his *Middle English Vocabulary,* designed to be used with Kenneth Sisam's *Fourteenth Century Verse and Prose.* His Early English Text Society edition of the *Ancrene Wisse* is a valuable addition to that series. He wrote a study of the art of the *Beowulf* poet that became a classic in its own right and changed the direction of *Beowulf* scholarship. His essay "Chaucer as a Philologist" explored new ground by directing critical attention to the hitherto overlooked use of regional dialect in Chaucer's *Canterbury Tales.* His studies of obscure or obsolete words and names showed clearly the interrelationship of history and myth and the importance of both to the study of literature.

Such achievement would be enough for most men, and if he had done nothing else, his place in the annals of literary scholarship would be secure.

But Tolkien did do something else. He wrote *The Hobbit* and *The Lord of the Rings*, and it is on these, and to a lesser extent on his invented mythology the Silmarillion, that his enduring reputation rests. His ability to combine scholarship with invention, to harness knowledge to imagination, did much to give his fiction its special appeal and to establish its enduring place in the literature of the twentieth century. His scholarly articles are models of painstaking criticism, displaying thorough and profound knowledge of the subjects under discussion. His creative manifesto is no less thorough. This, the clearest statement of his artistic *credo*, is his essay "On Fairy-Stories," first presented in 1939 as a lecture at the University of St. Andrews. In this essay, a wide-ranging discussion of the interconnections of fairy tale, myth, language, and the human imagination, Tolkien described what it was about fairy-stories that enchanted him. He called it *Faërie*, by which he meant both a spell cast and the altered and enchanted state the spell produced. It was the "Perilous Realm itself," and the special air of enchantment "that blows in that country" ("On Fairy-Stories" 114). It had little to do with fairies per se, something to do with magic, and even more to do with time. Fairy-stories, said Tolkien, "open a door on Other Time, and if we pass through, though only for a moment, we stand outside our own time, outside Time itself, maybe" (129). Not just an assessment of fairy-stories, this is also a very good assessment of the outstanding quality of Tolkien's own fiction. His own desire to pass through the door into Other Time, and thus to stand outside his own time and perhaps outside Time itself, led him to the creation of his own world of Faërie, Middle-earth.

For all his attraction to Other Time, however, he was also (though not enthusiastically) a man of his own time, living and working in a century particularly conscious of its own "modernity." For him the past, with its ancient griefs and glories, was a part of the present, woven into its fabric and deeply influencing its actions. And so his world of Faërie, clothed though it was in the magic of Other Time, reflected the dissociation, dislocation, and psychological ravagement of modern life quite as much as did that of the more obviously mainstream authors who were his contemporaries. Indeed, it can be argued that Tolkien was even more modern than his contemporaries, because through Faërie he grappled not just with his own time but with the mystery of time itself. His fiction, for all its magic, is in its outlook, its mood, its themes very much in tune with the work of such spokesmen for the fragmented present as T. S. Eliot and James Joyce, whose quasi-mythic heroes and antiheroes struggle to find a pattern in the broken pieces of a modern waste land.

Tolkien's own time was one of the most turbulent in history. Its wars, its use of technology in its most destructive aspects, its material progress and spiritual confusion, its avowedly "modern" ethos engendered in him a reaction that was in its own way equally modern: a nostalgic longing for a return to a lost past coupled with the knowledge that this was impossible save in the realm of the imagination. Tolkien wanted to stand outside his own time, to escape from what in the essay he called "progressive things like factories, or the machine-guns and bombs that appear to be their most natural and inevitable, dare we say 'inexorable,' products," to escape from "the rawness and ugliness of modern European life" (150). Dissatisfied with the present, like many in his generation, he wanted to travel back through time. This desire was made explicit in his unfinished time-travel story, *The Lost Road*, where he invested his hero Alboin with "the desire *to go back*. To walk in Time, perhaps, as men walk on long roads" (*Lost Road* 45).

Tolkien himself found ways to walk that long road, ways that informed both his life and his fiction. The first way was through language. His profession was philology, the study of the history of language, and his avocation (too serious to be called a hobby) was the invention of languages together with their concomitant invented cosmologies, mythologies, and histories. Language was for him the expression of the most profound and ancient beliefs of the human consciousness, both collective and individual. Language was for Tolkien the repository and conveyance of myth through time. He had an almost mystical belief in the relationship of language to human consciousness. In "English and Welsh," his Oxford O'Donnell lecture of 1955, he said:

If I were to say "Language is related to our total psycho-physical makeup," I might seem to announce a truism in a priggish modern jargon. I will at any rate say that language—and more so as expression than as communication—is a natural product of our humanity. But it is therefore also a product of our individuality. We each have our own personal linguistic potential: we each have a *native language*. But that is not the language that we speak, our cradle-tongue, the first-learned. Linguistically we all wear ready-made clothes, and our native language comes seldom to expression, save perhaps by pulling at the ready-made till it sits a little easier. But though it may be buried, it is never wholly extinguished, and contact with other languages may stir it deeply. (*Monsters and Critics* 190)

This is not a scholar speaking about an academic interest, but a singular individual expressing a deeply held belief. The phrase "psycho-physical" implies that language—not the aptitude for language but language itself—can be inherited rather than learned. Such a concept carries Tolkien's philological interest beyond the academic into the psychological, and beyond that into the frankly psychic. His belief in such inherited "native language" came out of personal experience. He wrote to W. H. Auden, "I am a West-midlander by blood (and took to early west-midland Middle English as to a known tongue as soon as I set eyes on it)" and, in the same letter, " I daresay . . . linguistic tastes, with due allowance for school-overlay, are as good or better a test of ancestry as blood-groups" (*Letters* 213, 214). In the obituary written for his old friend, C. S. Lewis said that Tolkien had "been inside language." He might better have said that Language—as a memory, a guide to the past and an inheritance from it—had been inside him.

Another way into the past for Tolkien was through dream. "In dream strange powers of the mind may be unlocked," he wrote in his essay "On Fairy-Stories," and the statement seems to have been founded on a personal experience. This was a recurrent dream that he called his "Atlantis haunting." In a letter to W. H. Auden he described it as "the terrible recurrent dream (beginning with memory) of the Great Wave, towering up, and coming in ineluctably over the trees and green fields" (*Letters* 213). The phrase "dream (beginning with memory)" connects memory with dream and suggests that memory may be one of the "strange powers of the mind" that dream unlocks, opening a way into past time. Both of the above quotations have as their common element an experience of inherited memory—in the first of language, in the second of a single powerful image—neither derived from personal experience but from some distant ancestral time and some distant ancestral level of the mind beyond the individual consciousness.

Language and dream connect to memory, and all three connect to time past. Time, as Tolkien envisioned it, was not a simple forward progression but a complex field of experience encompassing past, present, and future, a field of experience to which dream, memory, and language all gave access. These two triads—past, present, and future and dream, memory, and language—are strands that wind around one another to form a continuous theme throughout Tolkien's work. But while the theme is continuous, its expression is not always clear. Through his treatment of time he was attempting to embody and convey a complex psychological, philosophical vision, one that would encompass a whole mythic cosmology. He was not always wholly successful. He did succeed when he let the story have its way, when, as with *The Lord of the Rings,* the poetic energy of his narrative simultaneously transcended the vision and carried it along. He failed, or only partially succeeded, when, as in his half-finished time-travel stories, the vision took precedence over the story. And toward the end of his life his very concern to make all clear, to set his mythological world in order and rationalize its processes, led him from poetry to metaphysics and to that intellectualization of ideas that is the very antithesis of the story-teller's art.

An exhaustive study of all his fiction is beyond the scope of this book, but a close look at selected works, and a consideration of them in the light of some of their precursors in speculative thought, will show how Tolkien's treatment of time drew from the intellectual climate of his own time and developed as his mythology developed, over many years. *The Lost Road* and *The Notion Club Papers, The Lord of the Rings,* his poem "The Sea-bell," his last story *Smith of Wootton Major,* and the posthumously published works of the post–*Lord of the Rings* years all relate, to a greater or lesser degree, to this treatment of time. But like the treatment itself, their thematic relationship to one another and their importance as indices of Tolkien's response to his own time follow a rather complex line of development. What Constance Hieatt has called "Tolkien's extraordinary disorderliness, and his penchant for second thoughts and extensive revisions" (212) meant that Tolkien started, stopped, returned to, reconsidered, revised, and re-revised almost everything he wrote, and obviates the idea of a linear developmental sequence. Nevertheless, these works have a thematic coherence that is deeply engaged, as was their author, with the question of time.

Though on the surface Tolkien's fiction appears to reject the present in favor of an apparently romanticized past, at a deeper level it is very much informed by present time. His work could not have spoken so powerfully to his own century if he had completely succeeded in escaping it. The fact is that he could not escape and was in actuality both responding to and using the most typical aspects of his own age as essential elements of his fantasy. Like it or not (and the evidence suggests that he had, at least, mixed feelings) he was a man of his time, caught in it and struggling with it. And the more earnestly he tried to get away from it the more surely he reflected it. Over time this became one of the constant wellsprings of his imagination, and a hallmark of his fiction. For the profoundest exercise of the creative mind is to hold opposing ideas in tension, and thus to turn contradiction into paradox.

However, when the surface message—the apparent rejection of the present in favor of the past—does not balance the deeper level of immediate response to the present, the tension is unequal, and the result is not paradox but ambiguity. The conscious message and the unconscious response work against one another. Out of such ambiguity arises the sort of confusion, for example, that led many readers (much to Tolkien's concern) to miss the point that the hero of *The Lord of the Rings*, Frodo, fails in his quest. The same sort of mixed message leads readers enchanted with his immortal Elves to miss the point that Tolkien (who called them "embalmers of time") wanted their timeless beauty to make—that immortality is a prison, that a timeless world is a frozen world, that beauty preserved is beauty embalmed. Such confusion comes out of Tolkien's own struggle with time, with his rejection of the present in favor of the past coupled with his reflection of the ambiguous ethos of his own century with its characteristic swings between optimism and despair, discovery and disillusionment.

In a 1974 review of Roger Sale's *Modern Heroism*, a book that characterized Frodo Baggins as a modern hero, the eminent Christopher Ricks rejected Sale's view, called Tolkien "our Ossian," and dismissed him for his donnish retreat from modern life.[2] This is fairly typical of the critical attitude of the literary and academic establishment. With the exception of Sale and a few other early commentators, most notably C. S. Lewis and W. H. Auden, Tolkien has been persistently and narrowly read as a medievalist manqué, with the result that the message has all too often been confused with the medium. True, he created the idyllically rural Shire, an exercise in Edwardian nostalgia. But he also turned it (albeit briefly) into a dystopian mini-state worthy of Orwell or Burgess. True, he created Hobbits. But he put his Hobbits in a world that moved too fast for them, and then forced them to keep up with it. True, he is serious about dragons. But he knows they are there to be faced and killed. He is also serious about his much-misunderstood Elves. But these are the medium, not the message. They are the properties of his mythos, the setting, the dramatis personae. They provide the surface texture. Below that surface is a substrate of darker, flintier material, stained and spotted by the Age of Anxiety in which Tolkien lived and out of which he wrote.

This has been largely overlooked by those who saw the popularity of his work in the sixties and seventies simply as the response of a generation to an unusually appealing fantasy. The insight of the folklorist Katherine Briggs, who said that "These books [*The Lord of the Rings*] were felt at once by a surprising number of people to have something significant to say about our modern problems and to hold an implicit message for young people all over the English-speaking world" (401), has been largely ignored by contemporary critical theorists, who prefer their despair existential and their angst suburban. So contemporary a reading, however, must be approached with caution if it is not to reduce his work to a simple one-to-one correlation with the external events of his era. He vigorously rejected the early critical view that saw *The Lord of the Rings* as an allegory of World War II, with Gandalf and his forces as the Allies, Sauron and company as the Axis powers, and the Ruling Ring, the superweapon, as—what else?—the atom bomb. And quite rightly; the book was begun and the Ring conceived as its central artifact before that war, and years before Hiroshima. To subject it to such a reading is to ignore chronology and to reduce a rich and densely textured narrative to a political tract, at best a kind of extended *Animal Farm* and at worst a simplistic polemic. But the alternate critical posture—the one that says that as an author he is a temporal anomaly, displaced into the modern world but escaping through his fiction into an older and better one—is equally inaccurate.

A story need not be about a particular war in order to show its effects. Nor does it have to have a contemporary setting in order to mirror contemporary thought. Indeed, quite the contrary. The most effective commentary on an age or an event is as often as not oblique rather than direct, and the impact is no less powerful for being rerouted. The nursery rhyme of "Humpty Dumpty" says as much about the perils of kingship as does Lydgate's *Fall of Princes*, and *Huckleberry Finn* is as telling a piece of social commentary as *Das Kapital*. Tolkien is too often dismissed out of hand as an anachronism, a contemporary Pre-Raphaelite trying to pretend that the Renaissance and the Age of Enlightenment have not happened. On the contrary, any thoughtful reading of his work that looks below the surface will show that he is in fact quite a modern thinker, dipping into the past for the stuff of his story but reworking it for the age in which he lived and felt.

Yet it is part of the paradox of his work that his most immediate intention in writing it was that of escape. He began seriously to work at his mythology as a release from the exigencies, the monotony, and the horror of war. Many of the early parts were done, as Tolkien wrote to his son Christopher (at the time himself involved in another war), "in grimy canteens, at lectures in cold fogs, in huts full of blasphemy and smut, or by candle light in bell-tents, even some down in dugouts under shell fire" (*Letters* 78). He continued to work at it when he was invalided home from the war and kept on through the subsequent peaceful interim before another war and its own peace, through times bad and times good, and on and out into unexpected success and its aftermath of fame and fortune. At the beginning his focus was on the myth for its own sake. It was inevitably derivative, even imitative of other mythologies, and not always to its best advantage. But as his myth matured, it became more and more itself, acquired a stronger, less imitative and more independent tone. It became the instrument of profound reflection and the forging of a coherent vision of the pitfalls and possibilities inherent in the human condition.

While a writer's work is bound to develop by the mere process of writing, let alone the inevitable process of living, Tolkien's vision throughout his long life did not so much change as deepen.

Though the details altered and shifted, his work tended always to grow in the same direction, out of myth and legend into history, rooted in the past but flowering up almost in spite of him into contemporary expression. Though it has the quality of Faërie, though when we read it we pass through the open door into Other Time, his work is in Time and about Time. It is a long tale, as Sam Gamgee says of the tale of Beren and Lúthien, "and goes on past the happiness and into grief and beyond it" (*Two Towers* 321). His creative energies kept pace with the times, consciously and unconsciously recording for his audience their world and worldview, their defeats and renewals, their despairs and hopes. We write what we are, and Tolkien wrote not just out of his scholarship but out of himself and out of his response to this best and worst of times that is the twentieth century. Writing out of himself, he dared to be of a time not his own, and in so doing he made a profound and lasting comment on his own time.

Between Worlds and Times 1

I do not think that the reader or the maker of fairy-stories need even be ashamed of the "escape" of archaism: of preferring not dragons but horses, castles, sailing-ships, bows and arrows; not only elves, but knights and kings and priests.
—J. R. R. Tolkien, "On Fairy-Stories"

John Ronald Reuel Tolkien, born to English parents on January 3, 1892, in Bloemfontein, South Africa, was a product of one of the most difficult, contradictory times in modern history, his childhood spent in the Edwardian farewell to the nineteenth century and his adulthood coinciding with the two most devastating wars of the twentieth century. As the above epigraph makes clear, he endorsed the "escape" of archaism, for he was both a reader and a maker of fairy-stories. As such he was perforce a traveler between two worlds—the Primary World in which he lived and worked and the Secondary World of Faërie. As a traveler between worlds, he was also a traveler in time, shuttling restlessly between the grubby, smoke-stained present of his own century and the faërian past of his imagination. It is this very oscillation that, paradoxically, makes him a modern writer, for by looking backward his fantasy reflected the present, and the temporal dislocation of his "escape" mirrored the psychological disjunction and displacement of his century. Far from being a drag or a hindrance to his creative power, this continual dislocation, the shuttling between worlds, was a source of energy for him and is a significant factor in his fiction. It could be said of Tolkien, as A. N. Wilson said of C. S. Lewis, that "his writings, while being self-consciously and deliberately at variance with the twentieth century, are paradoxically in tune with the needs and concerns of our times" (ix). He and his work were the products of those times and are best read in the context of the cultural and personal history that produced them.

Cultural history provides context for any work of art, which, though it may transcend its own beginnings, must of necessity also be rooted in and derive from a particular time and a particular place. As the cultural historian Modris Eksteins observes in *The Rites of Spring: the Great War and the Birth of the Modern Age:*

> In modern society the audience for the arts, as for hobbits and heroes, is . . . an even more important source of evidence for cultural identity than the literary documents, artistic artifacts, or heroes themselves. The history of modern culture ought then to be as much a history of response as challenge, an account of the reader as of the novel, of the viewer as of the film, of the spectator as of the actor. (xiv–xv)

This argument is persuasive, but the inclusion of Hobbits, though striking, seems inapposite, out of place—or perhaps out of time—in a work purporting to chart the rise of modern consciousness. By their nature, Hobbits are a vision out of the past, a past deliberately out of step with the present time of their invention. They are Tolkien's earliest statement of nostalgia, of longing for a lost past. Bilbo Baggins and his world are unabashedly old-style recreations, fashioned out of Tolkien's familiarity with the children's and boys' literature of his generation and his own best memories of childhood. "The Shire," he wrote to his publisher, "is . . . in fact more or less a Warwickshire village of about the period of the Diamond Jubilee" (*Letters* 230). Yet the book caught on, and not only with children. It was more than just a good adventure story. It soothed the insecurities and appealed to the nostalgia of a reading audience living out what were to be its last days of peace, an audience whose own time was hurrying it into war.

And so Hobbits seem an odd example of cultural response to a period that encouraged the rebellion of Isadora Duncan and Nijinsky, the iconoclasm of Picasso and Braque, the innovation of Joyce and Eliot; a time that gave birth to surrealism, Bauhaus architecture, the twelve-tone system, and the spare ellipses of Hemingway and Pound. LeCorbusier dismissed Versailles as "nothing but decadence," and a whole generation followed his lead. Pound told his disciples to "make it new," and they did their best, sometimes to the detriment of clarity. "Astonish me," Diaghileff challenged Cocteau, and Cocteau obliged with sharply surreal, disjunct scenarios that shocked and disoriented as well as enchanted his audiences. Do Hobbits belong in such company?

Yes. They do. They are a response to a response, and thus a continuation of the dialogue. They are a regressive innovation whose very invention acknowledges what it tries to reject. If, as Eksteins argues, "Culture is regarded as a social phenomenon and modernism as the principal urge of our time" (xvi), then it is necessary in accounting for this to include the reaction as well as the action, to save all the phenomena, not just those that most happily fit the paradigm. If the period surrounding the Great War gave birth to modernism, it also engendered the reaction against it, the effort to ensure that "before" was not wholly lost in "after."

Such reactions are a personal response to cultural change. Thus personal history is a necessary context for art, for every work of art has a private as well as a public component and is just as deeply rooted in and as directly derivative of personality as it is of time and place. Enough has been written about the externals of Tolkien's life—his education, his love of language, his professorships, his marriage and children, and, above all, his creation of the most popular and influential fantasy narrative of the twentieth century—that there is no need to do more than mention them here. Nevertheless, without going deeply into biography, it is appropriate to begin a study of Tolkien's work with an examination of events that affected him deeply and that largely shaped his inner life, for it is the inner life that is the wellspring of art.

One event that affected him profoundly, according to his biographer, Humphrey Carpenter, was the death of his mother when he was only twelve years old. More than is the case with many fatherless sons, Tolkien's mother was the central figure in his young life. She gave him some of the most important, formative elements of his youth: the pastoral English countryside, the Catholic faith, and, by introducing him to Latin and French even before he began formal schooling, the beginning of his education in language. "The loss of his mother," says Carpenter, "had a profound effect on his personality. It made him into a pessimist. . . . Nothing was safe. Nothing would last" (31). Of course, this does not mean that Tolkien was perpetually sunk in gloom; he was a man of great warmth and humor, one who enjoyed life and participated in it with gusto. Nonetheless, a persistent theme in his work suggests that he had learned that time was a robber, carrying swiftly and irrevocably away all that was most precious. Such an intense, all-encompassing reaction was perhaps intensified by the fact that the death of his mother was the second such loss.

The first had occurred when he was even younger, barely four years old. An extended home-leave had brought the three-year-old Tolkien, his mother, and his younger brother to England in April 1895 while his father, detained by the press of business, remained in South Africa. Meant to be temporary, the visit lengthened when in November Arthur Tolkien fell ill and could not join his family. It became permanent when he died suddenly in February 1896. Thus the child Tolkien lost his father after nearly a year's temporal and geographic separation. A year is a long time for a child just turned four. It meant that he was too young to have many clear memories of his father, too young to comprehend the magnitude of his loss. While the death of his mother was a shock and a bereavement, a psychologist might speculate that this much earlier and therefore much less comprehensible loss (for in effect Tolkien's father simply disappeared from his life) might have had, though more submerged, an even profounder impact on his life and perhaps on his art as well. Several of his later stories include a relationship between a young man and an older father-figure who disappears suddenly and often without explanation.

Though they cause wounds and leave scars, such losses and their repercussions are usually borne with, and their effects woven into the fabric of everyday life. An appointed guardian, Father Francis Morgan, became a surrogate parent, and school provided the companionship of other boys Tolkien's age. In 1911, while he was a student at King Edward's School, Birmingham, Tolkien found the first of the formative fellowships with which his life was to be punctuated. It was an adolescent tea and poetry society, the T.C.B.S. (the T.C. stood for "Tea Club," and the B.S. for "Barrovian Society," from Barrows Stores, the place where they met). The membership was shifting, but the permanent nucleus consisted of Tolkien, Christopher Wiseman, Robert Gilson, and a later, fourth member, Geoffrey Bache Smith. The T.C.B.S. existed for a scant five years, from its inception as a study group in 1911 until half its membership was wiped out in 1916 by World War I. Its importance to Tolkien's life and work, however, greatly outweighs its brief existence or its slender membership.

Concurrent elements conspired to make the boys feel special— their youth and idealism, their community of interests—the threat of the approaching war made all experience more intense. Although the others scoffed at Tolkien's notion that they were a kind of latter-day Pre-Raphaelite brotherhood, there was undoubtedly among them a feeling that they had something important to contribute to the world. Tolkien observed that one especially vivid gathering during the Christmas vacation of 1914 had helped him to find "a voice for all kinds of pent-up things" (Carpenter 73). The boys remained friends when they went to university and when as young men they went to war in France, where two of them were killed.

Youthful patterns tend to persist, and the liking for literary fellowship was a prominent part of Tolkien's later life, which was warmed by several such groups. When he was at Leeds University he persuaded some of his fellow faculty members to meet regularly to read and translate Old Norse together. And of course when he was a professor at Oxford there was the Inklings, the informal group that included among others Tolkien, C. S. Lewis, Lewis's brother Major Warren Lewis, Owen Barfield, Charles Williams, and, in the second generation, Tolkien's youngest son, Christopher. Many of the Inklings were scholars; all of them were readers; most of them were writers. It was in many respects an adult replication of the T.C.B.S., for it too was a group of like-minded males who met to drink, talk, and read their work aloud to one another, though their preferred beverage was beer or whisky, not tea.

This attraction to fellowship was not mere conviviality, but a deeper impulse that set the personal against the cultural in Tolkien's world. This sort of fellowship became increasingly a bulwark against the onslaught of a century in which Tolkien felt less and less at home. The first two decades of the twentieth century changed forever the England he loved and shifted the pillars of his world. Every century has its own disruptions, but the twentieth has had more than most, filled to bursting as it has been with political, social, scientific, psychological, and technological upheaval.

Technology developed faster than society could keep up with it, going in one century from the dip pen to the computer, from kerosene lamps and horse-drawn conveyances to lasers and space shuttles. Above all, the century was broken in two by World War I, a new and devastating kind of war whose four-year entrenchment in the consciousness of Western Europe changed forever a culture and a world.

Tolkien's generation called it just The War (no serializing number necessary as yet), and after it was over The Great War. It was in their eyes the greatest war in history, "the War to end all wars." But the Great War did not end wars. Instead it challenged its survivors into another one, provoking endless military and social actions and reactions and leading cultural historians such as Eksteins to point out how art and culture both reflect and influence one another. Tolkien, a prime example of such influence, returned from the front with a clear vision of the horrors of war. It seemed to him, as to many, that very little had been gained and too much had been lost, that the gentle, civil, slow-moving world he knew had been swept away. He wanted it back. The fact that he never got it back, and that he knew in his heart that it was gone forever, only sharpened his regret and deepened his longing. And so while the avowed modernists, Pound and Picasso and their fellow-artists, were looking forward and trumpeting the value of innovation, Tolkien and others like him—reluctant modernists, if you will—were looking backward, finding new ways to escape into other times and other worlds.

Tolkien's Middle-earth is the best-known example of this impulse, but other serious writers of fantasy in this period were responding to the same escapist impulse. David Lindsay's allegorical Arcturan planet of Tormance, E. R. Eddison's imaginary medieval and Renaissance worlds of Mercury and Zimiamvia, and Mervyn Peake's grotesque, outrageous, unclassifiable Gormenghast all grew out of roughly the same post–World War I generation. All look away from the visible world to a more engaging—though not necessarily more pleasant, and certainly not contemporary—country of the mind. This retrogression is as much illusory as it is real. It is just as contemporary a response to cultural forces as that of the avant-garde: whether backward or forward, the very act of escape acknowledges that which it flees, and nostalgia, like modernism, must have a ground from which to turn away. Moreover, although Tolkien and those like him turned away from their own time, they did it by way of discoveries peculiar to the modern age, using an imagination born of nineteenth-century romanticism but kindled by the same intellectual surge that spurred Pound and Joyce and Einstein and Freud and Jung. H. G. Wells's *The Time Machine* anticipated Einstein's Special Theory of Relativity by ten years, but both arose out of the same climate of thought, one that looked outward to the uncharted possibilities of the universe.

That same climate of thought, the same cultural impulse also looked inward to the microcosm, the interior world of the unconscious. The publication in 1900 of Freud's *The Interpretation of Dreams* led the way into the uncharted possibilities of the mind, and psychology began the inward exploration of the unconscious that paralleled science's burgeoning exploration of the universe. Both the mind and the universe turned out to be more complex, more variable, and more irrational than anyone had dreamed. Or perhaps they *had* dreamed it. The new discoveries, the new theories suggested a relationship between the inner and the outer worlds, paired universes whose composition seemed far more akin to dream and nightmare than to the reassuring rationality of the Enlightenment and Newtonian physics. "Through the discoveries of Planck, Einstein, and Freud," says Eksteins, "rational man undermined his own world" (31).

Following science into the future or memory into the past, Tolkien and those like him were at once reactionary and avant-garde, turning their backs on the modernism that had turned its back on the past by using the century's own discoveries to escape it. Theories of quantum physics, theories of space-time, the concepts of the hidden activities and archetypes of the unconscious all contribute to this most contradictory of centuries, and no one living in it can hide from their implications. When Tolkien's fellow Inkling Owen Barfield wrote in *Poetic Diction* that "what [man] let loose over Hiroshima, after fiddling with its exterior for three centuries like a mechanical toy, was the forces of his own unconscious mind" (36), he was positing for his own generation and those to come the implications of the mind-blowing fusion of physics and psychology that was to be the detonator for the thought and philosophy of the twentieth century.

To anchor this characterization of Tolkien's work as both retrograde and modern, let us look at his chosen topic for his 1936 Sir Israel Gollancz Memorial Lecture to the British Academy, "Beowulf: The Monsters and the Critics." *Beowulf*, one of the oldest and most-studied epics in English, for decades the foundation of English syllabi, was hardly avant-garde in 1936. One might have wondered if anything new could be found to say about such well-covered ground. Tolkien found it and said it. He had the audacity to suggest to an audience of fellow scholars that *Beowulf* was a work of art. His lecture, later published as an essay, changed the direction of *Beowulf* studies. One of the most sensitive and poetic pieces of scholarship ever written, it was a work of art in defense of a work of art.

It is not inappropriate, then, to read the essay for what it can tell us about Tolkien's own sense of time as well as the creativity of the *Beowulf* poet. One of the most notable features of the essay is the repeated reference to time. The subject of the poem, says Tolkien, is "man at war with the hostile world, and his inevitable overthrow in Time" ("Beowulf" 18). He sees *Beowulf* as a "great temporal tragedy" (23) and Beowulf himself as a hero facing a monstrous foe "incarnate in time, walking in heroic history" (17). Like the Norse heroes and the monsters, the very gods themselves "are within Time, doomed with their allies to death" (25). Moreover, humanity's immemorial foe, the monsters of the poem, are also "within Time" and "within Time the monsters would win" (22). Time thus both encloses and supports the story, for Tolkien describes the battle between man and monster as a "contest on the fields of Time" (22).

"Time" is capitalized in these phrases, treated almost as if it were another character in the conflict. If not quite a character, it is an element as crucial in Tolkien's eyes to the outcome of the story as the characters themselves. Again and again the word and the concept reverberate throughout his argument. This overriding concern with Time is, as T. A. Shippey noted in *The Road to Middle-Earth*, "intensely Tolkienian" (24). It is a concern manifest no less in his critical than his creative work, for Tolkien's description of the *Beowulf* poet whom he so admired can easily be applied to himself: he, too, is "a learned man writing of old times, who looking back on the heroism and sorrow feels in them something permanent and something symbolical" ("Beowulf" 26). We might extend Shippey's comment to say that this overriding thematic concern with time is not only intensely but essentially Tolkienian, deeply embedded in his work and his philosophy.

Although it is a work of scholarship addressed to scholars, the *Beowulf* essay reflects Tolkien's imaginative as well as his critical faculty, coming at roughly the same period as "On Fairy-Stories" and his first time-travel story, *The Lost Road*. Taken together, all three reflect in their separate ways a desire to pass through that open door into Other Time. "When C. S. Lewis and I tossed up," Tolkien wrote in 1964, "and he was to write on space-travel and I on time-travel, I began an abortive book of time-travel of which the end was to be the presence of my hero in the drowning of Atlantis" (*Letters* 347). The result was *The Lost Road*, which marked the clear introduction into Tolkien's work of the idea of time as a road between the worlds of past and present, of everyday and Faërie, of waking and dream. It also conveyed the vision of the lost paradise and the longing to return to it that is embryonic in some of his earliest efforts and that became a more and more powerful element in his later fiction. The story was, as he said, "abortive" and was soon abandoned, but the ideas remained and found their way into much that came after. They became the underpinning for *The Lord of the Rings* and were reexplored in the later (and also abortive) *Notion Club Papers*. These ideas and their treatment in his work were the outward expression of a developing inner concern, a philosophical and psychological exploration of the relationship between the exterior, so-called "real" world and time and the interior, illimitable, but no less real time and space of the imagining, remembering, dreaming mind.

If the genesis of *The Lost Road* really was the casual toss-up that Tolkien made it seem, he certainly got the right side of the coin, being by virtue of personal inclination as well as academic interest a traveler in time. He was by profession a scholar, by vocation a philologist. His field was medieval literature and language, specifically Old and Middle English and the texts that give them voice. He was a scholar and philologist with a difference, however, for more than most of his colleagues he immersed himself in the language and brought the texts to life. As C. S. Lewis wrote in his obituary of Tolkien, "He had been inside language." But that very immersion bespeaks a powerful attraction to the world whose texts he read and taught, a desire not just to study it but to experience it.

"You can't go back," says one of his characters in *The Lost Road*, "except within the limits prescribed to us mortals. You can go back in a sense by honest study, long and patient work" (40). And Tolkien did, by honest study in Old Norse and Old English, by long and patient work on early texts such as *Beowulf* and *Sir Gawain and the Green Knight*. But that was not enough, and he found a way to go back through writing as well as through reading. Caught in, and not wholly at peace with, his own time, he used his own fiction to express his longing for the past and, finally, to take him back with it into a past half historical, half invented, wholly mythical.

As he recalled it, the impulse behind Tolkien's agreement with Lewis came for both men as much from the desire to read as from the desire to write. "L. said to me one day, 'Tollers, there is too little of what we really like in stories. I'm afraid we shall have to write some ourselves.' We agreed that he should try 'space-travel,' and I should try 'time-travel'" (*Letters* 378). And so they did. And in so doing declared themselves the audience for their own work, prime examples of Eksteins's thesis that art is as much response as it is challenge, no less the work of the viewer than of the doer. What Tolkien and Lewis wanted to read, and therefore needed to write, was not just tales of adventure but stories that lifted them out of their ordinary surroundings and their ordinary selves, stories that looked over the edge of reality, that took imaginative and philosophical risks, that reached for something beyond the story itself for which the story should be the vehicle.

In the case of Tolkien and Lewis the implementation of the impulse was typical of each man. Lewis seems to have lost little time in sitting down to write the first of his space romances validating the mythos of Christianity. It was published in 1938 as *Out of the Silent Planet*. Tolkien began methodically to work on *The Lost Road*, a time-travel story that he planned to weave into his own mythos of Middle-earth. After a promising first few chapters, however, he found himself more drawn to the myth than to the story and never completed it. This was not unusual; much of Tolkien's work was left unfinished at his death, a proliferation of prose and verse that frequently included several overlapping versions of the same story. Partly this was due to a stubborn perfectionism that prevented him from releasing work he had not polished to his satisfaction, partly from a habit of composition that sometimes kept several efforts going at once. But though he often put aside particular efforts, he never gave up an idea. Again and again in his fiction the same ideas appear—as motifs, as episodes, sometimes as individual speeches. These are the leitmotifs of his philosophy, the recurring figurations that give shape to the pattern. Though *The Lost Road* was never finished, it stands as the earliest explicit treatment of the reconnection of time present with time past and time future, a reconnection that occurs in a variety of forms throughout Tolkien's work.

As an integral part of Tolkien's fiction, time has first of all a practical function. The reader is kept constantly aware of the pattern of time which moves events and within which they move. In *The Lord of the Rings* it is a crucial factor in the success or failure of the central quest. If the Ring cannot be destroyed before Sauron's forces gain momentum, the whole enterprise will have gone for naught. Time can be length of years, as in the long disappearance of Gollum and the Ring, or it can be the space of a minute, as when the world momentarily comes to a halt in the instant of the Ring's destruction. Time brings Durin's Day, Bilbo's birthday, the "appointed hour" for Aragorn to reveal himself to Sauron in the Palantír. It coordinates the independent actions of the fragmented Fellowship as their adventures unfold on both sides of the river. Time brings round the sad anniversaries of knife wound and spider sting, of a finger and a treasure lost, the recurrent, unconsoling reminders of Frodo's sacrifice.

But as well as providing the essential framework of the narrative, time becomes the traveled road between past and present, connecting the two worlds. This interconnection appears in *The Hobbit* when Thorin Oakenshield walks into the guards' hut in Lake-town and announces himself: "Thorin son of Thrain son of Thror King under the Mountain! . . . I have come back" (208). And the guards are forced to realize that what they have dismissed as the forgotten past is suddenly with them in the present. It appears in *The Lord of the Rings* when a Rider of Rohan asks Aragorn, "Do we walk in legends or on the green earth in daylight?" and Aragorn replies, "A man may do both," observing that "not we, but those who come after will make the legends of our time" (*Two Towers* 37). It is explicit in chapters such as "The Shadow of the Past" and "The Council of Elrond," where the past must be recapitulated by Gandalf or Elrond in order to explain the present.

It is implicit in the whole of the Lórien section, where the present finds itself inhabiting the past, and it is explicit in certain episodes of that chapter, as when Frodo sees Aragorn standing on the mound of Cerin Amroth and knows that Aragorn is seeing things not as they are but as they once were, and again when Frodo and Sam look in Galadriel's mirror and see things that are and things that were and things that yet may be, though they cannot tell which are which. Each of these episodes emphasizes in its own way the motif so central to Tolkien's thought of the interpenetration and interdependence of all aspects of time. That motif extends beyond the simple concept of tense to a larger vision of contrasting concepts of time: as both fluid and static, linear and circular, mortal and immortal. In such a vision each concept is dependent on the other, while at the same time each dictates a separate perception of the self and of the world.

In addition, a typical characteristic of Tolkien's use of time is its frequent correlation with space, a characteristic that reviewers and critics have noted but have failed to put into its deepest context. "The field of Time" is more than a metaphor in his fiction. It is a working reality. The round of the year is a structural element in both *The Hobbit* and *The Lord of the Rings,* and within that round—at least on one plane—both Bilbo and Frodo travel across space and time. Less encompassing but no less significant examples of such correlation are scattered throughout the books. Approaching Weathertop on the fifth of October, Aragorn and his companions are "six days out from Bree." The measure is time, but the reference is a point in space. To be sure, this is a convention of expression, and on one level "six days out from Bree" is no more unusual than "a year after Pearl Harbor" or "the day before Waterloo." Nonetheless, when such expressions are read in the light of Tolkien's whole concern with time, they assume deeper significance.

In similar fashion, when Frodo awakes at Rivendell after his adventure at the Ford, his first impulse is to locate himself both spatially and temporally: "Where am I," he asks, "and what is the time?" Gandalf's answer is precise. "In the House of Elrond, and it is ten o'clock in the morning. . . . It is the morning of October the twenty-fourth, if you want to know" (*Fellowship* 231). The coordinates locate Frodo in time and space and give him the information he needs to reconstruct his journey. This space-time correlation is both characteristic and generic, not just of Tolkien or of his world but of the language that is the outgrowth and expression of both, for our language habitually interchanges prepositions for time and space: "after," "before," "ahead," "behind" are used equally for temporal or physical position.

Nothing could be more solidly realistic than this carefully detailed clock and calendar time, the days and seasons and years that measure the journeys and events of *The Hobbit* and *The Lord of the Rings*.[1] Sunset, moonrise, star time are meticulously noted and tracked. Breakfast-time, teatime, and dinnertime are missed and longed for. This is all part of an attention to and concern with time that at the other extreme, in the purely fantastic mode, successfully tries for and attains the stature of myth. An example of this other mode is Tolkien's early story "The Weaving of the Days and Months and Years," included in *The Book of Lost Tales I*, the first volume in Christopher Tolkien's edition of *The History of Middle-Earth*. This narrative is anything but realistic, relying almost entirely on mythic personification for its effect. The children of Aluin (Time), who are Danuin (Day), Ranuin (Month), and Fanuin (Year), weave for the gods the three invisible ropes that anchor and control the movements of Sun and Moon, binding the Middle-earth in the fetters of Time. The concept itself is surprisingly sophisticated, while the three figures who embody it are straight out of myth. They are primitive and mystical, and the world in which they appear is filled with and ruled by fantastic forces.

A story, wrote Tolkien, "grows like a seed in the dark out of the leaf-mould of the mind," what he called "one's personal compost-heap," and, he concluded, "my mould is evidently made up largely of linguistic matter" (Carpenter 126). For Tolkien, a philologist as well as a fantasist, the time component of his fiction was a function of language, of the words human communities have evolved and selected to express their perceptions of time, to name and process its shifting reality. His awareness that these words carry their own power to shape and to organize was itself one of the most formative influences on his fiction. In the languages he knew and loved best, the northern poesy of Old English and Old Norse, the words for *time* and *fate* are linked to one another and to a darkly beautiful worldview that saw each in terms of the other and both as ruling over the lives of men. Old English *wyrd* was "fate, destiny," to which all were subject. The fate-figures of Old Norse cosmology, the three Norns, were called respectively *Urth* (cognate with *wyrd*), *Verthandi*, and *Skuld*, names that are often loosely translated as Past, Present, and Future.

But it is at this point that equivalency breaks down, for the Norse words are verb forms while the English words, though they began as verbs,[2] have hardened into nouns. The contrast is between a static and a dynamic view of time, between picture and process. *Urth* and *Verthandi* are past and present participles respectively of Old Norse *vertha* (Old English *weorthan*) "to happen, to occur," while *Skuld* is the past participle of Old Norse *skulu* (Old English *sculan*), denoting external obligation or necessity, roughly equivalent to modern English *should*. But the present tense of *skulu* is in the preterite form, so that its past participle (it would be something like *shoulded* if it were translatable into English) carries a sense of pastness affecting futurity: "that which has already been determined." Thus *urth* is "happened," *verthandi* is "happening," and *skuld* is "must." The verbal nature of these words conveys a sense of process far more than does the nominative quality of the English time words. As terms, these are not discrete segments of some imaginary time line but continuous and continuing activities. They are, moreover, activities of a particular kind.

As Paul Bauschatz observes in *The Well and the Tree: World and Time in Early Germanic Culture*, the verb *vertha* derives from the Indo-European root **uert-*, denoting "turn, spin, rotate." He points out that

> The idea basic to *verða* contains this element of "turning," and probably represents some kind of change of location or reorientation in space . . . . Additionally the motion of "turning" or "changing position" found in **uert-* implies revolution or motion about an axis. Such motion suggests a return to an original beginning point (as in a revolving door), or at least an approximation toward such an orientation (as in a screw-like motion). Thus, one thing turning into something else will retain all or part of itself, or return at least partially to its original configuration. This antithetical nature of change and retention is found in the meaning of *verða* and the words related to it in the Germanic languages. When *Verthandi* and *Urth* are

semantically related, *Verthandi* becomes that which is in process of "turning" or "becoming," and *Urth* would be that which has "turned" or "become." (13–14)

Tolkien's close familiarity with Old English and Old Norse would have made him aware of such a perception of time, and it is safe to assume that the same impulse that inclined him toward those languages also inclined him toward their worldview—artistically and emotionally if not logically and rationally. Thus the idea of time as not just a linear progression but as a cycle, a "turning" or "return," was a philosophical concept with which Tolkien was comfortable on mythic as well as on purely philological grounds. Philosophically, it is not unlike the Eastern idea of reincarnation, with the concept of the soul's return to embodiment through a succession of lives.

But the concept, in the twentieth century at least, has its own particularly Western flavor, manifest in the renewal of interest in time as a subject, which was itself a symptom of the time that produced it. It was a time when poetic imagination embraced the cultural and historical philosophy of Friederich Nietzsche and rediscovered the cultural and historical philosophy of Giambattisto Vico, when Nietzsche's theory of Recurrence and Vico's idea of *ricorso*—both of which posited the perpetual return and repetition of the same events or configurations at intervals throughout human history—offered the only coherent explanation the century could find for the events that rocked and crossed it, explanations that could be said to elevate reincarnation from a personal to a historical plane.

Tolkien was not alone in responding imaginatively to this intellectual rediscovery, nor in seeing, through its lens, myth and philology as deeply interconnected. His contemporary and fellow mythmaker James Joyce was profoundly involved with the implications of time as cycle, as was another myth-suffused poet, T. S. Eliot. For them, and for Tolkien as well, history blends into myth in what Mircea Eliade has called the Eternal Return, the concept whereby the same event can—indeed must—cycle and recycle through mythic time, although in actual historical time the event has already passed. This way of looking at time—expressed philosophically by Nietzsche and Vico, poetically by Joyce and Eliot, philologically in the myth-embracing words of Old English and Old Norse—particularly suited Tolkien's own fantasy-oriented imagination. It was a way of seeing that marched in step with his idea of time-travel, allowing, as it must, for time-travel either forward or backward.

There are, of course, fictive as well as linguistic and philosophical precedents for this kind of travel, which has been for many generations one of the staples of fantasy fiction. H. G. Wells, the leading exponent of the genre, and still the best, sent his hero quite a long way into an imaginary future—all the way to the death of the planet, in fact—in *The Time Machine*, the novel that became a classic and set the standard for all subsequent treatments. Olaf Stapledon, Wells's obvious heir in the genre, took the readers of his *Last and First Men* and *Last Men in London* forward in time many millions of years.

The past has also had considerable appeal, in spite of the fact that time-travel backwards tends to be constrained by historical or legendary precedent. Nonetheless, Mark Twain, an author known for his more realistic fiction, wrote one of the best of the type. His Connecticut Yankee made a wry commentary on the romanticism of other Arthurians, and on his own time as well, when he chose to follow the long road back to King Arthur's Court. Though like Twain, Tolkien found the past to be dark, unlike Twain, he also found in it something worth saving and chose to follow his own Lost Road not just into the past but into successive pasts, each of which was the future of the one that came next. Moreover, he went further than most, right past history into his own mythology.

The commonalty among all these writers is that they all played hide and seek with their own time. They looked at the world around them, found it wanting in many respects, and—nostalgic or bitter, wry or romantic, as their fancy took them—dodged into imaginary worlds that turned out to be not much better. Wells and Stapledon both used time-travel as a platform for philosophical speculation. Twain used it for literary and social satire, debunking the romantics and making a devastating commentary on human nature. Tolkien used it as part of a long-term exploration and development of what became his own imaginative theology. A striking similarity among all these writers is that none manifested a very hopeful attitude toward the human race. The use of time to escape time, a simultaneous retreat from and comment on the present moment, seems to be typical of a certain quality of imagination, and Tolkien is eminently at home in such company.

But while he is at home with these writers in imagination and impulse, he differs from them in one important and profound way. This difference resides in his particular philosophical and theological inclination of mind. Most social commentary stops with society's relation to itself and its culture; or if it peers into the realm of philosophy, it often does so critically, with something of a grudge against God, a wish to demonstrate His nonexistence, or the impulse to redefine Him. It would be nearer the mark in Tolkien's case to say that he wished to redefine humanity and redefine the relationship of Creation to its Creator. Christopher Tolkien has commented that his father used his fantasy as "the vehicle and depository for his profoundest reflections," his "theological and philosophical preoccupations" (*Silmarillion* 7). In this regard, the truly fantastic elements of Tolkien's fiction are neither his Hobbits nor his Elves, but rather the varying perceptions with which he invested them, the space-time coordinates of the world he put them in, and the way in which he allowed each of these elements to relate to all the others. The structure that houses and shapes all of these is a space made of time, framed by time, and occupied in and by time.

To appreciate Tolkien's movement between the worlds, and fully to appreciate his special brand of time-travel and attitude toward time in general, we must see these in the context of his own time's ambiance and its unusually generative climate of thought, a climate that gave rise to speculation in science, in philosophy, and above all in literature. We must explore not just his own personal leaf-mould, but the general one of his time and culture. Ideas not really new but newly rediscovered or fitted into a new context were in Tolkien's time percolating through the literature of Western Europe and finding expression in works mystical, scientific, imaginative, and theoretical. A full grasp of their effect on Tolkien's thought and work will require another kind of journey back in time, to authors and works once well known and whose fame in some cases has been dimmed by the passage of time, ironically, the very subject of their concern.

Remembrance That Never Dies 2

We are all, *tous tant que nous sommes,*
little bags of remembrance that never dies.
—The Duchess of Towers

They are a mixed group, the writers whose work supplied fuel for Tolkien's imagination: a cartoonist, an aeronautical engineer, two schoolteachers, two playwrights, and a novelist—George Du Maurier, J. W. Dunne, Charlotte Moberly, Eleanor Jourdain, James M. Barrie, John Balderstone, Henry James. For all their apparent differences of profession, education, and position in life, they shared a common interest in the subject of time and time-travel. Moreover, all were typical of a new impulse to open the mind to unconventional experience. Common strands—thematic, conceptual, theoretical—link their work one to another and to Tolkien.

THE DREAM JOURNEY

First an artist and only late in life a novelist, George Du Maurier was for thirty years a cartoonist for *Punch,* and his social satire set the tone for an age. In the last six years of his life he wrote three remarkable novels that became the unexpected pinnacle of his creative achievement. Born in France in 1834 to a French father and an English mother, he was displaced from the Continent to

England when he was a child, returned to France for his school years, displaced again to England as a young man. He often returned to Paris as an art student, and in his maturity finally and permanently established himself in London in 1860. His biographer, Leonée Ormond, finds in these circumstances and in his family history not just the source of his posture as a social observer but also the wellspring of his psychological-cum-spiritual sensitivity as a novelist. "From the first," she writes, "George Du Maurier was subject to a conflict between his two nationalities. He was not only half-French and half-English, but the grandchild of a Frenchman exiled in England, and of an Englishwoman exiled in France. The aching nostalgia which characterized his personality had its roots as much in this family history as in his own memories of childhood" (8). He was, then, in a sense, always an exile, an emotional and psychological position that informed his life and his fiction.

This nostalgia, however, did not prevent him from being a lively and popular presence in the Victorian world of the arts. In Paris a friend and fellow student of Whistler (though they later had a rancorous falling-out, as did many with Whistler), in London a contemporary and admirer of Burne-Jones and Millais, in later life the friend of Henry James, Du Maurier was a man both typical of his time and curiously outside it. His cartoon drawings captured the fashions of current London society even as they punctured its vanities and mocked its follies. Readers of *Punch* saw themselves satirized and laughed at their foibles so quizzically pictured, so gently ridiculed. His weekly drawings pictured the superficialities of the moment. His books reached deep into the past and the unconscious. Based in memories of his own childhood, boyhood, and young manhood, they recreated a past he loved and mourned and gave it a special golden aura. Readers of his books found their dreams and buried hopes awakened and discovered in his pages strange aspects and aptitudes of the mind just then beginning to be explored.

Du Maurier's first novel, *Peter Ibbetson*, was published in 1891, when its author was already in middle life, a settled family man whose role as social satirist and identity as the *Punch* cartoonist seemed fixed and whose new role as novelist took both him and his audience by surprise. *Peter Ibbetson* was an immediate success, and his second novel, *Trilby*, published three years later in 1894, brought him even greater popularity and made him a fortune at the age of sixty. His third novel, *The Martian*, finished shortly before his death in 1896, was less successful. A more private reverie, it was perhaps a bit beyond—and therefore perhaps a bit disappointing to—an audience that had thought it knew what to expect from him.

Peter Ibbetson is about the power of dreams and the unconscious. Its immense success is an index of the direction of the popular thinking of the time. It was adapted for the stage, the Victorian equivalent of the movie version, and was, if anything, even more successful in that medium. Du Maurier's younger son, Gerald, the most successful actor of his day and a leading actor-manager in the West End, played one of his first small parts in the stage version of *Peter Ibbetson*. (This stage version was also notable as one of the early successes of the young John Barrymore, who played it for a year, both in New York and on tour.) First a novel, then a play, it was finally in this century a movie, although by the time it got to film it had been "adapted" almost out of all recognition. Nevertheless, it was still popular enough to be filmed twice, first as a silent film in 1921 and then in a soundtrack version with Gary Cooper in 1923.[1]

Some fifty years or so after the novel appeared, John Masefield wrote in an introduction to the collected *Novels of George Du Maurier:*

> One of the questions perplexing men had been that of the limitation of the mind. Towards the end of the nineteenth century, men were seeking to discover what limitations there were to the personal intellect; how far it could travel from its home, the personal brain, how deeply it could influence other minds at a distance from it, or near it. . . . This inquiry occupied many doctors and scientists in various ways. It interested many millions of men and women. It stirred George du Maurier, the writer of three novels, *Peter Ibbetson, Trilby,* and *The Martian.* (vii)

Masefield went on to analyze the phenomenon of the book's reception. "The new mind is usually assailed with every venom. When du Maurier published *Peter Ibbetson* he had been known as an artist for thirty years; his was not a new mind; and the book was not assailed, but perhaps it was imperfectly seen that the book was new, it was a discovery, a freshness, a thing till then unknown in our fiction" (viii). To be truly new, a thing cannot have been consciously anticipated, though its need may well have been unconsciously felt. And the newness that Masefield was at such pains to point out was not mere newness of style or of plot, but newness of subject matter. Accustomed as the reading public now is to a proliferation of fantasy, science fiction, psychological fiction, magical realism, the mind games of Kafka and Borges and Nabokov and Eco, it is hard to imagine how radically different and innovative Du Maurier's story must have seemed to an audience accustomed to Dickens and Trollope.

Peter Ibbetson is a story of the inner life, of the reality of dreams, and of the power of the mind to transcend observable reality. A boy and girl growing up in France, "Gogo" Pasquier and "Mimsey" Seraskier, are separated as children and meet years later in England, by which time their adult lives are established. He has become Peter Ibbetson and she the Duchess of Towers. She is now married to a faithless and abusive husband, and Peter is the adopted dependent of his equally unsavory uncle, the wicked Colonel Ibbetson. They meet only briefly before being parted again, this time for life, when Peter is committed to a lunatic asylum for the unpremeditated murder of Colonel Ibbetson. Cumbersome and arbitrary though it is, this plot device is necessary for Du Maurier's purpose, which is to separate the lovers in daily life so that they may meet in and share one another's dreams. Their dream life then becomes their primary mode of being, and their waking hours a secondary, merely interim existence.

In their shared dreams the lovers travel together back to childhood, revisit their old life and old haunts and, themselves unseen, observe the children they once were. Here Du Maurier moves explicitly into the realm of parapsychology, presenting the past and the present as intermingled or, perhaps more psychically, presenting them as a unified concept occupying the same dream space, differentiated only by limited observation and experience. The adult dreamers come to recognize that their present, dreaming selves were present in their own past, sensed by their childhood selves, who speak of being "haunted" by ghosts they cannot see, and which, of course, to ordinary perception do not even exist yet.

Having taken the step from observable reality with the lovers to interior reality with the dreamers, Du Maurier makes a greater leap from parapsychology to race memory. Taking ever-greater risks with probability, he sends his dreaming lovers beyond their personal past and memory into their ancestral past and family memory and history and finally as far back as they can go, back through race memory into a nineteenth-century dream of prehistory. Together they transcend the Paris suburb of their childhood to visit France in the ancien regime, to go back to the time of Napoleon, to Versailles and the Revolution and the taking of the Bastille, to the Renaissance of Villon, to the time of Charlemagne, and still on and back they go dreaming out into ancient starlight, into a Victorian vision of prehistory when only the earliest humans were awake, back to the Ice Age, the time of the mammoth and the cave bear.

This dream-life goes on for many years, during which time, though their real-world selves age, their dream-selves remain youthful and vigorous. The lovers' apotheosis comes when the Duchess, whose death precedes Peter's, returns after death in dream to reassure Peter of her continuing, though now unmanifest, presence in his life. She tells him what she now knows of the life beyond death, her realization that "sound and light are one" (Du Maurier 203), that "Time is nothing" (206), and "time and space mean just the same as 'nothing'" (207). She assures him that "We are all, *tous tant que nous sommes*, little bags of remembrance that never dies" (208), "tiny links in an endless chain" (210). It is a transcendental, almost Eastern vision, acceptable in the comfortable and material Victorian world of iron railways and plush furniture because it is not presented as any reality, or even as transcendent vision, but as dream.

To be sure, dream vision is not a new literary form, having been put to excellent use by Chaucer, Dante, Langland, and Lewis Carroll, to name only a few of its practitioners. It has always been useful for freeing authors and their readers from the constraints of ordinary reality, freeing them also from responsibility for whatever flights of fancy their imagination may lead them to. What made *Peter Ibbetson* new, even in this genre, was its suggestion that ordinary people could control their dreams and through them move through time and space; that they could, at will, exchange an outer for an inner reality and live fully in the experience of the latter. It validated the power of dream and the imagining mind over the actuality of the "real" world.

Even now it is an astonishing book. In 1891 it was a revelation. But while it struck its audience as new, it did not come entirely out of nowhere but was in many respects simply another manifestation of that reciprocity between art and society that Eksteins has characterized. The later years of the nineteenth century saw the emergence of a new wave of romanticism, a counter to Victorian industrialization and materiality. It was a wave that was to continue, against the odds and against technology, into the twentieth century. It was the legacy not just of the Romantics themselves, but also of their direct heirs, the Pre-Raphaelites. This next generation of romantics created in paint and print, out of their nostalgia for an idealized Middle Ages, a lush never-world of mists and magic, of spiritual, unattainable quests and sensuous and equally unattainable loves. The following generation took its readers boldly into that world, assured them of its reality, and held out the promise of its attainment. *Peter Ibbetson* was just such an effort. It grew out of the soil of a century culturally and sociologically at odds with itself in a time of unprecedented turbulence and change. The tempo seemed to have speeded up, so that each decade brought more newness than the one before it.

Seeing the nineteenth century from the perspective of the present, from above, as it were, presents a time-space panorama of the Waterloo victory and the Peterloo massacre, the coming of the railroad, the Crimean War, the beauty-worship of the Pre-Raphaelites, the horror of the Indian Mutiny, the rise of spiritualism, aestheticism, decadence. It was a century of contradictions, a century that spawned Jack the Ripper and Walter Pater, Victoria Hill and Oscar Wilde, Gilbert and Sullivan as well as Henrik Ibsen. In such a time the pendulum of thought swung as wide an arc as that of art and society. The same century that covered its sofas in plush velvet depended for its goods on the forced labor of children. It took increasing interest in the metaphysical yet tolerated the blacking-factory and the sweatshop; it introduced seances to the intellectual elite and the time clock to the working class. The same year that saw the publication of *Peter Ibbetson*, 1891, also saw the first performance of *Lady Windermere's Fan*. *The Time Machine* of H. G. Wells and the trial of Oscar Wilde were only four years away. Things were moving fast, too fast—though society stoutly denied it—to comfortably keep up. One predictable response to such speed is what William Empson calls "the pastoralization of experience," that escape phenomenon that occurs when a culture cannot keep pace with its own innovations and retreats for reassurance into nostalgia.

Peter Ibbetson emerged out of all of this, and without directly addressing any of it. It spoke indirectly but powerfully to the anxiety and anticipation, the optimism and disillusionment, the inseparable hopes and fears of its audience. Although its tone was quiet, the revelation of its content and treatment foreshadowed the coming psychological and spiritual revolution. By looking back into the past, it looked ahead to the revelations of Freud and Jung, dived deep into the personal unconscious and below it to the collective unconscious, mixed dream interpretation with telepathy, and took as a given that reality is within us as well as outside us. In his freedom to transcend the accepted laws of matter (laws which, though he could not know it, were soon to undergo revision) Du Maurier was typical of a new generation of romantics, imbuing their work with an atmosphere of dream that joined the contemporary and the atemporal, a blend that was Du Maurier's own special hallmark.[2]

Du Maurier's influence on Tolkien was in many respects a general one, though there are enough correspondences in their thought and work to invite comparison between them both as men and as writers. Du Maurier's first two books, *Peter Ibbetson* and *Trilby,* had much the same kind of appeal for his late-nineteenth-century audience that Tolkien's first two, *The Hobbit* and *The Lord of the Rings,* had for Tolkien's public in the mid–twentieth century. Both writers' later books lacked that same appeal; neither *The Martian* nor *The Silmarillion* entirely gratified the waiting audience's expectations. And there are other, more personal, comparisons. Both men were artists, though for Du Maurier art was a vocation, for Tolkien an avocation. Both were illustrators of their own works. Both, after gaining recognition in one field, achieved unexpected and late success in another. Both, for various reasons, were subject throughout their lives to moments of deep melancholy and to a persistent nostalgia for a lost past, a nostalgia that suffused their writing. And both, in their separate ways, without intending it or perhaps without even realizing it, spoke in much the same way to the dreams and hopes and fears of their time.

For example, the Duchess's report to Peter that in the life beyond death "sound and light are one" is a concept that strongly evokes Tolkien's marriage of sound and light in the creation story of *The Silmarillion.* Her notion of humanity as "links in an endless chain," "little bags of remembrance that never dies" recalls

Tolkien's treatment of his own Elves, immortal, endlessly reborn, keeping alive among themselves their memory of one another, their history, and the history of Middle-earth. Further similarities between Du Maurier and Tolkien certainly include their common interest in and use of time and dream. But perhaps Du Maurier's greatest gift to Tolkien was simply the opening up of new possibilities, a freeing of his authorial imagination to trust its own range and fully use its own strengths.

THE TRIANON ADVENTURE

Others saw those possibilities in a less literary context. The late nineteenth and early twentieth centuries were a time of increasing interest in the occult, in spiritualism, though these terms became so broad as to include almost anything not immediately verifiable by the rational faculty. As the Victorians declined and the new century loomed, the impulse to inquire into the hidden, unrealized potential of mind and soul gave rise to a proliferation of individual and concerted experiments in the occult whose practitioners included William Butler Yeats, A. E. Waite and his Society of the Golden Dawn, Aleister Crowley and his Order of the Silver Star, the Theosophy of Madame Blavatsky and Annie Besant, Rudolph Steiner's Anthroposophy, the explorations of Gurdjieff and Ouspensky, the uncommitted search for truth of Krishnamurti.[3] These deliberate investigators into occult and mystical disciplines were consciously searching for alternative realities. There were others, less consciously mystical, and certainly less deliberately concerned with exploring the occult. In 1901 two quite ordinary, and to all appearances quite unmystical, schoolteachers found themselves taking an unexpected walk into the past.

The women were Charlotte Moberly and Eleanor Jourdain, the principal and vice principal, respectively (Miss Jourdain subsequently became principal), of St. Hugh's Hall, later St. Hugh's College for Women in Oxford. Touring Versailles, the Misses Moberly and Jourdain had what they subsequently came to believe was a psychic experience. While exploring the grounds on August 10, 1901, the two women lost their way. They entered a lane that took them through a wood, past a kiosk or summerhouse, and across a small rustic bridge before bringing them by a circuitous route to the rear of the Petit Trianon. During this walk both felt an inexplicable depression, or feeling of discomfort, but neither spoke of it to the other. On the way they variously encountered or saw at a distance men in antique costume, whom they took at the time to be gardeners or grounds attendants. In addition, Miss Moberly saw, seated on the lawn below the terrace of the Petit Trianon, a lady in an old-fashioned, full-skirted summer dress. Though they both passed directly by the spot, Miss Jourdain saw no one. Entering the Trianon, they joined a guided tour that was in progress and then returned to Miss Jourdain's flat for tea.

It was not until some time later that the two women discussed and compared their experiences and revealed the curious mood of depression or discomfort each had privately felt. Miss Moberly speculated that she and Miss Jourdain "had 'entered within an act of the Queen's [Marie Antoinette's] memory,' when during her detention at the outbreak of the Revolution she 'had gone back in such vivid memory to other Augusts spent at Trianon'" (Coleman 17). Their conclusion was that the Trianon was haunted, that the wood, the kiosk, the rustic bridge, the figures of the men and the seated woman were no part of present reality, were from another time, were in fact ghostly manifestations from the time of Marie Antoinette and the French Revolution. In subsequent years they made several return visits but were never able to retrace the way they had taken or to rediscover the wood and the kiosk or to find the little bridge.

In 1911 they published their joint account of the experience, concealing their identities under the assumed names of Miss Morison and Miss Lamont, entitled simply *An Adventure*. As had *Peter Ibbetson, An Adventure* expressed the spirit of the time. But unlike the novel, it claimed to be actual experience: its events were not cloaked in fiction nor camouflaged as dream. Like *Peter Ibbetson, An Adventure* was enormously popular. It went through seven impressions of that first 1911 edition and has gone through at least five subsequent editions (one with a Note contributed by J. W. Dunne and one with a Preface by Jean Cocteau). The most recent edition was in 1988, evidence that interest in the subject continues.

Inevitably the story got about by word of mouth as well as through the book. C. S. Lewis's posthumously published *The Dark Tower*, itself a story of time-travel, refers to "the ladies of the Trianon," and Walter Hooper's Note in that volume cites their "notoriety in Oxford." Hooper also mentions a "retraction by one of the ladies involved," which he maintains was known to both Tolkien and Lewis (*Dark Tower* 93). Concrete evidence for the retraction and for Tolkien's and Lewis's knowledge of it has not been forthcoming; and whatever may have happened that day in 1901 (and there are arguments both ways), the consensus seems to be that the women themselves believed their experience and wrote of it in good faith. They may have been deluded, or have deluded themselves, but they were probably not frauds, not consciously perpetrating a hoax. It is important to remember that what they reported had as much to do with the quality of the things they saw and felt as with the events themselves. The mind and the memory can affect the meaning of events, and perception is as important a part of experience as factuality.

The account of the incident at the Trianon might best be seen as a kind of corroborating influence on Tolkien, affirming the possibilities inherent in the unconscious operation of the mind. Whether or not the events at Versailles really happened is less important to the present study than is the possible effect of such a story on so speculative an imagination as Tolkien's. Without necessarily either accepting or rejecting its actuality, Tolkien could have grasped the creative possibilities implicit in such an "act of memory," could have accepted such a validation of memory as a road into the past. Certainly the power of memory, both voluntary and involuntary, came to play an important role in his mythology.

THE EXPERIMENT

The twin phenomena of time and memory were not the private preserve of novelists and dabblers in the occult, but engaged other, more scientifically inclined, minds of the period as well. Einstein's Special Theory of Relativity postulated that time and space, far from being absolute, were relative to the position of the observer. Published in 1905, the Theory familiarized scientists and amateurs alike with the "fourth dimension"—that of time. Minds already prepared, so to speak, for this development by Wells's *The Time Machine* seized on the possibilities offered by Einstein's theory to imagine the bending of time into new configurations.

Not all were creative, like Du Maurier, or suggestible, like the Misses Moberly and Jourdain. J. W. Dunne, contributor of the Note to the 1931 edition of *An Adventure*, was another who took a special interest in time. Though coming from a different starting point, he managed to arrive at much the same place. Dunne was in no way a mystic, an occultist, or a philosopher. He was a military officer, an aeronautical engineer, a pilot, and the designer and builder of the first British military airplane. He was also the author of two children's books and a book about dry-fly fishing. The description given of him by J. B. Priestley in his book *Man & Time* captures a recognizable English type:

> He was a slightish man with a good big head; he belonged to the military section of Britain's old upper class, and had its staccato and not highly articulate manner in talk; he looked and behaved like the old regular-officer type crossed with a mathematician and engineer; and I repeat, he was as far removed from any suggestion of the seer, the sage, the crank and crackpot as it is possible to imagine. (244)

In addition to all of this, however, and far more important, Dunne was a dreamer. Not in the pejorative sense, as of one who is impractical, nor in the idealistic sense, as of one who is a visionary. He was simply a man who, when he slept, dreamed, and when he awoke, remembered his dreams. So far this is neither unusual nor noteworthy. What made Dunne's dreams remarkable was that they not only recollected waking experience, but they began to predict it as well. He noticed that an incident occurring in a dream might be followed rather than preceded by its occurrence in real life. Even this, at least as a literary device, is not unusual. Tales of prophetic dreams carrying portents or warnings are as old as Moses. Dunne's dreams were neither portents nor warnings; the recurrent images or incidents were for the most part unremarkable save that they were scenes or events of which he had no previous knowledge. Pondering this, he began to wonder if limitation to five senses might not have unnecessarily limited our perception of our world. He speculated whether memory might have a wider range, time, a more encompassing presence than we have assumed. Man of science and the modern age that he was, he set about to test the proposition. Hence the title of his book, *An Experiment with Time*. Not a revelation, not a discovery: an experiment.

The experiment was simple enough. He merely recorded, without editing or interpreting, whatever he dreamed as soon as he could after he dreamed it. He then kept alert for the reappearance of any element from the dream in his waking life. Once he started paying attention, he found that, far from being uncommon, the phenomenon occurred often. On the basis of his success, he enlisted the cooperation of friends to do the same thing with their dreams and found that they were often better dreamers (or perhaps just more open to the process) than he was. His conclusion was that this ability to dream ahead was no mark of singularity, no indication of occult faculty, of clairvoyance or prevision. The incidents ranged from the ordinary—a stopped watch, an old woman

tapping along a street with an upside-down umbrella—to the catastrophic—train derailments, plane crashes, volcanic eruptions. But they seemed to have little relation to the life of the dreamer and could occur days or weeks or, in some cases, years after the dream. They were predictions but not portents. Their importance resided simply in their reappearance in real life.

Dunne's account of these experiences comprises the first half of *An Experiment with Time*. The second half deals with the conclusions he came to and the philosophy he formulated on the basis of those conclusions. As the title of his book indicates, this philosophy is more concerned with time than with dream, which simply supplies the evidence from which he worked out his theory. That theory, in brief, is as follows: time, like space, is a constant, not the inexorable forward flow our human senses experience. We move across time as we move across space, and it is our movement, not time's, that creates the illusion of linear progression. Since all time, like all space, is always present, human memory, if it pays attention, can extend the range of observation and move forward as well as backward. Thus we can "remember" events that to less extended perception have not yet happened. Dunne offered an analogy that any train-traveler will recognize:

We are . . . seated in [a railway] carriage . . . now standing at a railway station. Looking from the windows on the side remote from the platform, we perceive another train at rest upon the rails. As we watch it a whistle blows, and we become aware that our train is beginning to pull out. Faster and faster it goes; the windows of the opposite train are running swiftly across the field of view; but . . . a doubt arises . . . we miss the accustomed vibration of our vehicle. We glance toward the platform windows, and discover, with something of a shock that it is the other train which is moving. (161–62)

His interpretation of this experience leads directly to his theory and makes use of some terms—*observer, field of presentation*—which are staples of his overall explication:

> the visual phenomenon of a window moves across the field of presentation, and attention follows that phenomenon. Again we judge that attention is fixed and that the field—*with the observer*—is moving; but afterward, in the light of other evidence, we reverse that judgment, and say that the field and observer must have been fixed, and that attention must have moved . . . . The phenomenon observed . . . moves across the field of presentation—followed by the focus of attention—until it disappears at the edge of the field . . . . *the field of presentation remains fixed with regard to the observer.* (162–63)

Dunne's theory is based on a simple extrapolation from this experience. Our primary awareness of time, like the train traveler's awareness of space, is bounded by our immediate field of observation. This Dunne calls Field 1, or Time 1. But if we think of ourselves observing that field, we are in a sense outside it, observing our observation. It follows from this that the second observing consciousness, since it encloses the first, must experience a larger field of awareness, thus a larger span of time. This larger span Dunne calls Time 2. To visualize the distinction, imagine a single individual, Observer 1, observing a scene. Now imagine someone observing that individual. Observer 2's field of attention will encompass Observer 1 as well as Observer 1's field of attention. Add Observer 3 to watch Observer 2 watching Observer 1. Each successive observer will encompass a larger field of attention, therefore a wider experience. These successively wider experiences Dunne calls Fields 2, 3, 4, and so on. Dreams are the triggers for this expansion. In sleep our limited waking awareness is suspended, making the wider fields of observation accessible to our wider awareness.

To illustrate these coexisting time schemes, Dunne drew a series of vertical time lines representing, from left to right, the sequence of past, present, and future. Observer 1 is represented by a

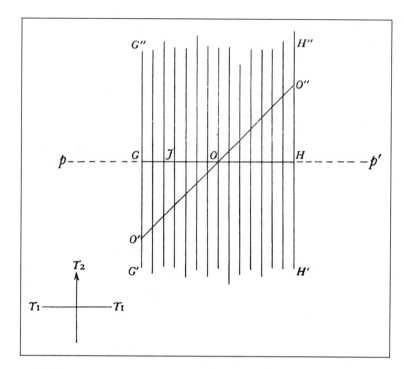

Figure 1

point on a tilted plane imagined as being at right angles to the page
and moving from left to right up and across the time lines. For
each progressively wider field of observation, another observer,
another point on another plane, is added. Two examples suffice
(see Figures 1 & 2).

The diagrams suffer from the limitation inherent in having to
explain time by means of space and may in the long run say more
about Dunne than about his theory. He takes many pages to labo-
riously explicate them, and the nonengineer reader is little wiser
at the end of his discussion. But for the present it is sufficient to
note the existence of such diagrams, for they will come up again in
a later context. To grasp the fundamentals of his concept, only two
sets of time fields are really needed. Call the inner, limited one
Time 1, or Field 1; and collectively call all the rest Time 2, or Field
2. If time is truly a field, it is simply the expansion of awareness
that makes one progressively conscious of larger and larger seg-

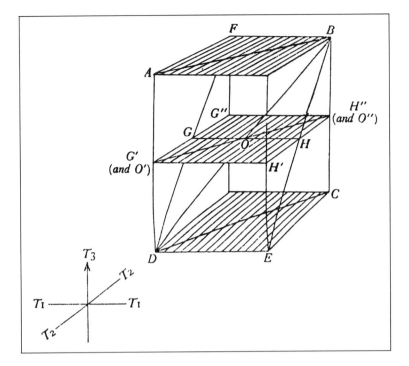

Figure 2

ments of that field. Dunne's system culminates in what he calls the "ultimate observer," or the observer at infinity. But "infinity" simply means the outermost observing awareness. This, he takes pains to remind his reader, "is nothing more magnificent or more transcendental than one's own highly ignorant self" (198). Only the increase in the field of awareness differentiates the ultimate observer from the primary one, or the ultimate individual from the waking self.

Thus far Dunne has extrapolated from observable reality while keeping within its theoretical limits. But this process of following awareness as far as it can go—and especially into the capacities of the unconscious or dreaming mind—is bound to lead from the apparently observable to the apparently unobservable but nonetheless theoretically possible. From thence it is an easy leap to implications that transcend the theoretical or psychological to enter the realm of the spiritual. Dunne is too conscientious an investigator not to follow that lead. "One's own highly ignorant self," he goes on to say, "is beginning to look perilously like a full-fledged *animus*" (198), that is to say, a soul.

In the final paragraphs of his book, Dunne sums up his philosophy, which he came to call "Serialism," as simply as he can: "Serialism discloses the existence of a reasonable kind of 'soul'—an individual soul which has a definite beginning in absolute Time—a soul whose immortality *being in other dimensions of Time does not clash with the obvious ending of the individual in the physiologist's Time dimension* . . ." He goes on to develop this idea.

> [Serialism] discloses the existence of a superlative general observer, the fount of all that consciousness, intention, and intervention which underlies more mechanical thinking, who contains within himself a less generalized observer who is the personification of all genealogically related life, and who is capable of human-like thinking and prevision of a kind quite beyond our individual capacities. In the superlative observer we individual observers, and that tree of which we are the branches, live and have our being. (236–37)

The combined notions of the animus, or soul, and of the superlative observer within which individual observers have their existence suggest that for Dunne successive awarenesses must have a spiritual component and that the animus is that element which the individual and superlative observers have in common. There is something very close to speculative theology here, tentatively approaching such nonscientific subjects as reincarnation and the immortality of the soul. One conclusion in particular is evidence of this and demonstrates Dunne's care in dealing with the implications. This is his conclusion, at the end of the first edition's discussion of the serial observer, that "observer 1 seems to be the only observer who dies" (163). The book's third, revised edition, while it follows substantially the same line of argument, has modified the language—though not the implication—of this provocative statement, so that it now reads "observer 1 seems to be the only observer who ceases to observe" (197). His ultimate conclusion, which takes him from time to transcendence and from diagrams to theology, is that his data and the argument derived from them are "proof of the unity of all flesh in the Super-body and of all minds in the Master-mind" (237).

Dunne's description of the serial, ultimate, and superlative observers recalls the words of the Duchess of Towers at the end of *Peter Ibbetson:* "We are all, *tous tant que nous sommes,* little bags of remembrance that never dies;" we are "tiny links in an endless chain." This likeness suggests that Du Maurier and Dunne—the one mystical and imaginative, the other empirical and investigative—may have arrived independently at the same vision. It is equally possible, however, that like many of his generation Dunne had read *Peter Ibbetson* and had consciously or unconsciously absorbed Du Maurier's ideas. Both men had in common a trust in the operation of dream and in the furthest implications of the dream state. Whatever the relationship of their work, it seems clear at least that both were part of the same surge of speculation, the same phenomenon of interest in alternative views of time.

It is easy to see also why Dunne would have been invited to contribute the Note to the fourth edition of *An Adventure.* The notion of two women becoming encompassed, as they saw it, within the memory of Marie Antoinette is perfectly in harmony with his theory. They reported suddenly finding themselves in a time and place that extended the boundaries of their immediate experience so that they felt and saw through another observer, thus widening their awareness of time. This shows, says Dunne, "that all our individual minds are merely aspects of a universal, common-to-all mind, which has for its four-dimensional outlook *all* the individual outlooks" (1931 ed. 34).

Like *Peter Ibbetson,* like *An Adventure, An Experiment with Time* grabbed the contemporary imagination. First published in 1927, the book went through three editions, the third, much-expanded edition coming out in 1934. But unlike the fictive dream travel of Du Maurier or the highly subjective and unverifiable experience of the ladies at the Trianon, Dunne's *Experiment* claimed to be scientific. The whole idea of experiment is that it should be repeatable. Try it yourself, Dunne told his readers. Anyone can do it. He bolstered his account with references to current theoretical and scientific speculation, invoking Einstein, relativity, the fourth dimension, and quantum theory. He captured the intellectual audience, where the Versailles story had captured the occultists.

Indeed, his theory became a kind of middle ground where both camps could meet.

It is important to remember here that the validity of Dunne's theory, like the veracity of the Versailles story, is not the point. The significance of both lies in their appeal to a certain kind of imagination at a particular moment in social and cultural history. Dunne's book is still sought by collectors and is a must for anyone exploring the history of the study of time, although later developments in quantum theory and later evidence about the nature of the universe have rather left him behind. Nevertheless, the book had a terrific impact when it appeared, though its influence was perhaps greater on literature than on science. Its message informs the opening lines of "Burnt Norton," the first of T. S. Eliot's *Four Quartets:*

> Time present and time past
> Are both perhaps present in time future,
> And time future contained in time past.
> If all time is eternally present . . .

The theory influenced at least two of J. B. Priestley's plays, *Dangerous Corner* and *An Inspector Calls*; it turned up as a theme in James Hilton's immensely popular novel *Lost Horizon* and as a subject for discussion in his later novel *Random Harvest*. It provided the theoretical rationale for Lewis's *The Dark Tower* and the metaphysical rationale for E. R. Eddison's Zimiamvian trilogy. It got a whole generation of writers interested in playing with time. Indeed, while it lasted, Dunne's theory was so current and popular a topic that *not* to understand it was a mark of singularity. A recent biography of Mervyn Peake, Tolkien's younger contemporary and the author of the Gormenghast trilogy, cites as evidence of Peake's unworldliness that "it was the era of Whitehead's Quantum Theory, and of Dunne's Theory of Time, but try as he would, Mervyn could not understand the very first things about either one of them" (Watney 63). Peake was not alone. H. G. Wells called *An Experiment with Time* "a really very exciting book" but observed that Dunne's further work would "carry conviction to many, but I doubt if it will be read as much as it is accepted" (*Nineteenth Century* 14–15). Wells's irony notwithstanding, he was correct about the acceptance. Dunne gave a whole generation of British writers permission to play with time and a way in which to do it; he affirmed and encouraged their interest at a point in the century when their own time seemed to be letting them down.

Of the influences on Tolkien so far examined, the least literary is that of J. W. Dunne. It is in many ways, however, the most immediate, or perhaps most practical, in its impact. There would be little doubt, even without corroborating evidence, that Tolkien and his Inkling friends had read and discussed Dunne, for it is very much the kind of thing that would have engaged their intellects. C. S. Lewis mentioned Dunne in his third space novel, *That Hideous Strength*, and, as noted, drew heavily on Dunne for *The Dark Tower*, citing him directly in the text of that story. Both Tolkien and Lewis owned copies of the revised and enlarged third edition of *An Experiment with Time*. Lewis's copy is in the Wade Collection of the Library at Wheaton College in Wheaton, Illinois. Tolkien's copy, in the possession of his son, Christopher, contains his interleaved notes and comments, jotted in the course of reading, on Dunne's ideas and the theory he derived from them. Tolkien's comments are not always in complete agreement with Dunne; nevertheless, they show a clear relationship between Dunne's *Experiment* and the mechanism Tolkien used in two time-travel stories, *The Lost Road* and *The Notion Club Papers*. In addition, two unattached pieces of paper bearing diagrams remarkably similar to the kind drawn by Dunne are among Tolkien's notes and rough drafts from the early period of the composition of *The Lord of the Rings*.

THE POET OF LOST TIME

Some writers had anticipated Dunne by decades. J. M. Barrie was juggling the accepted conventions of time and dream twenty years before Dunne published his *Experiment*. Barrie's *Peter Pan* played hide-and-seek with time, and its central character, the eternal boy, was emblematic of the time-travel impulse converted into time hoarding. This is the desire not to move but to stand still, not to speed time up but to slow it down, if possible to stop it in its tracks. It is Empson's pastoralization of experience on the personal rather than the cultural or historical level. It is the fear of leaving the garden of childhood. If one aspect of the time-travel impulse derives from longing for what is past, the time hoarding impulse derives from fear of what is to come.

A fate connected Barrie with George Du Maurier and his family. Du Maurier's five grandsons, the children of his daughter Sylvia, were the combined model for Barrie's Peter Pan and were informally adopted by Barrie when both their parents died.[4] George's son Gerald had two of his greatest successes in Barrie plays, doubling as both Captain Hook and Mr. Darling in *Peter Pan* and playing the tragic Harry Dearth in Barrie's *Dear Brutus*. More than familial circumstances, however, linked Barrie and Du Maurier. Both wrote in a mode that peered beneath surface reality; both were aware of the hidden recesses of the mind; both used fantasy to enable them to look into the world beyond the world. Du Maurier saw the brightness of that world, while Barrie saw the shadows. Nonetheless, their acquaintance with it put them both in the vanguard of a burgeoning literature of the fantastic.

The surface whimsy of Barrie's dramas all too often cloaks their darker aspects. *Peter Pan* has been sweetened and Disneyfied out of all recognition by Hollywood and the musical stage. But as Barrie conceived the story, it was a childhood dream of dark possibilities, of children's fears of grown-ups and of growing up. The paradoxical threat and attraction of adulthood were nightmarishly mingled in the character of Captain Hook. Barrie's Hook, on the surface a one-dimensional melodrama villain, became in performance one of the most telling psychological treatments of modern drama. By doubling as both Hook and Mr. Darling, Gerald Du Maurier achieved in each character the hidden implications of the other as they might appear to the mind of a child. Daphne Du Maurier described her father's performance as Hook:

> He was a tragic and rather ghastly creation who knew no peace, and whose soul was in torment; a dark shadow; a sinister dream; a bogey of fear who lives perpetually in the grey recesses of every small boy's mind. All boys had their Hooks, as Barrie knew; he was the phantom who came by night and stole his way into their murky dreams. He was the spirit of Stevenson and Dumas, and he was Father-but-for-the-grace-of-God, a lonely spirit that was terror and inspiration in one. (105)

Barrie achieved the same psychological duality in his *Dear Brutus,* in which Gerald Du Maurier again triumphed, not by playing two characters but by playing separately two aspects of one character: one as he really was and one as he might have been. *Dear Brutus* is thus only indirectly a play *about* time; rather, it is a play that uses time to make a point. Much more, it is a poignant story about second chances, about the opportunity (unavailable in linear time) to return to an earlier moment in life and make a different choice. Predictably, even with the second chance, the same opportunities are lost.

The most moving episode in the play is the idyll of the aging, alcoholic painter, Harry Dearth, and his dream-daughter, Margaret. In the wood of second chances he is young again and sober and hopeful. He and Margaret are merry in each other's company, unafraid of poverty or obscurity. Of Gerald Du Maurier's performance as Harry Dearth, his real daughter said, "It was the revelation of a living man, his hopes, his fears, his little ghosts and dreams, what he might have been, what he might become, a challenge and a confession in one" (177). Those hopes and dreams are lost all in a moment, when Dearth briefly (as he thinks) leaves the wood to get food for a tramp, and Margaret recedes into the shadows, crying, "Daddy, come back; I don't want to be a might-have-been." Of course he does not come back; he must reenter present time and present reality, and so father and dream-daughter are lost to one another. This is the dark side of time-travel, the bitter discovery not of the past as it was but as it might have been.

Peter Pan and *Dear Brutus* are among Barrie's most popular plays, probably because their deep waters are covered over by a surface of elfin whimsy. Even deeper is another of his dramas, *Mary Rose.* Here there is no distinction between surface and depth; the whimsy is dark, and the elfin laughter has a diabolic tone. It can be seen as a grown-up variation of the *Peter Pan* theme, in which the parent rather than the child goes away into Neverland. The play is a mood piece; its focus is on atmosphere rather than on action, and there is almost no plot. It is a frame story, beginning in the present, flashing back to scenes in the past, then returning to the present for the denouement, a final scene which, for all its slightness, conveys unbearable poignance.

A returned soldier comes to visit a house for sale, a house that he knew as a boy but has not seen for many years. His opening conversation with the housekeeper reveals that there is something "wrong" with the house. Though the word "haunted" is carefully avoided in the exposition, the feeling is conveyed: there is an empty room that the housekeeper will not enter; a door drifts open with no one behind it; there is the sense of an unseen presence. As the young man, Harry, waits in his chair (he insists later that he did *not* fall asleep, did *not* dream), his present experience merges with the past before he was born. He sees but is not seen by the previous occupants of the house, a man and wife and their curiously youthful daughter, Mary Rose. We learn from their reluctant conversation with her fiancé, Simon, that something is wrong with Mary Rose, that she has had a childhood adventure of which she is unaware, and that it has somehow changed her. While on a vacation with her parents on a remote island in the Hebrides, she disappeared and was not seen for twenty days. When she reappeared she had no knowledge that she had been away, no recollection of where she had been, and no awareness of the passage of time.

Simon accepts the story but goes ahead with the marriage, and a few years later the still-childlike Mary Rose brings him to her island, leaving on the mainland the baby Harry, whom she adores. Once again she disappears, having heard the fairy "call" that beckoned her the first time. But this time she is gone for many years, and when she does return, it is too late. The final scene is a meeting between the tremulous ghost of the girl Mary Rose, still searching for the baby she left behind, and the man Harry, who is her child grown up. She cannot recognize in him the child she longs for, and like a child herself, she sits on his knee to be comforted. For all its wistful quality, the scene has a kind of gossamer irony. Again she hears the "call"—though this time the script suggests the call of angels rather than fairies—and again she disappears, presumably this time forever.

The story is both fragile and disturbing, dependent for its effect on ambiance rather than action, on the interplay of light and shadow. To bring it off demands a special quality of theater, a light touch with the dark behind it. No stage magic is used, simply the awareness by the characters onstage of the unseen presence, the slow swinging open of the upstage door. The real magic is conveyed in the character of the arrested, forever-young Mary Rose and in her son's heartbreaking realization that there can be no recognition. The child she left behind her has now left her behind, and time, which should have carried her with it, has instead passed her by.

Time is as important a factor in *Mary Rose* as it was in Dunne's *Experiment* or in the Trianon adventure, but here it is an implicit, rather than explicit, part of the story. It is the fairy-tale time of Rip van Winkle enchanted in the Catskills, of Thomas Rymer carried off by the Queen of Elfland, the time warp that traps the adventurer in a frozen moment incapable of either rest or change. It was a theme that followed the child-enchanted, mother-haunted Barrie throughout his life. For all his whimsy, Barrie was deeply aware of the poignance and pain of being human, and he chose to clothe it in the dark magic of Faërie. Mary Rose's tragedy, deeper than Peter Pan's, is that because she did not grow, her child grew past her; her own development was halted while her child went on to become an adult. This is a not-uncommon fear and is not only mortals' fear of Faërie but parents' buried fear of their children—that they will grow up taller, different, *other* than they and will pass them by. It is the fear as well as the hope that every generation has for its own posterity.

Barrie's effect on Tolkien is documentable. Although perhaps no greater than that of *Peter Ibbetson*, and less immediate than that of *An Adventure*, his effect was more specific than either of these, in part because Tolkien disagreed with Barrie on several issues, and where we disagree there we are engaged. First, Barrie was a dramatist, and Tolkien faulted drama as an unfit vehicle for fantasy. He enjoyed the theater but found it to have distinct limitations in that area.

> Drama has, of its very nature, already attempted a kind of bogus, or shall I say at least substitute magic: *the visible and audible presentation of imaginary men in a story.* That is in itself an attempt to counterfeit the magician's wand. To introduce, even with mechanical success, into this quasi-magical secondary world a further fantasy or magic is to demand, as it were, an inner or tertiary world. It is a world too much. ("On Fairy-Stories" 141)

In a Note appended to the essay he does, however, concede the dramatic possibilities inherent in the "impact upon human characters of some event of fantasy, or Faërie, that requires no machinery" (160). And here he turns directly to Barrie for his example, specifically to Barrie's *Mary Rose*, wherein a disappearance into and return from Faërie is managed without machinery by the simple device of showing its effect on the humans involved. In a long, unpublished draft of the Note, Tolkien wrote an extended discussion of Faërie, of Barrie's dramatic use of it, and his own opinion of that use.

> By the dramatic form the human characters hold the stage, and it is upon their joy or suffering, victory or defeat, that attention is concentrated. If the Fantasy is taken seriously—it may be degraded to mere comedy—it must become allegory or devilry. This kind was attempted by Barrie. . . . Since Barrie was successful in making the Fantasy credible, the result leaned inevitably to the diabolic; but characteristically he shirked or sought to shirk his own dark issues, both in *Dear Brutus* and *Mary Rose*.[5]

These dark issues, and Barrie's handling of them, set Tolkien to thinking deeply, and rather to Barrie's disadvantage. Tolkien found it a flaw that the inhuman realm of Faërie, unlike the magical wood of *Dear Brutus*, is never shown in *Mary Rose*, and this he clearly felt to be an imaginative begging of the question. His unpublished Note addressed the issue directly:

> Stories telling how men and women have disappeared and spent years among the fairies, without noticing the passage of time or themselves appearing to grow older, are well-known and usually tragic or horrible, in so far as the human victims are concerned. But in the stories not only the human characters are presented, and the Fantasy also exists for its own sake: the fairies are in themselves interesting, and indeed their effect upon mortals is often only a way of indicating the strange powers of Faerie and its mode of being.

Mary Rose becomes his negative example.

In *Mary Rose* Barrie made a play on this theme, but no fairies were seen. Horrible suffering was inflicted on all those who loved

Mary Rose, but with this accumulating dramatic stuff nothing was done. It was as if Barrie, expending his art in making a notion of Celtic fantasy "credible" in the centre of the stage, and enchanted with his elvish heroine, had simply ignored the torment in the wings. Taken as a diabolic drama it is moving; that is if the producer says: the sufferings are the thing, cruel, valueless, purposeless; the fairies do not matter, except as being inhuman and malicious; no explanations are given, there are none. That at least is a theory. But not so Barrie. When I last saw the play Mary Rose walked out finally to the summons of the same elvish tones as those which had called her away before. But not so Barrie. In the printed play there is at the end a sentimental falling star, and the calling voices are angelic. Why? Why at any rate for Mary Rose? On any interpretation, realistic, fantastic, or allegorical, charming and elvish child as she may have been, her ghost is the least deserving of such (in this play) inappropriate mercy. (fol. 21r.)

It seems clear that Tolkien preferred the "diabolic" implications and "dark issues" that he accused Barrie of shirking. These might be formulated as a series of questions. Where do they go, those who disappear into Faërie? What do they see? Of what nature are the fairies who call to them, and why do they call to mortal beings? In his own work Tolkien found a way to answer these questions, or at least to address them, through the attitudes of his Elves toward Men and Hobbits and in the dark foreboding that Boromir brings to Lórien. He addressed these same questions in an early poem, "Looney," later revised as "The Sea-bell." Moreover, he added a postscript to his note with a perhaps deeper reflection on Barrie's treatment, one that carried implications for his own Elvish voices. "But B's meaning may have been: they suffered and died—that is human fate, and God's redress beyond the grave is not now my concern. But even for those entangled in 'Faerie,' pinned in a kind of ghostly deathlessness to the earth, God will grant release in the end" (fol. 21r.). Those "entangled in 'Faerie'" are trapped in timeless time, the consequence of living "pinned in a kind of ghostly deathlessness." At the probable time of the composition of the unpublished note, the time when he was writing the essay "On Fairy-Stories," Tolkien was beginning work on the new hobbit story that was to become *The Lord of the Rings*. He was seriously engaged in clarifying for himself the limits, both spatial and temporal, of his narrative world, exploring the Otherworld of Faërie and its intersection with the world of mortal men. Barrie's treatment of time, his oblique implication of time-travel, the "dark issues" that Tolkien accused him of skirting, the notion of living "pinned in a kind of ghostly deathlessness" were all to reappear, sea-changed, in Tolkien's cosmology.

A SENSE OF THE PAST

Not only Barrie, but writers of both lesser and greater notice framed concepts that fitted the growing cosmology of the age and that were to reappear in Tolkien's work. *Berkeley Square,* a play by John Balderstone with a plot derived from Henry James's unfinished story *The Sense of the Past,* is another time-travel story. A chain of coincidence stretches between Balderstone in the twentieth century and Du Maurier in the nineteenth, and Henry James is the connecting link. Of all the writers of his era, James was the most sensitive to time and culture and to their effect on one another. As has already been noted, he was a friend of George Du Maurier. The two men first met when Du Maurier illustrated James's *Washington Square.* James was not especially happy with the illustrations but came to know and like the illustrator. His biographer, Leon Edel, takes particular note of their relationship.

> [James's] friendship with George Du Maurier was a deeply attaching one. He found "something in him singularly intelligent and sympathetic and satisfactory." He liked walking to Hampstead from Piccadilly on a Sunday evening and sitting on a particular bench on the Heath with Du Maurier where their conversations could roam over Anglo-French subjects with an ease and affection that never diminished. The marriages of the Du Maurier sons and daughters and the career of Gerald Du Maurier on the stage commanded his interest and loyalty. (295)

Their conversations, it appears, ranged far beyond Anglo-French subjects and the marriages and careers of the Du Maurier offspring. Both men were accomplished raconteurs, but Du Maurier, especially, was a marvelous spinner of tales. One night he told James a fantastic story of a pair of lovers changed into albatrosses. They were shot and wounded; one resumed human shape and waited and watched in vain for the other. The germ of *Peter Ibbetson* seemed to be in this tale. And then there was the famous evening of 25 March 1889, when, walking with James through the streets of Bayswater, Du Maurier offered him "an idea of his which he thought very good—and I do too—for a short story." The story James then recorded dealt with a girl with a wonderful voice but no genius for music who is mesmerized and made to sing by a little foreign Jew "who has mesmeric power, infinite feeling, and no organ." *Trilby* thus acquired existence first as a note in James's scribbler. James decided he could not write it . . . . [but] then urged Du Maurier to tell it himself. Du Maurier tried, but instead wrote *Peter Ibbetson,* about a hero whose dreams become his only reality. Six years after their evening walk *Trilby* was published—with the results the world knows. (454)

More than mere coincidence, more than friendship, is in force here. A special cord vibrated between these two men, a cord whose fibers intertwined fascination with intuition about the mysterious, psychic, occult forces that play invisibly around the everyday life of ordinary humanity. James very nearly used Du Maurier's *Trilby* idea for a short story; he was a receptive audience for the albatross story that Edel suggests was the germ of *Peter Ibbetson;* and, of course, he himself wrote one of the most powerful of all tales of the supernatural, "The Turn of the Screw," with its provocative, unresolved mixture of the psychic and the psychological.

James's fascination with mystery and the supernatural led him to try his hand at a time-travel story. In the early days of 1900 he drafted the opening chapters of a story he called *The Sense of the Past.* It was to be the tale of a young American, Ralph Pendrel, who inherits an old house in London and therein, through a kind of reciprocity of time, exchanges places with an ancestor whose portrait hangs in the house. Ralph will step back into the past that is his ancestor's "present," while the ancestor comes forward into the future that is Ralph's "present." The exchange is not a complete one; the two men are to trade public identities but not consciousnesses. That is, while each will appear to be the other, he will retain his own memory and sense of himself. It is surely no accident that the turn of the century found James particularly conscious of time and writing about travel in time. But he may have been responding to more concrete stimulus. In *The Pop World of Henry James* Adeline Tintner offers evidence that James had received from H. G. Wells a copy of his *Tales of Space and Time* just at the close of 1899 (175). She suggests the immediate influence on James's story of some of Wells's tales. In one, "The Crystal Egg," people from two different worlds simultaneously look through similar crystals and by this means make contact with one another. Little is required to go from Wells's crystal to James's portrait as the medium of exchange. In another, "A Story of the Days to Come," a young couple from the future travel back to Victorian times, find life there unsatisfactory, and return to their life in 2100 (Tintner 276).

The concepts of identity exchange and of the present as the past's future form the basis for *The Sense of the Past*. The story, however, breaks off before the identity exchange has a chance to take place, just at the point where Ralph pauses at the entrance of the house, "before the closing of the door again placed him on the right side and the whole world as he had known it on the wrong" (Edel 505). James returned to the story, but not until 1914, a year whose ominous events, Edel suggests, "made him want to escape from a terrible present into a remote past" (505). This hyperawareness of time—first through the unfolding of a new century and second through the outbreak of a terrible war—seems to have had much the same effect on James that it was to have on Tolkien in the years between the wars—that is, to generate an impulse to escape the present. And since the future seemed even more inauspicious than the present, the obvious place to go was into the past. James's subsequent abandonment of the story, Edel suggests, related to his unease not just with the present, but with his own past. "*The Sense of the Past* remains a fragment of what might have been an extraordinary ghost-novel, James's ultimate discovery—had that been possible—of how to complete his journey into himself and his personal past" (505).

It remained for John Balderstone in 1929 to take James's fragment and turn it into a completed work. Balderstone's drama *Berkeley Square*, a less subtle, more boldly colored effort than James's original story, presents Peter Standish, a young American who develops a romantic nostalgia for the eighteenth century. From a distant relative he inherits a Queen Anne house in Berkeley Square in London and immerses himself so deeply in its history that he comes to think of that past as still in some way present, still accessible through the "inconceivable adventures of the mind." Balderstone updates James by citing Einstein's Theory of Relativity as the basis for the exchange, at first half in jest, as his hero quotes a limerick,

There was a young lady named Bright
Whose movements were quicker than light,
She went out one day, in a relative way,
And came back on the previous night.

and then attempts a serious explanation of Relativity and Simultaneity.

Suppose you are in a boat, sailing down a winding stream. You watch the banks as they pass you. You went by a grove of maple trees upstream. But you can't see them now, so you saw them in the *past,* didn't you? You're watching a field of clover now; it's before your eyes at this moment, in the *present.* But you don't know what's around the bend in the stream there ahead of you; there may be wonderful things, but you can't see them until you get around the bend in the *future,* can you? Now remember, *you're* in the boat. But *I'm* up in the sky above you, in a plane. I'm looking down on it all. I can see *all at once* the trees you saw upstream, the field of clover that you see now, and what's waiting for you around the bend ahead! *All at once!* So the past, present, and future of the man in the boat are all *one* to the man in the plane. Doesn't that show how all Time must really be one? Real Time with a capital T is nothing but an idea in the mind of God. (36)

Both the limerick and the time-as-space explanation recall so clearly not just Einstein but Dunne's theory (with the man in the boat as Observer 1 and the man in the plane as either the ultimate observer or the observer at infinity) that we must suspect a direct connection.

The action of *Berkeley Square*, which continues where James's story left off, relies on the commonalty of identity between the modern Peter Standish and his eighteenth-century ancestor. Where James contemplated trapping his modern man in the past, Balderstone instead has temporally distant relatives temporarily trade places (though we see only the journey into the past) and then resume their proper centuries. The effect of the play comes with the discrepancies between past and present. We are amused when twentieth-century Peter Standish raises eighteenth-century eyebrows for his habit of daily bathing and makes a hit at parties by tossing off bons mots quoted from nineteenth-century Oscar Wilde. We are moved when he falls in love with his eighteenth-century cousin Elizabeth, who is to marry his ancestral avatar, and when—leaving the century—he must leave her as well. His twentieth-century self knows that she will die three years after his return to the present.

The play is effective theater but lacks the haunting quality of either *Mary Rose* or *The Sense of the Past*. Essentially, it is the old mistaken identity plot in eighteenth-century dress, and the situations are stock confrontations out of *The Twin Menaechmi* or *Two Gentlemen of Verona*. Time is not the subject; it is simply the gimmick, hinging on the presence (or necessity) of an ancestor as the agent—the mode, the vehicle, whatever you want to call it—of the time travel. The protagonist uses neither machine nor dream as his way back; instead he participates in a quasi-mystical identification of blood and memory. Peter Standish can go back in time because there is another Peter Standish, an identical cousin, who is already there.

The Sense of the Past and *Berkeley Square* are in many ways the most like Tolkien's own work. Whether Tolkien had read James's story is moot. It remained a fragment, was not published until after James's death, and is hardly to be found outside an academic library. Tolkien did, however, see a production of *Berkeley Square* put on by students of the Oratory School, Oxford, in the academic year 1934–35 while his son John was a student there.[6] And his use of serial identity as a device for the time-travel of *The Lost Road* and *The Notion Club Papers* replicates both James and Balderstone so closely as to invite comparison. Moreover, it remained for Tolkien, in *The Lost Road, The Notion Club Papers,* and most of all *The Lord of the Rings,* to make for himself the "ultimate discovery" that James came near but never really found, that all writing is finally a journey into one's self, that any journey into the past must be in some sense a journey into a personal past.

THE SPIRIT OF AN AGE

All these writers were interconnected, though not always directly. Dunne wrote about the incident at the Trianon. Du Maurier traded story ideas with Henry James, and James supplied one to Balderstone. Both Dunne and James were correspondents of H. G. Wells, who might be said to have been the godfather of their speculative thought. Each was linked to one or more of the others, and together they formed a web of influence that established a tone for an age and combined to give Tolkien—in varying degrees and more or less directly—a template for his ideas.

George Du Maurier, J. W. Dunne, Charlotte Moberly and Eleanor Jourdain, James M. Barrie, Henry James, John Balderstone—and Tolkien—are in their various ways examples of Eksteins's assertion that culture is both challenge and response. Each embodied in some respect a response to a special time, a challenge to it, and therefore had an effect on it. The elements common to all of them—participation in memory, nostalgia for the past, dream or vision, recurrence of identity—are concomitants of a particular perception of time, a way of seeing it, relating to it, moving in it. They are, as well, particular characteristics of Tolkien's own time, and it was in that time and out of that time that the fictive framework of his world was created. This double perspective on an age and its discoveries about itself makes time both an external influence on and an internal element in his work. Much as he wanted to escape it, Tolkien was tied to his own era, and his work derives from and reflects that era. In no other time but the one he lived in could Tolkien have used time to escape time in the way he did.

Strange Powers
of the Mind

3

Words move into words, people into people, incidents
into incidents like the ambiguities of a pun, or a dream.
We walk in darkness on familiar roads.
—Richard Ellman, on Joyce's *Finnegans Wake*

Tolkien's use of time as a road between worlds and his characteristic mixture of contemporaneity and retreat are exemplified in *The
Lost Road*, the story that came out of his time-travel and space-
travel agreement with C. S. Lewis. Slight in itself, it nevertheless
is important as a precursor of the later *Notion Club Papers* and,
even more important, of *The Lord of the Rings*. A narrative of a
twentieth-century father and son who by means of racial memory
and serial identity dream themselves back through time, this fragment of a story (for Tolkien had scarcely begun before he abandoned it) has tantalizing, albeit only half-fulfilled, hints of a complex of time-travel motifs. It gestures toward *Peter Ibbetson*, with
its dream technique, and recalls the memory transfer of *An Adventure*. The time warp of *Mary Rose* is here, as is the identity-
exchange mechanism of *The Sense of the Past* and *Berkeley Square*,
as well as the conceptual framework provided by *An Experiment
with Time*. All this acknowledged, however, we must also recognize that what emerges from the mix is a new thing, for Tolkien
managed to transform these elements into something definitively
his own, stamped with his style and woven into a story that, had

he carried it to completion, might have made a distinctive contribution to the genre.

No certain evidence for the probable time of composition is available, and all of Tolkien's published references to it occur decades later, in letters written in the 1960s. Some attempt at dating is necessary, however, in order to fix the story's relationship to both the prevailing intellectual climate and Tolkien's later work. Circumstantial evidence can suggest an approximate time of composition. In reference to his father's account of the space-travel and time-travel bargain with Lewis, Christopher Tolkien comments: "I do not know whether evidence exists that would date the conversation that led to the writing of *Out of the Silent Planet* and *The Lost Road,* but the former was finished by the autumn of 1937, and the latter was submitted, so far as it went, to Allen and Unwin in November of that year" (*Lost Road* 8). We can work backward from the given time of the autumn of 1937. However rapidly Lewis wrote, however little he revised, it cannot have taken him much less than a year to write a book the size of *Out of the Silent Planet.* Tolkien wrote to Stanley Unwin in February 1938 that he had read it and that Lewis had also read it "aloud to our local club," where it was "highly approved" (*Letters* 29). If it was finished enough to be read by or to friends, even in draft, by the autumn of 1937, Lewis must have begun it sometime (probably early) in 1936. Presuming that Tolkien and Lewis set to work at or about the same time, and given Tolkien's more painstaking work habits, the partial narrative he submitted to Allen and Unwin was probably begun sometime in 1936.

In that same year James Joyce was at work on *Finnegans Wake,* his great, circular narrative of myth and human experience that would be published in 1939. This work—whose opening line, "riverrun, past Eve and Adam's, from swerve of shore to bend of bay, brings us by a commodious vicus of recirculation back to Howth Castle and Environs," is the continuation and recircling of its last line, "A way a lone a last a loved a long the"—is a story in the same vein as *The Lost Road.* Both deal with the interpenetration of historical and mythic time. The point here is not influence but confluence, suggesting strongly that Tolkien is not the simple "escapist" fantasy author he seems. Two very different writers working in widely different narrative modes responded to the same climate of thought, approaching time in the same mythic mode and arriving by different means at similar mythic ends. Unfinished though it is, Tolkien's narrative and his notes and outlines show that he had given enough thought to the project to develop a carefully worked out scheme of time-travel and to build a narrative structure of some complexity. His own account describes it best:

> The thread was to be the occurrence time and again in human families (like Durin among the Dwarves) of a father and son called by names that could be interpreted as Bliss-friend and Elf-friend. . . . It started with a father-son affinity between Edwin and Elwin of the present, and was supposed to go back in legendary time by way of an Eadwine and Ælfwine of circa A. D. 918, and Audoin and Alboin of Lombardic legend and so [to] the traditions of the North Sea concerning the coming of corn and culture heroes . . . . In my tale we were to come at last to Amandil and Elendil leaders of the loyal party in Númenor. (*Letters* 347)

Christopher Tolkien's dating of *The Lost Road* to 1936–37 indicates that it was written when his father was on the threshold of some of his most vigorous work. The Silmarillion mythology was maturing; *The Hobbit* was about to be published; the long essay "On Fairy-Stories" was setting out the theories of myth and language, of the careful creative process that Tolkien felt was essential for the making of what he called a Secondary World, which *The Hobbit* and later *The Lord of the Rings* would put into practice. From this central point, *The Lost Road*, Janus-faced, looks both backward and forward—backward to the high and far-off epic tone and time of the Silmarillion proper, forward to the more realistic, ordinary time and tone of the later work. Moreover, the centrality of time to both the plot and the theme of *The Lost Road*, and its emphasis on dream and memory, look ahead to the use of these elements in *The Lord of the Rings*.

But it has a contemporary historical context as well, and while it travels back to the past, its beginning in a present, and its relationship to that present's events, are also important. Like Henry James's *The Sense of the Past*, with which it also has other similarities, *The Lost Road* was written during a peacetime collecting itself for a war, a time when Europe knew that time was running out. It was a place in history where the present seemed balanced uneasily on the wreckage of the past, about to tip into an ominous future. A time-travel story conceived at such a time and by such an imagination as Tolkien's could hardly escape being colored by its author's awareness of the present and his apprehension of the future. Tolkien's own characterization of it as "a new version of the Atlantis legend" suggests that he did not set out to write a story with a happy ending.

The Lost Road is not a hopeful story. Wrath and ruin and the wreckage of a high civilization are in the offing as the narrative gathers momentum. The unfinished fragment breaks off with its protagonists on the threshold of a time journey that, if they had continued it, would have taken them deep into the past of Tolkien's mythic history and culminated in their presence at the downfall of his fictive kingdom of Númenor. The internal situation would thus have replicated the external historical circumstances of the time of its composition. Commenting on his father's creative mood in this period, Christopher Tolkien wrote: "When at this time my father reached back to the world of the first man to bear the name 'Elf-friend' he found there an image of what he most condemned and feared in his own" (Lost Road 77).

The importance of the name "Elf-friend," the English equivalent of Anglo-Saxon Ælfwine, of which Alboin and Elwin are respectively the Lombardic and the modern British forms, should not be underestimated, for it looms far larger in respect to the story's internal time scheme and to Tolkien's mythos as a whole than its appearance here might indicate. The name and the concept behind it grew with the mythology and put out branches. Ælfwine is Tolkien's later name for one of his earliest characters, Eriol the mariner who in The Book of Lost Tales comes to Tol Eressëa, the Lonely Isle, where he hears tales of the Ainur and the Valar. Both the name and the character underwent complicated modifications as Tolkien's vision grew and changed. "The 'Eriol-story'," says Christopher Tolkien, "is among the knottiest and most obscure matters in the whole history of Middle-earth and Aman" (Lost Road 23). Either his name or his character, or perhaps both,[1] were later changed to Ælfwine. The epithet "Elf-friend," as well as the concept behind the character, became one of the most recurrent elements in the mythology. Over the long length of Tolkien's work on his mythology, the name Ælfwine and the character who bore it became the emblem and embodiment of some of his most deeply rooted attitudes toward myth, language, history, and the participation of the unconscious in all of these. Even Frodo Baggins, a late arrival to the myth, yet in many ways the inheritor of its ramifications, acquires the epithet "Elf-friend" and over the course of *The Lord of the Rings* comes to embody, in his quiet way, more than a few of the characteristics of the Ælfwine character.

Of Ælfwine's original name, Eriol, Christopher Tolkien writes "That *Errol* (the surname of the twentieth century protagonists of 'The Lost Road') is to be associated in some way with *Eriol* (the Elves' name for Ælfwine the mariner . . .) must be allowed to be a possibility" (*Lost Road* 53). Worth noting also is the meaning Tolkien gave to the name *Eriol*, "one who dreams alone." It seems safe to say that the name and its meaning were to be intentionally associated with Alboin Errol, the dreaming hero of the opening chapters of *The Lost Road* whose first name is Latinized Ælfwine. Translated, then, his name describes both his character and his function in the story: *Alboin-Ælfwine* = "Elf-friend," *Errol-Eriol* = "One Who Dreams Alone."

There is also a strong possibility that the very concept of the Ælfwine character may have been a formative as well as a connecting element in Tolkien's story. Christopher Tolkien writes of his father's process of composition:

> With the entry at this time of the cardinal ideas of the Downfall of Númenor, the World Made Round, and the Straight Road, into the conception of "Middle-earth," and the thought of a "time-travel" story in which the very significant figure of the Anglo-Saxon Ælfwine would be both "extended" into the future, into the twentieth century, and "extended" also into a many-layered past, my father was envisaging a massive and explicit linking of his own legends with those of many other places and times: all concerned with the stories and the dreams of peoples who dwelt by the coasts of the great Western Sea. (*Lost Road* 98)

This seems to suggest that the "very significant figure of the Anglo-Saxon Ælfwine" was to be the "thread" that would link Tolkien's own legends with those of other times and places. It further suggests that through this character's extension into both the "many-layered" past and the twentieth-century "future," Tolkien intended all the father-son characters of his time-travel story—the

Elwins and Alboins—to be in some way avatars of Ælfwine. It would thus be his consciousness that framed and unified the whole schema. Given the probable time of composition, it seems not only possible but highly probable that this presentation of myth and history as seen through one overarching consciousness that spanned the centuries was influenced by J. W. Dunne and that Tolkien found in *An Experiment with Time* the ideal mechanism by which to effect time-travel without magic or machinery.

This expansive concept was never to be realized, however. Four chapters into the narrative the story stops abruptly. Yet it is not altogether lost, for we can reconstruct the concept and realize at least the shape of what Tolkien envisioned. In addition to the completed chapters, Tolkien left an outline sketch of the story, some uncompleted fragments obviously meant to be part of it, as well as a note on the chapters yet to be written, suggesting how and where the uncompleted fragments might have fit in.

> It cannot be shown whether my father decided to alter the structure of the book by postponing the Númenorean story to the end before he abandoned the fourth chapter . . . but it seems perfectly possible that the decision led to the abandonment. At any rate, on a separate sheet he wrote *"Work backwards to Númenor and make that last,"* adding a proposal that in each tale a man should utter the words about the Eagles of the Lord of the West, but only at the end would it be discovered what they meant. (*Lost Road* 77)

We can deduce from this that the original concept was elaborated on and the cast of characters shifted around so as to change from a direct passage back to Númenor—the sequence of the story as we have it—to a serial return, working back through many identities of fathers and sons and many periods of history. Christopher Tolkien describes

> a rapid jotting down of ideas for the tales that should intervene between Alboin and Audoin of the twentieth century and Elendil and Herendil in Númenor, but these are tantalizingly brief; "Lombard story?"; "a Norse story of ship-burial (Vinland)"; "an English story—of the man who got onto the Straight Road?"; "a

Tuatha-de-Danaan story, or Tir-nan-Og"; a story concerning "painted caves"; "the Ice Age—great figures in ice"; and "Before the Ice Age: the Galdor story"; "post-Beleriand and the Elendil and Gil-Galad story of the assault on Thu"; and finally, "the Númenor story." (*Lost Road* 77–78)

A rough outline for the projected structure of the book gives evidence that the story had already grown beyond its first rapid jotting and was hardening into a definite sequence and shape. "Chapter III was to be called *A Step Backward: Ælfwine and Eadwine*—the Anglo-Saxon incarnation of the father and son, and incorporating the legend of King Sheave; Chapter IV 'the Irish legend of Tuatha-de-Danaan—and oldest man in the world'; Chapter V 'Prehistoric North: old kings found buried in the ice'; Chapter VI 'Beleriand'; Chapter VIII (presumably a slip for VII) 'Elendil and Herendil in Númenor'" (*Lost Road* 78). Some of these episodes, in particular, the "painted cave" and "Ice Age" sequences, recall the dream journeys described by Peter Ibbetson in his visits to the past with the Duchess of Towers. The fact that both Du Maurier and Tolkien take their heroes as deep into prehistory as the Ice Age is especially noteworthy.

Noteworthy, too, is the "English story of the man who got onto the Straight Road." An extended note suggests that Tolkien was thinking of this particular episode as being "best of all for introduction to the Lost Tales: how Ælfwine sailed the Straight Road" (*Lost Road* 78). Unlike many of the others, this story idea comes from no historical or legendary model. It is not Lombardic or Anglo-Saxon or Irish, but pure Tolkien. Its reemphasis of the importance of the Ælfwine character recalls the story's title, *The Lost Road*, and raises a question about the relationship between the Lost Road and the Straight Road. Are these different roads, or one road with different modifying adjectives? Humphrey Carpenter's opinion that the Lost Road is indeed the Straight Road to the Ancient West, lost when in the sinking of Númenor the world is bent (171), would fit with Tolkien's original conception of *The Lost Road* in which Alboin and Audoin travel directly back to Númenor and witness its downfall, after which the world is rounded away from the Straight Path. A possible second meaning, which does not contradict Carpenter's interpretation, is that the Lost Road is also time, leading back into the past, lost as humanity has lost touch with its past. In this event, the recurrent identities would provide the mechanism for the journey back, thematically linking the concept of time as a road with the concept of Ælfwine and serial identity. Character is thus not merely a function of plot but an essential of the theme.

The first two chapters, set in Tolkien's present England, do not introduce Edwin and Elwin as advertised but a father called Oswin (Anglo-Saxon "God-friend") and his son, Alboin. Their conversation about their own names, about the meaning of names, and the relationship of language to history takes up the opening pages. We learn that Alboin has dreams in which he seems to remember fragments of an unknown language. Here we have, cloaked in modern dress but plainly set up by name and situation, a dreaming Ælfwine. Alboin and his son Audoin form the first active father-son pair, for Oswin's importance (except as progenitor) immediately fades behind that of his son and grandson. In *The Lost Road* as Tolkien left it, two subsequent chapters are set in Númenor and seem meant to follow directly after the first two. In these we are given another father-son pair, the Númenorean Elendil and Herendil (rather than, as previously announced, Amandil and Elendil). In the serial structure that Tolkien subsequently envisioned for *The Lost Road*, all the father-son pairs, whatever their particular period and personae, were to be seen as links in a chain, or as travelers on a road on which they would be both before and behind one another. Between the two father-son pairs stretches the road, whose reality will be established by the succession of characters who travel it into the past.

The metaphor of time as a road leading back into the past is one whose familiarity renders it almost invisible. Tolkien made it visible and took care to make road a prominent image in the text and the context of his story. Alboin wants to "walk in Time, perhaps, as men walk on long roads" (*Lost Road* 44). He has "scattered tales and legends all down Audoin's childhood and boyhood like one laying a trail" (46). Such metaphors and similes express an apparently simple space-time equation so taken for granted that we do not become aware of its implications until someone like Tolkien— or Einstein—comes along to make us take a good look at what we are saying. If we pay attention, we discover that we have been speaking in the concepts of quantum physics for quite a while without realizing it. The implicit puzzle and paradox of space-time, its reflexive, recursive nature, are already present in the common, everyday expressions we use so often and know so well that we no longer hear them.

Tolkien heard them. A long, unpublished note headed "Elvish time" is tucked in among the manuscripts from about this period. This note explores the shift and switch of language as it tries to express what Tolkien saw as the confused and confusing human impulse to think of time in terms of space. It moves from an analysis of such expression in the English language to a consideration of alternate concepts as expressed in Tolkien's invented Elven worldview. The development of his Elven languages provided Tolkien with a way of moving beyond his native tongue to try out another way of looking at time. The note on "Elvish time" has strong implications for his use of time and space in *The Lost Road* as well as in his later work.

Our language is confused using *after* or *before* both (in certain circumstances) of the *future*.[2] We sometimes think and speak of the future as what lies before us, we look ahead, are provident, forward-looking, yet our ancestors preceded us and are our fore-fathers; and any event in time is *before* one that is later. We speak as if events and a succession of human lives were an endless column moving forward into the unknown, and those born later are behind us, will *follow* us; yet also as if though facing the future we were walking backwards, and our children and heirs (*posterity!*) were ahead of us and will in each generation go further forwards into the future than we. [*penciled in:* "A widow is a *relict*, one left behind by a husband who goes on."] As far as a single experiencing mind goes, it seems a most natural transference of spatial to linear language to say that the past is *behind* it and that it *advances* forwards into the future, that later events are *before* or in *front* of earlier ones. At the point where the individual ceases the survivors go on further go ahead of him. All living creatures are in one mass or column marching on, and falling out individually while others go on. Those who do so are *left behind*. Our ancestors who fell out earlier are further behind, behind us forever.

Having worked his way through this confusion of concept and diction, Tolkien turns to the time concept of his Elven mythology.

> In Elvish sentiment the *future* was not one of hope or desire, but a decay and retrogression from former bliss and power. Though inevitably it lay *ahead,* as of one on a journey, "looking forward" did not imply anticipation of delight. "I look forward to seeing you again" did not mean or imply "I wish to see you again, and since that is arranged/and or very likely, I am pleased." It meant simply "I expect to see you again with the certainty of foresight (in some circumstances) or regard that as very probable—it might be with fear or dislike, *'foreboding.'*" Their position, as of latter day sentiment, was one of exiles driven forward (against their will) who were in mind or actual posture ever looking backward.
>
> But in *actual language* time and place had distinct expressions.

Here the text breaks off. Like *The Lost Road* itself, the note is incomplete. Its ending, just as it seems about to move into actual Elven language theory, is tantalizing, but the perspective revealed by what is actually there is worth close attention. The apparently contradictory prefixes—*pro*vident, *pos*terity, *fore*fathers—and the contradictory uses of *after* and *before* are, as Tolkien points out, indicators of confusion of perception and, therefore, confusion in expression of time. He was trying to work out in terms of actual vocabulary the linguistic paradoxes contained in our unexamined, unwitting space-time lexicon and its unrecognized implications about our attitudes toward such concepts as past and future. And he, like everyone, saw it in terms of space.

Two pictures of humanity as a moving column are contrasted. In the first, the column advances into the future ahead of it, trailing behind it as followers those born after; in the second, it faces toward the future while being displaced backwards into the past by those who succeed it and go ahead of it, each generation moving further forward in time than the one behind (not before) it. These two pictures are then placed against the more consistent vision of Tolkien's Elves, who, facing toward their past, are backed into the future by those who follow. Men are *pro*ceeding into the future, while Elves are *re*ceding into it.

While this discussion has long-range importance in terms of Tolkien's handling of Men and Elves in the Silmarillion and *The Lord of the Rings*, its immediate importance to *The Lost Road* lies in its deliberate directional analogue, which presupposes a road or path for the columns of humanity to move along, whichever way they may be facing. The deliberate presentation of time as space leads directly to the title metaphor of the story and to the road references within it, wherein time is treated as space that really can be traveled, as a road back that can be rediscovered through the recurring father-son pair in their serial identity. What was explored as theory in Tolkien's note was to become fictive reality in the projected adventures of the Errols.

A side effect of this serial method of time-travel is that it prolongs by extending backwards the father-son relationship, which in the real world is bound to dissolve with the passing of the father. In the case of the Errols this is particularly poignant, for Oswin's late marriage has made him older in relation to his son's age than most fathers. In another, and certainly a deliberate, road reference, the narrative tells us that "He [Oswin] would have liked to accompany Alboin a great deal further on the road, as a younger father probably would have done, but he did not somehow think he would be going very far" (*Lost Road* 42). Fathers die and leave their sons. As Oswin sees it, the road has only one direction: it goes forward, and he, the forefather, will fall out, while his successor, Alboin, will go on. Though he does not use the road metaphor, Alboin's feelings mirror his father's. "I wish life were not so short," he muses, and thinking of his aging father, he reflects: "I want him for years. If he lived to be a hundred I should be only about as old as he is now, and I should still want him. But he won't. I wish we could stop getting old" (42).

The feelings of both father and son are captured in an Anglo-Saxon verse that Alboin remembers from one of his dreams and reports in a conversation with his father:

Thus cwæth Ælfwine Wídlást:
Fela bith on Westwegum werum uncúthra
wundra and wihta, wlitescéne land,
eardgeard elfa, and ésa bliss.
Lýt ænig wát hwylc his longath síe
thám the eftsíthes eldo getwæfeth.

Alboin translates for his father:

> "Thus said Ælfwine the far-travelled: 'There is many a thing in
> the West-regions unknown to men, marvels and strange beings,
> a land fair and lovely, the homeland of the Elves, and the bliss
> of the Gods. Little doth any man know what longing is his whom
> old age cutteth off from return.'" (44)

Almost immediately he regrets the last two lines, with their
implications of mortality and their poignant nostalgia. His father
looks up "with an odd expression. 'The old know,' he said. 'But
age does not cut us off from going away, from—from *forsith*. There
is no *eftsith*: we can't go back.'" Alboin's wish to "stop getting
old," to keep his father "for years," and his father's rueful comment that "there is no *eftsith*: we can't go back" are exactly the
desires to be satisfied in the projected time-travel sequences. They
are Tolkien's desires as well as his characters', and they will be
realized for him as well as for them through the overarching consciousness of "Ælfwine the far-travelled."

Further evidence of the centrality and growing importance of
the Ælfwine figure is to be found in a prose note attached to a
poem that Tolkien apparently wrote and rewrote and for which
Christopher Tolkien postulates a "continuous development" involving "many texts, both manuscript and typescript" (*Lost Road*
98–104). It seems in its development to have become more and
more focused on a specific character. First published in 1927 as
"The Nameless Land," the title was later changed to "The Song of
Ælfwine." An "intermediate version," according to Christopher
Tolkien's best guess, was written at "about the time of *The Lost
Road*," and thus would seem to be associated with the time-travel
theme and with the longings of Ælfwine to travel the lost road.
Christopher Tolkien also includes a "final" version, which he suggests is later and "might be associated with *The Notion Club Pa-
pers* of 1945." Appended to this final version is a prose note by
Tolkien that tells of Ælfwine the mariner who found the "straight
road" and came at last to Elven-home. The note ends by attributing to Ælfwine, with almost no change, the verse assigned in *The
Lost Road* to Alboin. The prose translation of the verse is also almost exactly the same as Alboin's, except that "Gods" is changed

to "Valar." Whether he is called Eriol or Errol, Alboin or Elendil, the Ælfwine figure is the connecting link between the present and the past, the consciousness that spans the centuries and moves freely over the field of time.

The autobiographical aspect in all of this cannot be overlooked. Humphrey Carpenter called *The Lost Road* "a kind of idealised autobiography" (171), and Christopher Tolkien commented that "Alboin's biography sketched in these chapters is in many respects closely modelled on my father's own life—though Alboin was not an orphan, and my father was not a widower" (*Lost Road* 53). Several elements contribute to this impression. The similarity between Tolkien's interests in language and myth and the nearly identical interests of both Alboin and Audoin is plain. Moreover, it seems clear that Tolkien, both a son and a father, drew at least in part on his own feelings for his portrayal of the father and the son. Even more revealing is Christopher Tolkien's observation that Tolkien "was concerned above all with the relation between the father and the son, which was cardinal" (*Lost Road* 75). It does not take much effort to imagine that the recurring relationship threading the projected sequences of *The Lost Road* derived, at least in part, from Tolkien's awareness of his own loss of a father when he was very young.

It would unfairly limit the story, however, to read it solely in the light of Tolkien's life and family circumstances, for this would give it more importance as autobiography than as fiction and shift attention unprofitably from the story to its author. Over against this objection, it must be acknowledged that there is a general psychological and intellectual sense in which all fiction can be said to be autobiographical. In this sense, Tolkien's characters' expressed interest in history, and in "northern languages and legends," could legitimately be placed in the larger context of his own expressed interest in languages and legends, in history, and in the persistence of race memory. What seems like a fairly typical father-son conversation early in the story turns on a discussion of language, with Alboin defending to Oswin what he calls "language-atmosphere." By this he means a genealogical inherence in language like that in race and culture, the idea that "echoes come through" from earlier languages into the present tongue, somewhat like recurrent facial features in a family line, or the identifying characteristics that a society passes on to its posterity. These same ideas and attitudes toward race, history, and language were expressed again years later in a letter from Tolkien to his son Christopher:

> I read until 11:50, browsing through the packed and to me enthralling pages of Stenton's *Anglo-Saxon England*. A period mostly filled with most intriguing Question Marks. I'd give a bit for a time-machine. But of course my mind being what it is (and wholly different from Stenton's) it is the things of racial and linguistic significance that attract me and stick in my memory. Still I hope one day you'll be able (if you wish) to delve into this intriguing story of the origins of our peculiar people. And indeed of us in particular. For barring the Tolkien (which must long ago have become a pretty thin strand) you are a Mercian or Hwiccian (of Wychwood) on both sides. (*Letters* 108)

The clear idea in both the story and the letter is that "things of racial and linguistic significance" are not linked by cultural association only but are combined deep in the blood and the ancestry so that body and mind remember. In another letter, this one to W. H. Auden, Tolkien wrote that "linguistic tastes, with due allowance for school overlay, are as good or better a test of ancestry as blood-groups" (*Letters* 214). Language is the signpost not just to the historical but also to the ancestral past. Given this expressed belief in the persistence of familial, racial, historical memory, it is not unreasonable to suppose that Tolkien might have felt a familial, racial, historical identification with his characters and his subject. In the same letter to Auden, speaking about *The Lord of the Rings*, Tolkien wrote:

> if you want to write a tale of this sort you must consult your roots, and a man of the North-west of the Old World will set his heart and the action of his tale in an imaginary world of that air and that situation: with the Shoreless Sea of his innumerable ancestors to the West, and the endless lands (out of which his enemies mostly come) to the East. Though, in addition, his heart may remember, even if he has been cut off from all oral tradition, the rumour all along the coasts of the Men out of the Sea. (212)

If this statement is true of *The Lord of the Rings*, imbued in all its imaginary detail with the air and situation of the North-west of the Old World, it is even more true of the consciously historical and legendary *The Lost Road*.

Tolkien's idea that the "heart may remember, even if [it] has been cut off from all oral tradition" suggests that his own heart had some familiarity with "the rumour all along the coasts of the Men out of the Sea." A detail worth noting is that among the historical Ælfwines, on whose name Tolkien based his frame-consciousness, the Ælfwine character, one, like Tolkien and son, was also a Mercian. This Ælfwine figures briefly but poignantly in Tolkien's play for voices, "The Homecoming of Beorhtnoth, Beorhthelm's Son," first published in *Essays and Studies* in 1953. Though they are necessarily tied to actual history, the few lines Tolkien wrote about him may reflect, however lightly, his own attitude toward the figure. Searching among the slain on the battlefield of Maldon, the young minstrel's son Torhthelm exclaims, "And here's Ælfwine: barely bearded and his battle's over," to which the old *ceorl* Tidwald replies, "He was a brave lordling, and we need his like: a new weapon of the old metal." This last phrase undoubtedly refers to this Ælfwine's descent from an old and noble Mercian line but might also suggest the multiple identities, "new weapons of the old metal," with which Tolkien had invested his own Ælfwine. Taking shape out of such a consciousness, so formed out of a blend of natural affinity, historical, literary, and racial consciousness, *The Lost Road*, if it is to be seen as autobiography at all, must be on so grand a scale that it dwarfs the genre. Tolkien's great design, had it come to fruition, would have interwoven selected episodes of Western history with suggestions of his own personal and familial history and made it all the epilogue to his own mythology. Genealogy is folded into history, and both are imagined into myth, making out of autobiographical fiction a history of a culture and an age.

But the very way in which these elements are woven into the story contains perhaps the most personal and deeply mysterious autobiographical element of all, Tolkien's "Atlantis" dream. In the story, the characters' dreams act as the mechanism for their time-travel, and their gateway to the road back. The function of dream in the narrative is directly linked to the *Eriol-Errol* surname of

Alboin and his family and to their recurrent identities. It seems reasonable to connect this to the fact that Tolkien himself had at least one recurrent dream through which he felt some unfathomable connection to the past. This was the already-mentioned "Atlantis" dream of being overwhelmed by a huge green wave: "What I might call my Atlantis-haunting. This legend or myth or dim memory of some ancient history has always troubled me. In sleep I had the dreadful dream of the ineluctable Wave, either coming out of the quiet sea, or coming towering in over the green inlands. It still occurs occasionally, though now exorcised by writing about it. It always ends by surrender, and I awake gasping out of deep water" (*Letters* 347). The Downfall of Númenor, the cataclysmic event toward which Tolkien's *The Lost Road* protagonists are moving, and in which they are to participate, culminates in that continent's submergence under the sea, overwhelmed by huge waves. In his myth-history Tolkien called this episode the *Akallabêth*, or *Atalantie*. As Tolkien evolved them, both words mean "the downfallen," one in Númenorean, the other in a language he called Adûnaic.

Caution must be exercised in postulating relationships between invented languages and real ones, and Tolkien staunchly and quite rightly defended the integrity of his nomenclature against the associative impulses of readers who found Anglo-Saxon or Norse (or Welsh or Irish or Latin) correspondences, insisting that "where the resulting names have analyzable meanings (as is usual) these are relevant solely to the fiction with which they are integrated. The 'source,' if any, provided solely the sound-sequence (or suggestions for its stimulus) and its purport *in the source* is totally irrelevant except in the case of Earendil." He concludes that "It is therefore idle to compare chance-similarities between names made from 'Elvish tongues' and words in exterior 'real' languages, especially if this is to have any bearing on the meaning or ideas in my story" (*Letters* 380).

These statements are in specific reference to *The Lord of the Rings*, but the general import has to do with his languages as a whole, and any respector of his work should take them seriously. Nevertheless, some correspondences seem to go beyond "chance-similarities." In a note appended to the "Atlantis-haunting" letter quoted above, Tolkien observes disingenuously that "It is a curious chance that the stem √*talat* used in Q[uenya] for 'slipping, sliding, falling down,' of which *atalantie* is a normal (in Q) noun-formation, should so much resemble Atlantis" (*Letters* 347n). Curious indeed, if it can be called chance. But to insist that this resemblance is chance requires a remarkable ability to compartmentalize ideas. The near-identical correspondence of these words to one another appears too close for mere coincidence,[3] especially in light of Tolkien's expressed desire to make "a new version of the Atlantis legend" (*Lost Road* 7). Whatever the intentionality, conscious or unconscious, of this particular name association, we can at least safely agree with J. S. Ryan that "Tolkien has left for others to ponder a remarkable nexus of actual literary, linguistic and cultural association much more potent than many of his 'invented names'" (22).[4]

Chance or design, conscious or unconscious correspondence, this linguistic similarity alone hardly qualifies as autobiography, but Tolkien's own comments on his "Atlantis complex" bring it closer to home. The letter to Auden in which he describes the dream as "beginning with memory" links dream to memory and both to their use in *The Lost Road*. Tolkien's own notion that his Atlantis dream was both a race memory and a family inheritance is transferred to the dreaming Errols and becomes the central mechanism of the story. The most curious aspect of the whole business is the fact that Tolkien learned only long after the writing of *The Lost Road* (the letter citing the information as "recent" was written in 1955) that his dream *was* inherited and that—as with the Errols—the inheritor was a son—Tolkien's second son, Michael. This is autobiography, to be sure, but autobiography on a transpersonal, psychospiritual level. It extends coincidence into synchronicity and deepens the unconscious implications of the story. It cannot be overlooked, of course, that this particular dream type—the overwhelming of the dreamer by a towering wave—is a fairly common manifestation of anxiety and would probably be seen as such by a psychologist. But, as with the Trianon adventure and Dunne's theory, the importance of the dream to Tolkien's fiction is not its "real" meaning (if such can ever be determined) but its effect on his imagination.

A problem arises, however, when we move from autobiography, whether written consciously or unconsciously, to the mechanics of narrative. Dream as true vision, or as the revelation of the personal or the collective unconscious, is one thing, and it is clear that here Tolkien was comfortable with such use of dream narrative. But dream as a narrative frame is quite another thing, and in "On Fairy-Stories" he expressed serious reservations about it. The problem, as Tolkien saw it, was not with the dream per se—that is itself valid—but with the awakening, with the realization that it *was* a dream, a vision, not a waking reality. He was, of course, writing directly and specifically about fairy-stories, but his opinions come out of a life of thought about literature in general, and mythic literature in particular, and would certainly have had an immediate bearing on his own work. Of dream as frame he said:

> At the least, even if the reported dream was in other respects itself a fairy-story, I would condemn the whole as gravely defective: like a good picture in a disfiguring frame. It is true that Dream is not unconnected with Faërie. In dreams strange powers of the mind may be unlocked. In some of them a man may for a space wield the power of Faërie, that power which, even as it conceives the story, causes it to take living form and colour before the eyes. A real dream may indeed sometimes be a fairy-story of almost elvish ease and skill—while it is being dreamed. But if a waking writer tells you that his tale is only a thing imagined in his sleep, he cheats deliberately the primal desire at the heart of Faërie: the realization, independent of the conceiving mind, of imagined wonder. ("On Fairy-Stories" 116)

The fact of waking wraps an explanatory frame around the very element that must remain unexplained—the experience of enchantment—instead of allowing it to stand on its own.

A few authors have been able to bridge the gap and have given precedent for Tolkien's own efforts. George MacDonald was one. W. H. Auden praised MacDonald's dream novels *Phantastes* and *Lilith* for their avoidance of "incoherence and mechanical allegory," the two extremes that he called "The Scylla and Charybdis of Dream Literature" (vi). This is especially true in an age when the dream can no longer be a valid allegorical vision, as it was in the Middle Ages, but must be looked at psychologically as the encoded revelations of the personal unconscious. Few writers can navigate between the rigidity of allegory and the incoherence of the unconscious and manage to avoid both, as MacDonald was able to do.

A. N. Wilson wrote of MacDonald that he was "the missing link between Spenser's *Faerie Queen* and the writings of Freud and Jung":

> [MacDonald] seems to have had the supreme gift, in his fairy stories, of writing unselfconsciously about the subconscious: not only describing what it is like to be in a subconscious dream-state, but also, without any spelling-out of the obvious, highlighting the meaning of these mentally subterranean journeyings. One of MacDonald's favourite sayings came from Novalis: "Our life is no dream, but it ought to become one, and perhaps will." He is the great chronicler of the inner life, the mapper-out of what takes place when the subconscious is allowed free range and—in dream or fantasy—tell us stories about ourselves which with our conscious minds we would not necessarily understand or might not be strong enough to bear. (46)

This sounds easy, but it isn't. Only a very few writers can meld the conscious and the unconscious as smoothly and seamlessly as the actual dreaming mind. Lewis Carroll could do it. Dostoevsky could do it. George MacDonald could do it, and in this connection both his commentators, Auden and Wilson, might well have mentioned that he does it as well or better in his two children's romances, *The Princess and the Goblin* and *At the Back of the North Wind*, than in his adult novels (with the latter book in particular doing an especially good job of contrasting the spiritual dullness of waking life with the spiritual reality of dream-vision).

Another who could achieve this blend of conscious and unconscious was David Lindsay, whose *Voyage to Arcturus*, admired by both Tolkien and Lewis, takes dream vision to its uttermost and may be one of the most fantastical books ever written. "I dream with open eyes," says one character at the beginning of the book, "and others see my dreams" (2). The actual truth of this is not made apparent until the final pages of the story, when the whole of the story and its central character, the vigorous, incarnate, and embodied Maskull, are revealed as the waking dream of the real hero, Nightspore, who represents the struggling human soul. Having journeyed into wakefulness, Nightspore realizes that he must do it all over, must reenter the dream state and make the dream journey yet again.

Tolkien learned from these masters, and both their skill and their metaphysics informed his own work. Knowledge of his reservations about dream as the frame for fantasy makes it an education in authorial sleight-of-hand to see with what quiet skill Tolkien, rather like Carroll having Alice follow the White Rabbit, eases the dream aspect of *The Lost Road* into the reader's consciousness—or rather, eases the reader's conscious unconsciously into the enchantment of the dream. Tolkien's story lacks Carroll's edge-of-madness whimsy and is closer to the visionary ultrareality of MacDonald.

What Tolkien most disliked, and was particularly careful to avoid, was the rude awakening, the usual abrupt reentry into the real world, that dispels the magic. Carroll's Alice awakes to a scurry of leaves and evening coming on and runs home to tea. Keats's knight-at-arms, deserted by La Belle Dame sans Merci, awakes alone and bereft "on the cold hill's side." The waking reality calls the dream into question. Unlike Carroll and Keats, Tolkien wanted something subtler, a dream that would call the waking reality into question, as do the deeper reflections of MacDonald's dream novels. And so it does. Tolkien's dream narrative manages to suggest dream without identifying it, as if Carroll had left Alice down the rabbit hole.

Dream is handled in two ways in *The Lost Road*, and we must distinguish between them before we look at how they are related. The first way is both the most apparent and the least significant. This is the part of the story in which waking characters report or refer to dreams they have had and thus convey necessary information to both characters and readers. The second way, in which dream becomes itself a narrative technique, deliberately blurs the distinction between dream and waking and between past and present realities. But there is no clear signal of this blurring as the story begins in present reality, with Oswin Errol going into the garden in search of his son. His repeated calls are at first unanswered, until he hears "a young voice" sounding like "someone asleep or just awakened." Alboin is lying outstretched on a wall overlooking the sea, and Oswin comments that he "must be deaf or dreaming" (*Lost Road* 36). In its first context this appears to be no more than a parental complaint, a throwaway comment. But at the opening of chapter 3 in Númenor the same scene and lines are repeated with only slight variation by another father-son pair, Elendil and his son Herendil.

And now each father's comment that his son is dreaming (both nearly the same age and both stretched out on sea walls) takes on new significance, becoming, in fact, a link. We are not told, then or later, whether they really are dreaming or not (both boys insist they are awake). Nor are we told what they dream. But we know of Alboin that he dreams a lot and that his dreams take him into strange country. The similarity in the episodes is too close to be accidental, and the echoes of dialogue between the two convey the impression of parallel or overlapping time, of two events occurring simultaneously in two apparently different worlds. Beyond the repetition of scene and character and dialogue, the emphasis in both episodes on the boys' dreaming suggests the possibility that each may be dreaming the other. And in that case, we have been in a dream from the beginning of the story, and the whole of the story is to be seen as dreamed reality.

From here it is only a small step to see it as the sort of dream experience described by Dunne in which Observer 2 can range freely from past to future (Field 2) while Observer 1, whose field is limited to the present, sleeps. If that is the case, Tolkien's projected amplification of the structure to include other father-son pairs and other tales extends but does not alter the concept. This is not to suggest that *An Experiment with Time* was the sole inspiration for *The Lost Road*, or that Tolkien set out to write a time-travel story in order to illustrate Dunne's theory. But given the fact that Tolkien had read Dunne, it seems more than possible that Dunne's theory and Tolkien's line of thinking intersected, and that the one offered the other a viable theoretical structure for the time-travel story whose genesis was the conversation with Lewis and whose antecedents stretched back to the dawn of Tolkien's mythology.

The structure of the narrative does not establish the dream connection until the appearance of Herendil in chapter 3. What, then, is the meaning of chapter 1's title, "A Step Forward: Young Alboin"? In what sense and for whom do the events recounted constitute a step forward? If they are simply the conversations between Alboin and his father Oswin, and/or Alboin's dreams of strange language and strange country, the title seems to make little sense. But if both chapter title and chapter are to foreshadow the dreaming

Herendil, if *his* is a step forward through time and dream into Alboin's present memory—though not perceived as such until chapter 3—then the title does make sense. It becomes a fictive demonstration of Dunne's theory as described in *An Experiment with Time*, turning it from principle to practice and underscoring the Field 2/Time 2 dream structure of the narrative.

Dream memory and road motif work together. In chapter 2 Alboin is poised on the threshold of the journey back to Númenor. In Tolkien's projected revision, whereby the story was extended by the inclusion of the other tales, the third chapter was to have been the story of the Anglo-Saxon incarnation of the father-son pair and was to be titled "A Step Backward: Ælfwine and Eadwine." Christopher Tolkien's considered opinion is that the titles for chapters 1 and 2 were added at this time, when this second version was taking shape. The repetition of the word "steps" in chapters 1 and 3—both forward and backward—fits with the road motif. Within the dream memory, as in Dunne's theory, the road stretches in both directions, with stops along the way.

The projected chapter 3 was part of a revised outline for the structure of the book and would have included, in addition to the Anglo-Saxon episode, the list of episodes sent by Tolkien to Allen and Unwin: "the Irish legend of Tuatha-de-Danaan—and oldest man in the world"; "Prehistoric North: old kings found buried in the ice"; "Beleriand"; "Elendil and Herendil in Númenor." Of these the only one that went beyond outline was the Anglo-Saxon episode, which after "some very rough notes and abandoned beginnings," according to Christopher Tolkien, developed into an actual, though (again) uncompleted, narrative. It begins as Ælfwine awakens on a bench in an Anglo-Saxon hall. Here it is notable that he "felt he had been dreaming; and for a moment the English speech about him sounded strange" (*Lost Road* 83). It seems clear that Ælfwine's awakening from a dream was to be coincident with the falling asleep of his Alboin counterpart, and that sleep and dream, as before, were to be the vehicles of transition from one time to another.

Tolkien's handling of the transition both in this unfinished fragment and in the completed chapters of the earlier version is of a piece with his stated position on dream and fantasy. Dream does not frame the story; rather, it inhabits it. In chapter 1 Alboin has dreams of an earlier reality. He is the first in the narrative to speak the line about the eagles of the Lord of the West, as he stands looking out to sea. Dark clouds are coming up over the sunset, "stretching huge wings southward and northward, threatening the land. 'They look like the eagles of the Lord of the West, coming upon Númenor,' Alboin said aloud, and he wondered why" (38). Note that it is possible for Alboin to remember the words, envisioned by Tolkien as the links between the episodes, without understanding them, possible for him to be who he is—that is, it is possible for him to have a Númenorean identity—without being aware of it.

In chapter 2 Alboin—no longer "Young Alboin" but now grown and himself the father of a son, Audoin—falls asleep in his chair. It is not said that he is dreaming, only that he passes "out of the waking world." In this sleeping state, in "a wide, shadowy place," he hears a voice and sees a figure whose face reminds him of his father. "I am with you," says the figure. "I was of Númenor, the father of many fathers before you. I am Elendil, that is in Eressëan 'Elf-friend,' and many have been called so since." The connection is clear. But Elendil's statement that he is "with" Alboin seems vague. With him how? With him where? Part of his blood and ancestry as "the father of many fathers before him," certainly, but also as part of his collective memory, and most certainly of his dreaming.

I suggest that in this state the figure of Elendil operates as what Dunne called the ultimate observer, within whom the other observing consciousnesses are contained. Dunne's discussion of the ultimate observer's participation in fields of observation clarifies the idea:

It is not surprising that [analysis] has brought to light no law which *compels* the ultimate observer to direct his attention to any particular phenomenon in any particular field. That such attention is, as a matter of plain fact, habitually directed during waking moments to phenomena in Field 1 is obvious enough; but the theory leaves us with habit as the only compulsion in the matter. . . . But habit keeps [attention] in field 1, and in that field all images relate to the past. Nevertheless, the habit was no *law*. It could be overcome. By determinedly refusing to attend to those readily proffered images, attention in field 1 could be completely discontinued. And, in the rare instances when this was successfully effected, attention in field 2 was free to slip away along associational tracks extending elsewhere than in the Time 1 "present moment." (195–96)

The conversation that takes place between the dreaming Alboin and what I will call his Elendil self—Dunne's ultimate observer—uses language so like that of Dunne and refers to concepts so similar that it is difficult not to see a direct connection. Elendil speaks first, addressing Alboin:

"You may have your desire."

"What desire?"

"The long-hidden and the half-spoken. To go back."

"But that cannot be, even if I wish it. It is against the law."

"It is against the *rule*. Laws are commands upon the will and are binding. Rules are conditions; they may have exceptions."

"But are there ever any exceptions?"

"Rules may be strict, yet they are the means, not the ends, of government. There are exceptions . . . . To each, under the rule, some unique fate is given, and he is excepted from that which is a rule to others. I ask if you would have your desire?"

"I would."

"You do not ask how, or upon what conditions?"

"I do not suppose I should understand how, and it does not seem to me necessary. We go forward as a rule, but we do not know how." (*Lost Road* 48)

The similarity between the ideas presented in this dialogue and those expressed in Dunne's discussion quoted above scarcely needs pointing out. In each text the apparently ineluctable forward motion of time is called into question by a distinction between law and something less binding. In Dunne it is *habit*; in Tolkien it is *rule*. Further, the point is established in both arguments that whatever the mechanism, whether habit or rule, it can be changed. The premise of Tolkien's intellectual engagement with Dunne's ideas is supported by his own jotted comments on the passage from Dunne's book just cited: "What does 'observer (?at infinity)' think of our efforts to understand Exp. with Time?" And further: "More than *habit* required?"

The dialogue between Elendil and Alboin supplies Tolkien's answers to his own questions. If we read it in the light of his jottings, we may imagine that Elendil speaks as the "observer (?at infinity)" and Alboin, in his protests about the impossibility of going back in time, speaks to "our efforts to understand Exp. with Time" as it bears on the narrative. Further, Tolkien's replacement of the word "rule" for Dunne's word "habit" seems to answer his own jotted question: "More than *habit* required?"

A point of importance in both texts is that the conventional perception of the forward movement of time is reduced from the status of law to that of custom, whether imposed from without, as with a rule, or developed from within, as with a habit. But just here is where the difference between Tolkien and Dunne, rather than the similarity, becomes noticeable. For Dunne the capacity to move around in time is as easy as breaking a habit; we are habituated to the view of time as forward-moving, but we are not bound by it. For Tolkien, at least in the context of the story, time-travel is not available on those terms. It is not the result of an effort of will to overcome habit but is something "given," conferred on selected individuals as an exception to a rule. "We go forward, *as a rule*," says Alboin, "but we do not know how" (emphasis added). The implication is that we assume a forward motion of time, without examining by what agency this is contrived. If we can go forward, we may also go backward, but we go in neither direction through our own striving or at our own volition.

As Tolkien left it, the English chapters of the story broke off at a point where Audoin, returning from a long walk with the intention of telling Alboin about his own Dreams, sees his father sitting by the fire, apparently (the text specifies that "He seemed") asleep. The narrative continues:

> Audoin was creeping out of the room, heavy with disappointment. . . . As he reached the door, he thought he heard the chair creak, and then his father's voice (far away and rather strange in tone) murmuring something: it sounded like *herendil*.
>
> He was used to odd words and names slipping out in a murmur from his father. . . . He turned back hopefully.
>
> "Good night!" said Alboin. "Sleep well, Herendil. We start when the summons comes." Then his head fell back against the chair.

"Dreaming," thought Audoin. "Good night!"

And he went out, and stepped into sudden darkness. (*Lost Road* 52–53)

Since this is followed immediately by the first Númenorean chapter, the obvious intent of the sequence is to show that Audoin has stepped into another time. We know already that Alboin has accepted Elendil's invitation for himself and Audoin to go back. Alboin's "We start when the summons comes," coupled with Audoin's step into darkness is clearly meant to be the transition from one world to another.

The next chapter will introduce Elendil and Herendil, into whose consciousness Alboin and Audoin will have entered. Tolkien's subsequent decision to postpone the Númenorean episode to the end and to interpose other time-travel sequences would not have changed the nature of the transition, only the names and times. Instead of Elendil and Herendil, his travelers would have awakened (as in the fragment cited) into the Anglo-Saxon Ælfwine and Eadwine and then presumably worked their way back through the times and episodes sketched out, finally arriving at Elendil and Herendil and the Downfall of Númenor. A note by Christopher Tolkien gives a revealing sidelight on the nature of the transition and its implications: "Since the Númenorean episode was left unfinished, this is a convenient point to mention an interesting note that my father presumably wrote while it was in progress. This says that when the first 'adventure' (i.e. Númenor) is over 'Alboin is still precisely in his chair and Audoin just shutting the door'" (*Lost Road* 57).

Unlike the faërian time warp of Mary Rose or Rip van Winkle, whose moments in fairy-land cost them (though each in a different way) days and years of their real lives, the whole adventure in Númenor, which might possibly encompass days or even weeks of Númenorean time, takes no time at all out of the present-day lives of Alboin and Audoin. This same approach was used years later by C. S. Lewis in his *Chronicles of Narnia*. The whole adventure of the first book in that series, *The Lion, the Witch, and the Wardrobe*, occurs within the single moment in which the four children dodge into the empty room and into the wardrobe to escape the housekeeper, who is showing a party of sightseers around the house.

When they emerge from the wardrobe after all their time in Narnia, the housekeeper and visitors are still approaching.

There are other precedents for this than fairy tale and folktale. On a more psychologically realistic level, this is precisely the way dreams operate. The dream time stretches out to cover apparently endless time and space within the unconscious processes of the dreamer during what to the conscious observer are the documentably brief intervals of dreaming sleep. And on a technical level this is precisely the operational principle of Dunne's theory, which provides for the dream to free the dreamer's awareness and enable it to move freely over the field of time. Observer 2 can go anywhere, for any length of time, while Observer 1 sleeps on, fixed in one place and caught in one time.

Tolkien's expanded outline, with its interpolation of a multiplicity of other episodes, would have complicated but not markedly distorted this concept. Too little of the story is available for us fairly to imagine, let alone experience, how effective his design would have been had he stayed with it and carried it through. All the evidence points to the figure called Ælfwine—"Elf-friend" in all its various forms—as representing the unifying consciousness that was to tie the whole, far-flung enterprise together. Whether as Tolkien would have used it, that consciousness could have successfully combined his modern-day Errols with actual historic Lombards and Anglo-Saxons, mythic Tuatha de Danaan, legendary prehistoric Ice Age men, and wholly fictional Númenoreans we shall never know. It might not have come off. But then again, it might have, and the result would have been time-travel on an epic scale, a dream of myth and history combined as Tolkien saw them as being, as they might once have been.

But the project was dropped when it was scarcely more than well-begun, and that was the end of that idea for quite a while. First of all, the manuscript of *The Hobbit*, which according to Humphrey Carpenter had been abandoned uncompleted, was submitted to Allen & Unwin in 1936. Requested to finish it so that it could be considered for publication, Tolkien set again to work. On August 10, 1936, he wrote, "*The Hobbit* is now nearly finished, and the publishers clamouring for it" (Carpenter 180). After a favorable review by Stanley Unwin's ten-year-old son Rayner, the book was accepted.

But that led to even more work, not so much of a creative as of a mechanical and technical nature. Carpenter paints a picture of "difficulties and disappointments," of the "machinations and occasionally the downright incompetence of publishers and printers" (181). The redrawing of the maps, the checking and altering of the proofs were done with Tolkien's painstaking, time-consuming thoroughness. The book was published on September 21, 1937, and a few weeks later Tolkien met with Stanley Unwin to discuss a possible successor. He submitted to Allen & Unwin several short narratives, *Mr. Bliss, Farmer Giles of Ham,* "Roverandom," as well as the multiple texts of the Silmarillion and chapters of *The Lost Road.* None was quite what the publishers were looking for, which was essentially more about Hobbits. Of *The Lost Road* the Allen & Unwin reader reported that it was "a hopeless proposition," though it was "immensely interesting as the revelation of the personal enthusiasms of a very unusual mind" containing "passages of beautiful descriptive prose." The conclusion was that on the whole it would be "difficult to imagine this novel when completed receiving any sort of recognition except in academic circles" (Hammond 265). The publishers' lack of interest in his time-travel story, combined with their request for more Hobbits, may well have prompted Tolkien to drop the project, for during the next seven years his creative powers were bent to the "new *Hobbit*" which became *The Lord of the Rings.* Nevertheless, the time-travel idea lay in the back of his mind, and when he came to a halting place in the new book, it surfaced again.

Over a Bridge of Time 4

In Faërian drama you are in a dream
that some other mind is weaving.
—"On Fairy-Stories"

In a letter to an inquiring reader of *The Lord of the Rings* Tolkien
stated that "The real theme for me is about something much more
permanent and difficult [than war]: Death and Immortality, the
mystery of the love of the world in the hearts of a race 'doomed'
to leave and seemingly lose it; the anguish in the hearts of a race
'doomed' not to leave it, until its whole evil-aroused story is complete" (*Letters* 246).

So portentous a theme is not immediately apparent to someone
reading *The Lord of the Rings* for the first time, and perhaps not
even the second or third time. But a careful look will reveal evidence to support Tolkien's statement, though that evidence is sometimes buried, often ambiguous, and occasionally deliberately obscured. Toward the end of *The Fellowship of the Ring*, Sam, Frodo,
Legolas, and Aragorn—two Hobbits, an Elf, and a Man—have a
conversation about time (404–5). It is a small episode, hardly two
pages in length, and in relation to the plot it is unimportant. But in
relation to the theme described above of Death and Immortality,
and to Tolkien's use of time to explore and develop that theme, it
looms large and deserves a close examination.

The situation is this: the Company is on its way down the Great River. The time is a week after their farewell to Galadriel and the Elves of Lórien. A puzzled Sam Gamgee is counting on his fingers in an effort to reconcile his recollection with present observation. He has just seen a new moon in the evening sky and remembers very clearly that the moon was on the wane when they came to Lórien. How much time can have passed between the two moons? The narrative supports his memory, for it describes a "fast-waning moon" as the Fellowship flees Moria and a "sickle moon" when they arrive in Lórien the following night. And now, says Sam, quite bewildered, "up pops a New Moon as thin as a nail-paring, as if we had never stayed no time in the Elven country."

It would be Sam who would notice something like this, that earthbound gardener whose work is tied to the rhythms of time. And it would be Sam of all the Company who would want to make the reckoning come out right. "Anyone would think," he exclaims with some heat, "that time did not count in there!" This is precisely the issue, both of the ensuing debate and of the question of time in Tolkien's world. Either more time has passed than Sam can account for, or else no time has passed at all. Either way, Tolkien finds it important enough to call to our attention, and we must ask ourselves—why? The answer is there, but buried, and will take some digging to bring to light.

Two phrases in Sam's outburst deserve special attention: "in there," and "time did not count." The phrase "in there" seems at first like a throwaway, just what anyone would say about a place in the woods. But it immediately establishes a contrast with an implied "out here" and has the effect of setting Lórien off from the rest of the world. Just as important is the question of whether or not time "counts" in Elven country. If it does count there is no need to raise the question. If it doesn't count we must wonder why not. Sam's outburst fits his character, but to be effective, his frustration must be to some purpose, and that purpose is not immediately, or even eventually, obvious. Moreover, the word "count" is ambiguous. It could mean "count" in the sense of "matter"—that is, time does not count in Lórien because it flies when you're having fun—or it could mean "count" in the sense of "add up." The word could mean both, of course, and perhaps it does. But if that is the case, we must be prepared for equal ambiguity in the explanation.

Tolkien's narrative gives a variety of answers, all of them plausible, each a little different from the others. The nature of Lórien is the crux of the question, and Lórien is hard to pin down. Without doubt it is meant to be a real place. It is on the map. Travelers arrive by the road and on their two feet. And yet it is extraordinary in some way. It is isolated from the ordinary world not just by its inaccessibility, but also by that indescribable quality that Sam calls Elven magic and that Tolkien called Faërie—an air of enchantment, an atmosphere, an ambiance. We are told that Lórien has a strange reputation, that people are afraid to go in for fear they will be changed when they come out. It is most certainly, in some indefinable but recognizable respect, "in there." But until Sam raises the question there is little to suggest that "in there" is outside natural law.

And yet there are anomalies, clues, shifts of perception unobtrusively woven into the narrative that, when assembled, evoke echoes of other experiences, other treatments of time, and suggest that there is a difference. Frodo is the first to feel it. When he first enters Lórien it is plain that the quality of his experience changes: "As soon as he set foot upon the far bank of Silverlode, a strange feeling had come upon him, and it deepened as he walked on into the Naith: it seemed to him that he had stepped over a bridge of time into a corner of the Elder Days, and was now walking in a world that was no more. In Rivendell there was a memory of ancient things; in Lórien the ancient things still lived on in the waking world" (*Fellowship* 364). A parallel but more explicit passage from an earlier draft reads: "As soon as they pass Silverlode into Angle Frodo has a curious sense of walking in an older world—unshadowed." The draft goes on to note that "Evil had been heard of . . . but it had not yet stained or dimmed the air," and that "it was winter, but nothing was dead, only in a phase of beauty" and "there was no smell of decay" (*Treason* 241). The phrase "an older world" in place of "Elder Days" and the fact that in a dead season—winter—nothing is dead and that in a wood full of fallen leaves there is no decay mark Lórien as a type of Eden, a world before Evil—though it has been heard of—has yet stained the air. This is what Mircea Eliade calls *"illo tempore," "that time,"* that high and far-off mythic time "in the beginning." Christopher Tolkien contrasts this with the published passage in *The Fellowship*, where, as he notes, "the 'undecaying' nature of Lothlórien is expressed in terms less immediate" (*Treason* 241). Tolkien has refined and tempered the language to suggest a meaning rather than to state one.

But overt or covert, the quality of Frodo's sensations has always to do with his sense of the past. This sense of having passed a barrier, the image of time as a bridge, the sense of being "in a world that was no more," all these recall the sensations experienced by Henry James's time-traveler and Balderstone's dramatic counterpart Peter Standish; they evoke the perceptions reported by the ladies of the Trianon, their feelings of having crossed over into another time, of experiencing things as they used to be. Once established as something peculiar to Lórien, this quality of experience is sustained throughout the Company's stay there. Indeed, it is elaborated. At the hill of Cerin Amroth Frodo feels that he is "in a timeless land that did not fade or change or fall into forgetfulness. When he had gone and passed again into the outer world, still Frodo the wanderer from the Shire would walk there, upon the grass among the *elanor* and *niphredil* in fair Lothlórien" (*Fellowship* 365–66).

This seems at first to be a simple imaging of Frodo's desire to stay in Lórien. Taken literally, however, the passage conveys a more complex meaning, actualizing Dunne's theory of time as static field rather than linear progression. Though the narrow concept of the observer in Field 1 will perceive Frodo as leaving Lórien and moving on, the wider omnichronous awareness of Observer 2, or "observer at infinity," with a wider field of time to survey will retain the impress of Frodo's presence in Lórien even after his immediate experience takes him beyond it. This concept is extended, a few paragraphs later, to include Aragorn. Catching sight of Aragorn standing on the hill, Frodo sees that "He was wrapped in some fair memory: and as Frodo looked at him he knew that he [Aragorn] beheld things as they once had been in this same place" (*Fellowship* 366). The same complexity of perception is conveyed here, though Aragorn's vision connects him with the past rather than the future, with "things as they once had been in this same place." But the principle is the same. Aragorn is in the position of Observer 2; he is in two places at once, not in memory merely, but in his present field of attention. Or rather, he is experiencing one place at (apparently) two different times through the multiple awareness of Observer 2. A further elaboration of the concept is to be seen in Frodo, who, as he looks at Aragorn and comprehends his dual experience, becomes a kind of third observer watching Observer 2.

"Memory." "A world that was no more." "A timeless land." "Things as they once had been." Every carefully wrought phrase suggests that Lórien is a refuge from linear time, an island where the past still somehow exists in the present. Treebeard puts it less lyrically and more bluntly:

> *Laurelindórenan!* That is what the Elves used to call it, but now they make the name shorter: *Lothlórien* they call it. Perhaps they are right: maybe it is fading, not growing. Land of the Valley of the Singing Gold, that was it, once upon a time. Now it is the Dreamflower. Ah well! But it is a queer place, and not for just anyone to venture in. I am surprised that you ever got out, but much more surprised that you ever got in. That has not happened to strangers for many a year. It is a queer land. . . . They are falling rather behind the world in there, I guess . . . . Neither this country, nor anything else outside the Golden Wood, is what it was when Celeborn was young. (*Two Towers* 70)

"A queer place." Hard to get out of but even harder to get into. "Fading, not growing." "Falling rather behind the world." No doubt about it. However pleasant it may be, experience in Lórien is of a different order from the rest and respite that the Hobbits got in the house of Tom Bombadil or from their long recovery from stress in the House of Elrond. Sam remarks, "It's wonderfully quiet here. Nothing seems to be going on and nobody seems to want it to" (*Fellowship* 376). How right he is. And for as long as they are in Lórien (and that is hard to determine, for them as well as for the reader) the Company feels this sense of escape from the world, of an unexpected pause, of time-out. We are told that they "remained some days in Lórien, so far as they could tell or remember" (373), and yet "they could not count the days and nights they had passed there" (386). Tolkien is making sure we get the point without telling us what it is.

Furthermore, the sensations experienced by the Company at their departure from Lórien emphasize the atmosphere of "pastness" and contrast this with their sense of a return to the present and of an actual physical progress into the future. These impressions are not unlike the images used by Tolkien in his note on

"Elvish time" to convey the perceptual and linguistic space-time confusion of ordinary language. Recall his citation of the use of both *after* and *before* to refer to the future, his example of human lives as "an endless column moving forward" wherein those born after us are *behind* and *follow* us, yet his comment that it is "also as if though facing the future we were walking backwards and our children and heirs were ahead of us and will in each generation go further forwards into the future than we."

Now look at the perceptions of those about to leave Lórien. As the Company and the Elves picnic on the hythe just before they depart, Galadriel appears to Frodo to be "present and yet remote, a living vision of that which has already been left far behind by the flowing streams of Time." Though she is a presence out of the past *before* their time, she nevertheless appears to be *behind* the Company as they move out and away into the "flowing stream." As they fall in ahead of her she drops back into the past. And when they are launched and out in the current,[1] Galadriel watches from the shore: "As they passed her they turned and their eyes watched her slowly floating away from them. For so it seemed to them: Lórien was slipping backward, like a bright ship masted with enchanted trees, sailing on to forgotten shores, while they sat helpless upon the margin of the grey and leafless world" (*Fellowship* 393). The earliest manuscript version of this last line, although shorter and terser, has the same image: "Lórien was slipping backward like a green vessel masted with trees sailing to forgotten shores, while they were cast again on the grey, never-halting water of time" (*Treason* 284).[2] This expresses much the same idea, but the metaphor is fuzzy, and Tolkien did well to fix it. The replacement of "never-halting water of time" with "leafless world" clarifies the image. Otherwise the green vessel Lórien is sailing (but on what?) to forgotten shores, while the Company is also sailing on the water of time, which is different. Nonetheless, the original phrase made clear what its replacement does not, that the river is equated with time and that the Company is once again *in* time and *outside* Lórien.

Just as important, however, is the surreal quality of the whole picture, which is central to Tolkien's intent. The Company is on the water, moving. Galadriel is on the shore and still. Yet they feel as if it is *she* who is moving away from *them*. This is precisely the reverse of Dunne's illustration of the two trains in the station. In

Dunne's example the observer is at rest but experiences the illusion of motion, whereas here the observer is in motion but experiences the illusion of being at rest. The point in both instances is that the perception is dependent on the observer's field of attention.

Tolkien's jotted comment on the relevant passage in *An Experiment with Time* shows his awareness of the concept: "Note that the idea of motion is instinctive and does not depend on 'rational' thought about evidence. The sensation of motion can be dispelled and recaptured in the train experiment, even though intellectually we *know* we are not moving. I have even waited in such circumstances for the sensation, *knowing* that I was not going to move." This is precisely the Company's experience when they see Galadriel "floating away" and Lórien "slipping backward." They know that this is not the case yet feel (not depending "on rational thought about evidence") that it is the case. Tolkien has here successfully used the language of space in the service of a particular concept of time, for Lórien, while remaining physically motionless, is yet temporally "sailing on to forgotten shores," moving not through space but through time. Or perhaps in Dunne's terms, not through time but through a "field of attention."

All evidence indicates that not until completion of what Christopher Tolkien calls the fourth phase of the first part of *The Lord of the Rings*, when the story had been rewritten into something like its final form and the Company had left Rivendell, did any mention of Lothlórien enter the text. The first appearance of the name occurs in a draft of "The Ring Goes South," part of an extended advance in the narrative that Christopher Tolkien has dated as subsequent to August 1940 (*Treason* 67). Here an exchange between Gimli and Gandalf about the Mirrormere ends with Gandalf saying "We must go down the Morthond into the woods of Lothlórien." In *The Fellowship* as published this was changed to "into the secret woods," but the concept of Lórien had entered Middle-Earth (*Treason* 167), and with it the opportunity for this new story to explore, like its predecessor *The Lost Road*, the nature of time.

There is no doubt that the exploration owed something to Tolkien's previous work on *The Lost Road*. But it also was predicated on the nature of Elves as Tolkien envisioned them in the Silmarillion. The two major races of his mythology, Elves and Men, embody alternative aspects of and attitudes toward time. In the earliest version of his creation story "The Ainulindalë" (the Music of the Ainur), the creator-figure Ilúvatar declares that "The Children of Men dwell only a short time in the world alive, yet do not perish utterly for ever, whereas the Eldar [the Elves] dwell till the Great End [*draft text reads:* "whereas the Eldar dwell for ever"] unless they be slain or waste in grief" (*Lost Tales I* 59, 61). This passage and the concept it embodies change very little from this earliest version written between 1918 and 1920 to the text as published in *The Silmarillion,* which reads:

> the Children of Men dwell only a short space in the world alive, and are not bound to it, and depart soon whither the Elves know not. Whereas the Elves remain until the end of days, and their love of the Earth and all the world is more single and more poignant therefore. . . . For the Elves die not till the world does. . . . But the sons of Men die indeed, and leave the world. . . . Death is their fate, the gift of Ilúvatar, which as Time wears, even the Powers shall envy. (41–42)

The concept is not just philosophically complex; it is also theologically troublesome in its relationship to its author's personal belief. Tolkien was a devout and orthodox Catholic whose religion was founded on the affirmation of victory over death and the promise that all men shall live in Christ. Yet here he seems to be subverting or contradicting his own faith by presenting death as the positive and its opposite, continued life, as the negative. The problem is more apparent than real, however, for Tolkien is contrasting his fictive concept of death with an immortality that, for all its seeming attractions, is finally mere longevity, certainly not the eternal life promised in the Gospels. Hints that he envisioned some sort of spiritual apotheosis that would encompass the mystery of what happens to his Men after death are to be found in scattered references to the Second Music, "when the songs of the Ainur shall be sung aright" and the Children of Ilúvatar shall join in the singing.

It can be seen, then, that the period spent by the Fellowship in Lórien represents a significant intersection of the attitudes toward time of Elves and Men. The incursion of Men (and their smaller relatives Hobbits) into a land inhabited by Elves and permeated by their relationship to time was an opportunity for Tolkien to compare and contrast those attitudes and to explore their basis in experience and their relationship to one another within the same world.

Recall the departing Company's vision of Galadriel slipping backward. The effect of all this is to convey an impression of two kinds of time. One, that of Lórien itself, is of time stopped, the pristine moment caught and held in crystalline suspension, time-out. The other, as the Company looks back at Lórien, is of time leaving itself behind. No wonder Sam is confused. No wonder he has trouble believing the evidence of his senses. Neither the reader nor Sam can tell if Lórien's special quality of timelessness is a quality only or whether it has some kind of actual reality. The debate that Sam's outburst sets off, a discussion about time in Lórien among himself, Frodo, Aragorn, and Legolas, is addressed to this very question. But since no reliable omniscient narrator has the final word, since each answer comes from the point of view of and expresses the perception held by the species of the particular character speaking, the debate is never satisfactorily settled.

Frodo has an important role in the debate, one commensurate with his central position in the story and with his role as a Hobbit and an Elf-friend. Tolkien made it clear that he intended Hobbits to be a subvariety of humankind, not a different species altogether. Therefore, Frodo speaks to some degree for both Men and Hobbits. Taken in the context of the sequential relationship between *The Lord of the Rings* and *The Lost Road*, the epithet "Elf-friend," while it is a courtesy title informally bestowed by Gildor, recalls Tolkien's Ælfwine/Eriol character, the encompassing Field 2 observer and traveler through time. Thus Frodo is invested with associations that suggest that he may be unusually sensitive to the mood and ambiance of Lórien. Moreover, much of its timeless quality is conveyed to the reader through Frodo's perception. In the debate, he takes Sam's statement that "time didn't count" literally and ventures an explanation. "In that land, maybe," he proposes, "we were in a time that has elsewhere long gone by. It was not, I think, until Silverlode bore us back to Anduin that we returned to the time that flows through mortal lands" (*Fellowship* 404).

Much is suggested by this. For one thing, his phrase "mortal lands" implies a contrast with immortal—that is, Elven—lands, just as Sam's "in there" implies an "out here." For another thing, the image of time as a river carries a weight of metaphoric connotation. Although it seems to be Frodo's contribution to the conversation, the concept is not new to the story. Tolkien first tried it out in the rejected passage in which the river is referred to as the "never-halting water of time." In the text as published it has already been mentioned by Legolas. As they are departing Lórien, Gimli breaks down in tears at his loss of Galadriel. "Alas for Gimli son of Gloin!" he cries, mourning his bereavement. "Alas for us all!" replies Legolas. "And for all that walk the world in these afterdays. For such is the way of it: to find and lose, as it seems to those whose boat is on the running stream" (*Fellowship* 395). It is no accident, moreover, that this conversation is held on a river, thus physically proximating the actuality of water to what appears to be the metaphor of time.

The familiarity of the image slides the actual import of both Legolas's and Frodo's words past the conscious level of understanding; it evokes the old "time and tide" aphorism and the meaning embedded in such association. When Galadriel tells Frodo that if the Ring is destroyed "the tides of Time will sweep [Lórien] away" (380), we accept the metaphor before we examine it; the phrase seems dramatic but not actual. A closer look, however, reveals the true import: real Time will wash over Lórien and sweep away its timeless perfection. So then, in Frodo's explanation we have mortal, passing time—the river Anduin—and immortal, suspended time—Lórien, the Edenic world of the Elder Days, which Anduin bypasses. Frodo knows Paradise when he sees it, but leaving he knows also that he has lost it. Like Galadriel it is receding inexorably into an unrecoverable past as he and the Company, once more subject to the time that flows through mortal lands, move with equal inexorability into the future.

Just as familiar as the time-as-water motif is the *Mary Rose* time warp that Frodo's explanation implies, wherein the mortal is taken into the timeless fairy land for a spell, to be returned unchanged to a changed real world a month or a year or a lifetime later. One of Tolkien's objections to Barrie's handling of the theme, that it pushes the faërian element to the periphery, is answered here in his own treatment, in which he takes his mortals (and his readers) into the faërie land to show them the other side of the experience and then takes them out again to show the difference.

But here Legolas, a full-fledged Elf and thus presumably even better qualified than an Elf-friend to speak for Elven lands and times, disagrees. "Nay," he says, "time does not tarry ever, but change and growth is not in all things and places alike. For the Elves the world moves both very swift and very slow. Swift, because they themselves change little, and all else fleets by. Slow, because they do not count the running years, not for themselves" (404–5). His explanation introduces subjective experience as a valid measure of time. The issue is not *whether* time counts, but *how* it counts. Elves count time differently. Or rather, they do not count at all, "not for themselves." Mortal men may count the running years, but immortal Elves don't bother, anymore than mortal men would bother to count the swift-moving minutes that make up the daylong lifetime of a mayfly.

A note by Christopher Tolkien is apposite here for its bearing on Legolas's line about the running years. He writes, "The phrase as my father wrote it was 'because they *need* not count the running years,' but in copying I missed out the word *need*. Looking through my copy, but without consulting his own manuscript, he wrote in *do*, and *do* survives in *FR* (p. 405)" (*Treason* 366). The difference is minor, but "need" might have conveyed more precisely the options open to Elves in the matter of time. At any rate, it is clear that Legolas, and the Elves in general, see time as experience, as something contingent on perception, and thus as a variable rather than a constant. But, he concedes, "beneath the sun all things must wear to an end at last" (*Fellowship* 405). Swift or slow or changeable, however time may be seen to pass, it is real and it does pass, even in Lórien.

Frodo is not persuaded and sticks to his notion of an actual time difference between Lórien and the rest of the world. He argues that while, yes, all things do wear to an end, "the wearing is slow in Lórien." He offers Galadriel as the agent for this. "The power of the Lady is on it. Rich are the hours, though short they seem, in Caras Galadon, where Galadriel wears the Elven-ring" (405). This is a more equivocal view than his first answer, however, for on the one hand he concedes that time is tied to perception—rich hours *seem* short—but on the other attributes this not to perception but to the power of Galadriel and the Elven-ring. This raises more questions than it answers.

Aragorn, descended through many generations from the long-lived Númenoreans and with a faint strain of Half-elven blood, takes a middle position, reconciling both views. He agrees with Legolas that time has indeed passed, but explains to Sam and Frodo that they have experienced it like Elves rather than like Men. "In that land you lost your count," he tells Sam, echoing Sam's own word, but giving it a specific meaning. "There time flowed swiftly by us, as for the Elves. The old moon passed and a new moon waxed and waned in the world outside while we tarried there" (405). This seems reasonable; the Company has simply lost track of time but has not lost time itself. His phrase "the world outside," however, recalls Sam's "in there" and reinvokes the fairy tale concept of Lórien as set off from the ordinary world, perhaps with laws of its own. The question is still unresolved.

Seeking fact instead of opinion, we leave the narrative proper and turn to Appendix B at the end of *The Lord of the Rings*. Here we find support for Aragorn's position, noting that "The Tale of Years" records with reassuring exactness that the Fellowship arrived in Caras Galadon on January 17 and left Lórien by way of the Great River on February 16. They thus spent one month in Lórien. But if this is the case, why has Tolkien gone to such lengths to raise the question of time at all? Something about the differences in perception between Men and Elves seems to be worth our attention. At this point all we can know for certain is that something is at least qualitatively—if not quantitatively—different about time in Lórien but that in some way the two aspects are related. Unlike the treatment of time in *The Lost Road*, wherein there was to be a clearly plotted regression, more seems to be going on here than our author will allow to meet the eye, and for a writer known for scrupulous attention to the calendar, this raises new questions. What might be behind this apparent concern with the nature of time coupled with so deliberate an avoidance of a definite answer?

Some clues to the puzzle lie in the manuscript versions of the debate, the rough drafts, revisions, riders to revisions, fair copies, and final typescripts. Versions of this episode are multiple, and not easily disentangled, for it is plain that Tolkien was trying out a variety of approaches to what was evidently a problematic issue, one he found difficult to resolve. Christopher Tolkien's account of this stage of composition describes and organizes the tangle, and the reader is referred to his admirably ordered and lucid discussion in *The Treason of Isengard* (363–69 passim). "The conversation concerning Time in Lothlórien," he says, "was developed in several competing and overlapping riders, and when I came to make my copy my father evidently instructed me to set the passage out in variant forms." He gives an orderly sequence of the variants and presents a coherent picture of changes abandoned and changes made. His conclusion, after a look at the evidence, is that Tolkien, having tried out all the options (and the various chronologies he worked out show the pains he took), decided to have no time difference between Lórien and the rest of the world.

This decision notwithstanding, the question remains as to why the possibility was considered at all. The issue has as much to do with the nature of the problems encountered as it does with the final outcome. For the present purpose it will be useful to focus on the shifts and changes in order to get as clear a picture as possible of their directions and what they imply about Tolkien's use of time. This must necessarily overlap Christopher Tolkien's consideration of this same evidence but will have a somewhat different function and will seat the revisions in the context of the larger issue of time.

The early drafts of the time-debate underwent multiple and, as Christopher Tolkien says, competing reworkings and make clear what the published text does not: that time was a far more central issue to the whole of Tolkien's mythology than this rather low-key discussion among friends seems to suggest. Anyone who has done any writing and come up against a technical sticky place knows how many ideas can be tried and discarded before a final settlement is made. I do not propose to look at all the ideas Tolkien considered and rejected. But I hope that a fair sampling of the *kinds* of changes contemplated, the contrast between what was kept and what was discarded, will illuminate the issue.

Unpublished drafts of Sam's speech introducing the question try out a number of variations on the same idea. One has two penciled additions: the first, "in Lórien doesn't count"; and the second, "I mean that our time [*struck out:* here]" which Tolkien tried as alternates to Sam's outburst as published: "Anyone would think that time did not count in there!"[3] These are minor changes and do little to alter the general idea, though the addition of "our" to modify "time" suggests either that at this point there were two distinct time schemes or that Tolkien was considering an implied contrast between subjective and objective measurement. Other phrases tried out include "time slowed down" and "we came straight on" (that is, without ever stopping in Lórien). These seem so similar as to be nearly interchangeable. Note, however, that each phrase implies a change in experience. "Time slowed down" challenges the clock. "We came straight on" questions the duration of their stay. Either may have been too explicit, for both were discarded in favor of the more neutral and more ambiguous "time did not count," with "our" omitted.

Unlike Sam's, Frodo's speeches go through major changes. His reply to Sam about being in a time gone by and returning to mortal lands and mortal time is in one draft assigned to Aragorn (called Trotter in the manuscript; hereafter referred to as Trotter-Aragorn). This is a big shift. Since Trotter-Aragorn has been to Lórien before (as Frodo has not), his voice would give the speech more weight. Its reassignment to Frodo weakens the authority of that explanation. And while in all the draft versions Legolas's speech is the same as the version in the published text, Frodo's reply to him varies between attributing the phenomenon to Galadriel's "power" or to her "will," a nice distinction, and one that has some bearing on the issue as it relates to the Elves. The final text retained "power" and by so doing suggested that the time factor is a consciously imposed condition that takes some effort.

One draft replaces Frodo's "rich hours" in Lórien with "days and nights and seasons," omitting the adjective and citing more objective phenomena. Days and nights and seasons can be observed; hours are human inventions with no real existence except on the clock. But the subjective rich hours went into the published version. Still another draft has Frodo trying out an uneasy compromise between subjectivity and objectivity. "Slow for us there might time have passed, while the world hastened. Or in a little while we could savour much, while the world tarried." This is a bad mix. The hastening or tarrying of the world seems to be external and objective, while the phrases "for us" and "savour" are a recognition of subjectivity. The explanation vacillates between magic and psychology, without coming down in favor of either. This draft, too, was discarded.

Whether published text or rough draft, the clearest, most definitive statements seem always to be given to Trotter-Aragorn, who, in the text as published, not only tells Sam what really happened, but explains to him how he came to be confused. His speeches are therefore worthy of special attention as pointers to the direction of Tolkien's intent. The same draft that tries out the alternatives to Sam's "time doesn't count" speech has Trotter-Aragorn first saying "whether we were in the past or the future or in a time that [struck out: is and] does not pass [struck out: passes not] I cannot say." This speech is then reworked to read "whether we were in some time that [struck out: is long gone] or in some place where time does not pass, I cannot say." In one draft his "time flowed swiftly by us as for the Elves" is followed contiguously by the explicit statement "for we did not change." And just to make it clear what that means, the word "change" is struck out and replaced with the word "age" so as to read "for we did not age." Here is the *Mary Rose* motif plain as day and given by an authority. But it was omitted from the published text.

Those trial efforts that do not make it into print are revealing, not just for what they say but for the fact that, finally, they are not allowed to say it. Whatever he tried out, Tolkien seems in general to retain the least explicit words and expressions, so that Sam's question does not get a full and satisfactory answer. Indeed, some answers appear to be contradictory: for example, Legolas's statement that time moves slower for Elves as against Trotter-Aragorn's statement that Sam lost his count. Most of these multiple, overlapping, occasionally competing revisions suggest that Tolkien was not just grappling with the technical problem of juggling two times but wrestling with the more difficult problem of how to convey the quality without explaining the concept. Hence Trotter-Aragorn's equivocal "whether" and "I cannot say." Rewriting in order to say better what needs to be said is difficult enough. Rewriting in order to find a better way *not* to say what needs to be said, but to establish it nonetheless, is a far more difficult assignment.

The most striking revision of all, one also noted by Christopher Tolkien, appears in a draft of the preceding chapter, "Farewell to Lórien," in which two canceled sentences and Tolkien's note on their cancellation reinforce speculations about whether time does or does not pass and supply the rationale for the debate in all its versions. As the Company prepares to leave Lórien, their Elf-guide Haldir announces, "I have just returned from the Northern Fences . . . and I am sent now to be your guide again. [struck out: There are strange things happening away back there. We do not know the meaning of them. But]." Above the canceled words is penciled the provocative comment "This won't do—if Lórien is timeless, for then *nothing* will have happened since they entered"[4] (*Treason* 286). Tolkien's mind here is plain. It "won't do" to have an Elf in a timeless land report things happening in time. Sam was righter than he knew when he observed that nothing seemed to be going on in Lórien, and probably even more right when he added that nobody seemed to want it to. The crucial phrases, Tolkien's "if Lorien is timeless" and Trotter-Aragorn's equally telling "some place where time does not pass" make the issue plain, though they do not explain how, or even if, Tolkien resolved it. For the difficulty then arises of how to reconcile exterior time and Lórien timelessness.

His "this won't do" note shows that he was well aware of the difficulty. He tried several ways of solving the problem. One way is particularly noteworthy, for it provides unmistakable evidence that Tolkien was working with the time theory of J. W. Dunne. Tucked in among the notes of composition for this stage of the narrative are two penciled diagrams with an unmistakable likeness to those in Dunne's *An Experiment with Time*. One, on a torn-off scrap of paper labeled "Chart illustrating 'Two Times,'" consists of a horizontal line drawn from left to right, marked at the left with the letter O and labeled "Line of Origin." A series of vertical lines descends from this horizontal, and crossing these is a line angling obliquely down from "Line of Origin" labeled "Mortal Time." Cutting through these, angled sharply up to touch "Line of Origin" and immediately slanting down away from it again, is a double line labeled "Lórien Time" (see Figure 3). The second diagram, while similar, is much less clear, and simply shows a line labeled "Lórien Time" crossing other angled, horizontal, and vertical lines (see Figure 4).

The resemblance to Dunne's own diagrams illustrating his time theory is unmistakable. Obviously, at some point in his consideration of the Lórien/mortal time discrepancies, Tolkien tried to work out the practicalities in terms of the Field 1/Time 1–Field 2/Time 2 concept proposed by Dunne. This further implies that, whether or not he finally succeeded, at some point at least Tolkien envisioned his mortal Men (and mortal Hobbits) in the position of Dunne's Observer 1 and his immortal Elves in the position of Observer 2, thus conferring on Elves, as Legolas's explanation shows,

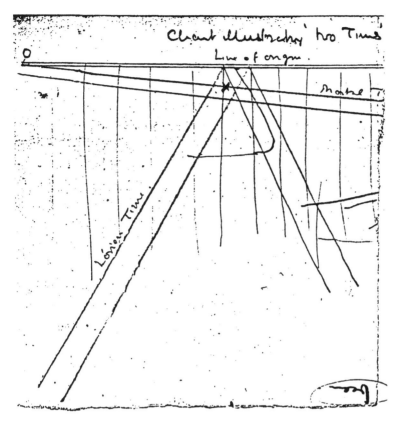

Figure 3

a wider (or longer) perspective of time. Both Men and Elves, then, become parts of the series and parts as well of the wider field of attention that encompasses the whole field of Time. Whether Tolkien succeeded or not is less important than that he made the attempt, for it demonstrates clearly that such a difference in time was in some way important to the whole picture.

Something in Tolkien's vision of the story required both mortal time and Elven timelessness, yet the narrative structure demanded that outside Lórien time should go on as usual. This is not an impossible paradox, but the practical difficulties of trying to balance chronology against timelessness would strain the most limber imagination, as Tolkien's notes for this section show. He drew up carefully worked-out chronologies charting the Company's progress

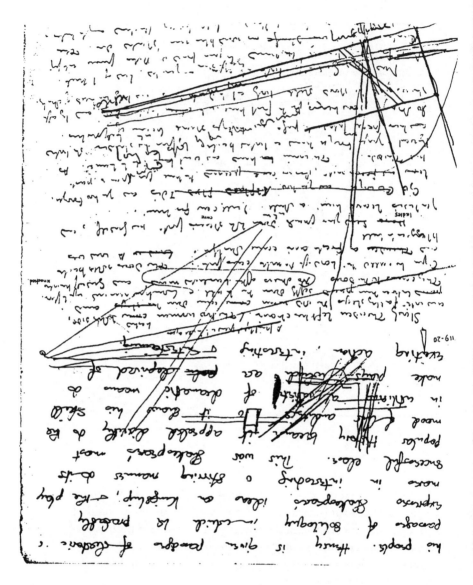

Figure 4

day by day against the calendar. A note on what Christopher Tolkien has labeled time-scheme "I" reads "Dec. 15 onwards time at Caras does not count," and a note at the bottom reads "from here to leaving Caras *time* [underscored twice] does not count." A note between January 14 and January 15 reads *"time ceases,"* and at the bottom of time-scheme "II" is written "Does time cease at Lórien or go on faster? So that it might be *Spring* or nearly so?" And on another page, "Why have any difference of time?" and "If Lórien time is not different then no need for Sam to see moon." And finally, in rather vigorous script, as if a decision had been reached, "Better to have *no* time difference." The interior argument these notes and time schemes reflect must have been a lively one, with the outcome in doubt right up to the final surrender. But if the final decision was to have no time difference, and there was no need for Sam to see the moon, we must wonder why Tolkien put the debate in the text at all. Sam does see the moon and he does raise the question. Tolkien's theme, if not his plot, needed two kinds of time, however that was to be managed.

We can return now to the theme of Death and Immortality introduced at the beginning of this chapter, the theme that would require a difference of time in Lórien important enough to be noticed but too important to be made explicit. If this last seems a paradox, it is one the author himself endorsed. "The significance of myth," as he said of *Beowulf*, "is not to be pinned on paper by analytical reasoning. It is at its best when it is presented by a poet who *feels rather than makes explicit what the theme portends*, who presents it incarnate in a world of history and geography" ("Beowulf" 15; emphasis added). No great stretch of imagination is required to apply these words to the significance of Tolkien's own myth as well as to *Beowulf*, for if anything is to be learned from this investigation of the revisions and rough drafts it is that Tolkien also consciously avoided pinning the significance on paper and chose to make implicit rather than explicit what his theme portended.

Death and Immortality, mystery and anguish and doom are the portents of the theme, to be presented incarnate in a world of history and geography and—more important—in time. For death depends upon time and time upon death. Where there is no time, there can be no death. Without the death of each moment to make way for the next, there can be no time. A race "doomed" to die and a race "doomed" to live might have something "permanent and difficult" to teach each other about death and immortality and about time and timelessness. Elves and Men will live in the world at different speeds, as it were, and their intersecting paths must involve a shift, on some level, from time to timelessness. The task facing Tolkien was to make this operative while keeping it implicit, to convey a sense of "other" time while staying in the narrative present.

Equally important is what that "other" time might signify and how the contrast between Men and Elves would further the theme. Tolkien's association of both races with Death and Immortality, and all of these with mystery, anguish, and doom, seems simple and clear enough until you look at it closely. The mystery of love of the world in the hearts of Men doomed to leave it is easy enough to understand, for we have all had some experience of loving and losing. But to understand the anguish in the hearts of Elves doomed not to leave it—that is, not to die—is a bit more difficult, since for most of us death, though inevitable, is seldom seen as desirable. Tolkien gave a rather cryptic hint of his fictive position on this in a letter to another reader, in which he explained that *The Lord of the Rings* "is mainly concerned with Death, and Immortality, and the 'escapes': serial longevity, and hoarding memory" (*Letters* 284). The first part of the statement is an almost exact repetition of Tolkien's phrase in the letter previously quoted and, like it, seems straightforward. Death and Immortality are the two supporting pillars of the theme. But the last three terms are nowhere near so clear and require thoughtful investigation.

First, what are "the 'escapes'"? And how are they linked to Death and Immortality? A clearer hint can be found in "On Fairy-Stories." Here Tolkien tells us that one of the gifts of Fantasy is escape. He lists many kinds: escape into another world, escape from pain, from hunger, from sorrow. In his view these are minor, preliminary escapes that lead to the final, the Great Escape, the Escape from Death. As mortals, we naturally desire escape from death, and we find it—temporarily in the fairy tale happy ending, eternally in the salvation promised in the Gospels (which Tolkien called "true" fairy tale). But having made the point, Tolkien goes on to stand it on its head so as to introduce the other Escape, observing with a perfectly straight face that "the human-stories of the elves are doubtless full of the Escape from Deathlessness." Elves and Men are mirrors of one another; they embody one another's deepest wishes and tell escapist stories about one another. Here is the clue to the "mystery" of Men and the "anguish" of Elves. Each has what the other wants and wants what the other has. Just as humans dream of es-cape from death, Elves dream of escape from deathlessness. One race must let go of life and the world; the other cannot relinquish its hold.

And so we are shown Lórien, where there is no death, where even the leaves do not decay when they fall on the ground, and where, though the seasons cycle, time appears to stand nearly still. Lórien seems to be an island of preservation amid a general decay. Thus Frodo, entering Lórien, feels that he has stepped over a bridge of time into a corner of the Elder Days, that he is in "a timeless land that did not fade or change or fall into forgetfulness." The Elves are living in a greatly slowed, if not altogether arrested, time, one in which past and present coexist. They cannot escape from deathlessness. But why should they want to? The answer is not spelled out in the text, which seems to imply the opposite. When the timeless beauty of Lórien is described, it is as enchanting to the reader as it is to Frodo:

> All that he saw was shapely, but the shapes seemed at once clear cut, as if they had been first conceived and drawn at the uncovering of his eyes, and ancient as if they had endured for ever. He saw no colour but those he knew, gold and white and blue and green, but they were fresh and poignant, as if he had at that moment first perceived them and made for them names new and wonderful. (*Fellowship* 363)

This is a child's clear view of a new-made world; it is Tolkien's childhood memory of the countryside of Warwickshire as he saw it when he came from South Africa, before the encroachment of the industrialization he hated. It is Empson's pastoralization of experience, that reaction to an accelerated pace of forward movement that drives modern sensibility to retreat into nostalgia. It is Eden before the Fall. For contrast, put this description of Lórien—which Frodo must leave and lose—next to this picture of the Shire to which he will return:

> Many of the houses they had known were missing. Some seemed to have burned down. The pleasant row of old hobbit-holes in the bank on the north side of the Pool were deserted, and their little gardens that used to run down to the water's edge were rank with weeds. Worse, there was a whole line of the ugly new

houses all along the Pool side, where the Hobbiton road ran close to the bank. And looking with dismay up the road towards Bag End they saw a tall chimney of brick in the distance. It was pouring out black smoke in the evening air. (*Fellowship* 349–50)

Which seems better—the "new" Shire or the "old" Lórien? Given the two pictures as Tolkien presents them, it would be difficult indeed to cast a vote for the new Shire. And yet that is precisely what Tolkien, on a rational level, wanted, though on an emotional level his heart was with the past. For Lórien has not changed nor will not change, whereas the ruined Shire will rise out of its ashes. Sam will work his magic; new trees will grow; the Shire year 1420 will be *annus mirabilis*. The point being made is that the seeming good must pass in its time and the seeming bad may carry within it the seeds of a new life.

Confirmation of this is easier to find in Tolkien's comments on his world than in his picture of the world itself. His letters to readers of his story spell out what his narrative only hints at, and that obliquely. He may have exalted Elves and things Elven in his story, but in his often lengthy expository letters he took a different view, calling them "embalmers" of time and explaining that: "They wanted to have their cake and eat it: to live in the mortal historical Middle-earth because they had become fond of it . . . and so tried to stop its change and history, stop its growth, keep it as a pleasaunce" (*Letters* 197). The notion of having your cake and eating it may be a clue to the puzzle of the second and third terms in the passage quoted earlier, "serial longevity" and "hoarding memory." The first of these, "serial longevity," is the most puzzling. "Serial" by itself is plain enough, but seems an inappropriate modifier for "longevity." The second term is clearer, for "hoarding" fits well enough with "memory," being precisely what memory is supposed to do: to hoard, to keep. But "serial" also recalls Dunne, whose serial observer acquires a wider and wider field of time. In line with this, it recalls Elendil-Ælfwine of *The Lost Road*, whose reincarnation from age to age might appropriately be called serial longevity. And now one phrase can illuminate the other. Ælfwine's reincarnate, serial longevity implies the hoarding of memory by his avatar, Alboin. Memory, moreover, is the one human faculty wholly concerned with the past, whose entire effort and effect is to bring the past into the present. Both in respect of their serial longevity and their hoarding memory, the Elves come close to having their cake and eating it too.

Throughout the narrative, the attributes of long memory and knowledge of the past are repeatedly associated with the Elves. In the face of Elrond is written "the memory of many things." The eyes of Celeborn and Galadriel are "the wells of deep memory" (*Fellowship* 369). Since Elves, if by misfortune they are killed, return in the same body, the term "serial longevity" might well be applied to them. And because of this serial longevity, theirs is an especially hoarding kind of memory, keeping stored the experience of the untold years of the past. This in itself is not a flaw, unless it inhibits the acceptance of the present, as Tolkien explains:

> But the Elvish weakness was in these terms naturally to regret the past, and to become unwilling to face change: as if a man were to hate a very long book still going on, and wished to settle down in a favourite chapter. Hence they fell in a measure to Sauron's deceits: they desired some "power" over things as they are (which is quite distinct from art), to make their particular will to preservation effective: to arrest change, and keep things always fresh and fair. (*Letters* 236)

But it is just here that Tolkien falls foul of his own ambivalence about the passage of time. For all his stated philosophical position, he cannot help imbuing his narrative with a mixed message, a rueful rationale for change covering a deep nostalgia for what has passed and is passing. In spite of all its Hobbit jollity, its mushroom and pipeweed, its victories and celebrations, *The Lord of the Rings* is suffused with a sense of transience and loss. The Shire changes, the Ents never find the Entwives, Frodo loses his Ring, his finger, and himself and cannot really go home. "However the fortunes of war shall go," Theoden says to Gandalf, "may it not so end that much that was fair and wonderful shall pass forever out of Middle-earth?" (*Two Towers* 155). It does so end, and all the renewal and rejoicing do not put back what was lost. Theoden speaks for Tolkien, but so does Gandalf, when he replies to Theoden: "To such days we are doomed."

The fact is that like his Elves, Tolkien hoarded memory. He, too, regretted the past; he, too, was unwilling to face change and wanted to arrest history, to keep hold of the past in the present. He, too, wanted escape from what he called "the Robot Age," escape from "the 'grim Assyrian' absurdity of top-hats, or the Morlockian horror of factories" ("On Fairy-Stories" 148, 150). And so, in a sense, he subverts his own message, surrounding his Elves and their lands with an aura of such golden nostalgia that their appeal is almost impossible to resist. But he also knew that real escape is impossible. We are where we are, and we cannot go back to where we were; we can only long to. Tolkien is susceptible to the Elven impulse and yet capable of seeing its fallacy, subject to the confusion of the heart that feels one thing and the head that knows another. And so there is a concealed sting in Lórien's beauty. Its timelessness is not the unspoiled perfection it seems. Rather, that very perfection is its flaw. It is a cautionary picture, closer in kind to the Ring than we'd like to think, shown to us in all its beauty to test if we can let it go.

The Lord of the Rings is, among many other things, a story about the ability to let go. The Ring is the obvious example, the clearest picture of the possessiveness engendered by possessions, and the corruption that grows with the desire to keep. It is easy to see the Ring as evil, and while Frodo's inability to give it up is both unexpected and inevitable, what happens to him appears to be an extraordinary tragedy, not something the reader can readily identify with. The timeless beauty of Lórien is the deeper example. It is more difficult to recognize as such, because, unlike the Ring, Lórien and everything about it in the narrative make us want to keep it, make us want, like Frodo, to stay there. We love Lórien, as, quite clearly, its author loved it. The beauty of Tolkien's Elves and their Elven lands blinds us to their significance in his world and his narrative.

Nonetheless, this very sense of passing and loss that on one level Tolkien mourned, on another level he celebrated. For to be capable of living is also to be capable of dying, and without death there can be no rebirth. Elves preserve. Men grow and die and grow again. It is in this respect that the contrast between Elves and Men is of such importance to Tolkien's vision. But while the contrast itself is apparent to any reader of Tolkien's work, it is a safe bet that many readers mistake its overt purpose and consequently appreciate the wrong values in each culture, valuing immortality above mortality and Elves above Men.

This message is nearly always implicit, but oftentimes it is so well hidden that it is easy to miss. A good example is the brief conversation between Legolas and Gimli as they enter Minas Tirith after the Battle of the Pelennor Fields. As in the debate about time, Tolkien presents his meaning in the form of argument between his characters, and without offering editorial opinion. Gimli speaks first:

> "It is ever so with the things that Men begin: there is a frost in Spring, or a blight in Summer, and they fail of their promise."
> "Yet seldom do they fail of their seed," said Legolas. "And that will lie in the dust and rot to spring up again in times and places unlooked for. The deeds of Men will outlast us, Gimli."
> "And yet come to naught in the end but might-have-beens, I guess," said the Dwarf.
> "To that the Elves know not the answer," said Legolas.
>
> *(Return of the King* 49)

As with the earlier discussion about time in Lórien, this discussion about the things that Men begin seems to end irresolute. It starts out critical of the works of Men and ends with no disagreement that they will fail of their promise. Most of the words carry negative connotations—"frost," "blight," "dust," "rot." We cannot but remember that in Lórien there is no decay, no rot; but we ought to remember that there is no growth either. If the key word in the conversation is "seed," that potential which must fall into dust and rot in order to germinate "in times and places unlooked-for," the key concept is time, without which there can be no growth. This will be true of Minas Tirith, just getting over the ravages of decline and war. It will be true of the Shire, whose urban blight will give way to new growth. It will be true of the rise and fall of any of the "things that Men begin," those deeds that will outlast Elves and Dwarves, about whose end "the Elves know not the answer." It will not be true of Lórien. "They are falling rather behind the world in there." And with that we are led back to *verthandi*, to the "happening" world as opposed to the timeless Lórien "where *nothing will have happened*" since the Company entered. And we are led back to Tolkien's initial problem with the dual presentation of Time and Timelessness.

To write about Time is easy enough; indeed, the sequency of English grammar makes it difficult not to write about time. But to write about timelessness brings with it, as we have seen, some sticky technical problems, not the least of which is the concept itself. For of course one cannot really picture timelessness, even fictionally, in a primary world of time, and using the tools of time, one of which is language. If Tolkien had succeeded in creating actual timelessness, his Elves and all their lands would be suspended in midstep, unable to finish a song or twist a rope or see a Hobbit. The narrative would stop dead, and the concept be compromised, in the very act of presenting it. But within the limits of linear narrative, Tolkien uses his Elves and Lórien to illustrate the dangers of trying to arrest time. Human as we all are, it is hard to face death, hard to accept loss, hard, therefore, to find consolation in the Escape from Deathlessness. Swift's Struldbrugs illustrate the danger in one way; they grow old but cannot die and are imprisoned in decay and impotence. Tolkien takes the tougher way. His Elves do not grow old, they do not die, they keep their strength and their beauty. And thus they illustrate by their very preservation the danger to faith in a fallen world of clinging to the present, which inevitably becomes living in the past. Over against this, his Men—and his Hobbits—illustrate, with the consequent pain and loss of all that seems most precious, the absolute necessity of letting go, of trusting in the unknown future, of having faith in God.

Tolkien condemns the Shire to near-destruction by urban blight before he allows it to be renewed. He condemns Frodo to almost equal destruction of body and self. He gives him pain and loss and describes his ordeal and his voyage oversea as a kind of purgatorial experience. But for his Elves in all their beauty he reserves a deeper despair, and that is no destruction at all. They are sentenced to be bound to the world through all its changes, powerless to let go and to go on. Sam's instinct is right. Time does not count in Lórien. Nothing is going on and no one wants it to. Lórien's beauty is crystallized. It is frozen. And in its perfection is its flaw.

Frodo's pain, but also his salvation, are contingent on his obligation to move and his ability to change. "You have grown, Halfling," the envious and bitter Saruman will tell him as the story draws to its close. "Yes, you have grown very much." He has grown, and in so doing he has outgrown his world. Like the Shire, like Minas Tirith, like all Men and all their works, he cannot stay in

the moment, however good it seems, but must move on. Having
known the Edenic bliss of Lórien, Frodo, like all humanity, must
love it and leave it, must continue his journey down the flowing
stream of Time toward his unforeseen destination, going ever on
and on but never There and Back Again.

*Over a
Bridge of
Time*

Where the Dream-fish Go   5

I've got a very Briny Notion
To drink myself to sleep.
Bring me my bowl, my magic potion!
Tonight I'm diving deep.
down! down! down!
Down where the dream-fish go
—Arry Lowdham

Seven years passed after he abandoned *The Lost Road* before Tolkien turned again to the subject of time-travel. In those seven years another major war had come and gone, ending with a detonation that exploded forever the world that had existed before. The privations and disruptions of World War II gave way to a disturbing new world that brought with it yet greater disruption. The rapid changes of the postwar world made it even less to Tolkien's liking than the prewar world had been. The terrible new war and its daunting aftermath of a brave new world he found hard to recognize may have turned his mind more forcibly than ever back to the past. In that interim he had begun the "new *Hobbit*," which was quickly to develop into *The Lord of the Rings*. When he returned to time-travel, his new version, *The Notion Club Papers*, showed, in its similarities to (and even more by its differences from) *The Lost Road*, how much his imagination and his skill as a storyteller had grown. If the idea came from *The Lost Road*, the improvement came from his labor on *The Lord of the Rings*. Indeed, these three, *The Lost Road*, *The Lord of the Rings*, and *The Notion Club Papers*, have a deeper relationship than mere chronology. A complex reciprocity of ideas and techniques, of the interrelated concepts of time and dream, language and memory, links them one with another.

In a letter dated December 18, 1944, Tolkien wrote to his son Christopher, "I have been getting a lot of new ideas about Prehistory lately (via Beowulf and other sources of which I may have written) and want to work them into the long-shelved time-travel story I began" (*Letters* 105). More than new ideas about prehistory distinguish this version from the predecessor on which it builds. Again there is time-travel back to Númenor. Again the mechanism is dream. Again modern identities merge with ancient ones. But the differences are notable. For one thing, *The Notion Club Papers* is closer to science fiction than to historical fantasy. The tone of the new narrative is more overtly contemporary, more "modern"—more, shall we say, timely?—than the earlier story. A fascination with the past is still paramount, but there is a cautious venture into the future as well, for the narrative present of the story is postdated forty or so years beyond the time of its composition, from the forties to the eighties of the twentieth century. This projected future is mere epilogue, however; the past is still the focus, still more exciting, more immediate than either the narrative present or its future.

There were other energies at work as well, however, generated out of the very present from which Tolkien recoiled, unleashed by the new postwar world about which he had many reservations. These energies, together with a new time, a new setting, and a new cast of characters, revitalized the old idea of time-travel. He was not, to be sure, the only serious writer working in a time-travel mode. In 1943 T. S. Eliot had published his *Four Quartets*, whose view of time, of past, present, and future as simultaneous experiences, was certainly evocative of, if not directly influenced by, the theories of J. W. Dunne. The principle of simultaneity that drives the *Quartets* is exemplified in the lines from "Burnt Norton": "Time present and time past / Are both perhaps present in time future / And time future contained in time past." In his own fashion, and without consciously imitating Eliot, but responding, surely, to the same climate of thought, Tolkien would cast his new time-travel story in much the same mode. And though his aim was not, as was Eliot's, overtly religious, it was deeply mythic and contained within it something like Eliot's vision of humanity's eternal return. For Tolkien felt, as Eliot said in "Little Gidding," that

> We shall not cease from exploration
> And the end of our exploring
> Will be to arrive where we started
> And know the place for the first time.

This interest in time-travel had reawakened at a time when Tolkien's work on *The Lord of the Rings* had run out of energy. Christopher Tolkien refers to "a long halt between October 1944 and the summer of 1946, after Book IV was completed." At that point in the narrative Tolkien had encountered "a most awkward error" in the synchronization of the movements of Frodo and Sam east of the river with the events west of the river in Rohan and Gondor,[1] and the difficulties involved in rectifying the error had brought the story to a standstill. The pause in work on *The Lord of the Rings* and the reappearance of the idea of time-travel may be mere coincidence. Nonetheless, it is worth noting that at a point when he was having problems with time and chronology Tolkien's imagination found itself returning with renewed interest to his time-travel idea.

Nearly two years is a long halt indeed, but the blank spot had provided an opportunity for work on "the long-shelved time-travel story." Over a year later, on July 21, 1946, Tolkien wrote to his publisher, Stanley Unwin, apologizing for his failure to finish *The Lord of the Rings* and introducing the new project:

> I have in a fortnight of comparative leisure round about last Christmas written three parts of another book, taking up in an entirely different frame and setting what little had any value in the inchoate *Lost Road* (which I had once the impudence to show you: I hope it is forgotten), and other things beside. I hoped to finish this in a rush, but my health gave way after Christmas. Rather silly to mention it, till it is finished. But I am putting *The Lord of the Rings*, the *Hobbit* sequel, before all else . . . (*Letters* 118)

In the interval between the time when Tolkien wrote to his son in 1944 and the time he wrote to Unwin in 1946, his "long-shelved time-travel story" took shape as *The Notion Club Papers*, a rethinking and reworking, as the letter to Unwin indicates, of "what little had any value" in *The Lost Road*. The story's development was less rapid, however, and its final shape less fixed from the outset than Tolkien's statement to Unwin suggests. Its unfinished state makes it impossible to do more than speculate on what Tolkien finally intended for his Notion Club, and the evidence, both internal and external, is confusing and complex. It is clear, however, that the story had a longer history and underwent more changes than Tolkien's letter to Unwin would suggest.

First of all, a story of such length could not easily have been dashed off in the "fortnight" of leisure time that Tolkien so offhandedly mentioned to Unwin. According to Christopher Tolkien's account of the matter in *Sauron Defeated*, "the quantity of writing constituting *The Notion Club Papers*, and the quantity of writing associated with them, cannot by any manner of means have been the work of a fortnight" (145). Moreover, though this scheme was later rejected, Tolkien's early drafts divided the story into two distinct parts, Part One being "The Ramblings of Ramer," or "Out of the Talkative Planet," and Part Two "The Strange Case of Arundel Lowdham." For Part One, Christopher Tolkien cites manuscripts "A," "B," and "C" and a final typescript "D"; for Part Two he cites a manuscript "E" and a final typescript "F"; both "E" and "F" end, he says "at the same point, with the next meeting of the Club arranged and dated, but never written" (146–47). The history of composition suggests that between the original conception of Part One and the development of Part Two the focus and perhaps the direction of the story underwent a change. There is certainly a shift in the major character from Ramer to Lowdham and a commensurate shift in energy, for the "Ramblings" of Part One seem to be all talk and no action. In contrast, the unfolding of Part Two's "Strange Case," the characterization of its major figure, Arundel Lowdham, and its thunderous climax pick up the pace considerably.

Part One has more to do with space than time and concerns itself with space-travel as both a literary genre and an actual possibility. This segment concentrates largely on the mechanics of space-travel narratives and the possibility of space-travel by means of dreams. As the story stands, "The Ramblings of Ramer" constitutes a long introduction to what then develops as the real business of the story, which is "The Strange Case of Arundel Lowdham." In support of this, Christopher Tolkien cites instances in which ideas and information introduced in Part Two were inserted back into the late drafts of Part One. He also cites a slip of paper, which he says was "undoubtedly written before my father began the writing of the manuscript E" (that is, at the beginning of the composition of Part Two), on which are written the words "Do the Atlantis story and abandon Eriol-Saga, with Loudham, Jeremy, Guildford and Ramer taking part." He continues:

> The words with which this sketch begins, "Do the Atlantis-story and abandon Eriol-Saga . . .", are remarkable. . . . "Part One" of the *Papers* (not at this time conceived to be so) had reached the stage of the completed manuscript B . . . and at this stage Harry Loudham was not seen as contributing greatly to the discussions of the Notion Club: a maker of jokes and interjections. Above all, he had no especial interest in the question of Atlantis or in names from unknown worlds. . . . Only when the manuscript B was completed (and the text of "Part One" of the Papers very largely achieved) did the thought enter: "Do the Atlantis story." (*Sauron* 281)

This explains the shift from Ramer to Lowdham already mentioned, and accounts for the "adjustments and additions" that Christopher Tolkien says were subsequently made to Part One in order to expand Lowdham's part in that segment. And it is possible that the concentration on Ramer's dreams in Part One may have reawakened Tolkien's interest in "the Atlantis story" that is the focus of Part Two. But what Tolkien meant by *Eriol-Saga* is unclear. Such jottings by writers are often shorthand reminders of more extensive ideas, and if the Eriol-Saga was indeed abandoned, Tolkien's note must remain a mystery. However, the name *Eriol* itself may provide a clue. Earlier in his commentary for *The Notion Club Papers* Christopher Tolkien had written that "From the beginning of this history [*The History of Middle-Earth*] the story of the Englishman Ælfwine, also called Eriol, who links by his strange voyage the vanished world of the elves with the lives of later men has constantly appeared" (*Sauron* 279). Ælfwine was to have been one of the receding time-travel identities of Alboin Errol, and the receding identities themselves were to have been an integral part of the time-travel concept of *The Lost Road*. As we have seen, "Ælfwine, also called Eriol" (also called Elendil) was in *The Lost Road* the "Elf-friend" figure within whose consciousness past and present, myth and history were encompassed. Thus, the reference to "the long-shelved time-travel story I began" in Tolkien's letter to Christopher and the mention of *The Lost Road* in the letter to Stanley Unwin offer persuasive indication that the Eriol-Saga was to have been some replication of the serial time-travel device of *The Lost Road*.

When he wrote "Do the Atlantis story and abandon Eriol-Saga," it is possible that Tolkien may have considered going direct to Atlantis-Númenor, for the Atlantis story does indeed provide the climactic scene of *The Notion Club Papers* and carries his twentieth-century time-travelers directly back to Númenor. But then—again as with *The Lost Road*—Tolkien apparently changed his mind. Evidence against the abandonment of the Eriol-Saga is provided by his retrieval from *The Lost Road* of one of its unfinished fragments, the Anglo-Saxon story and its addendum of King Sheave, for reuse in *The Notion Club Papers*. And the narrative promises more such episodes, though it stops before these can be realized. Moreover, Tolkien's sanguine expectation, expressed in the letter to Unwin, that he could finish "in a rush" may have been because he planned to incorporate into the new story some of the time-travel episodes that he had projected but never written for *The Lost Road*. Reconstituting Tolkien's original intent is difficult enough, let alone reconstructing his changes of plan along the way. But we may safely look to Christopher Tolkien for the most educated guess. He writes:

> But when my father wrote "Do the Atlantis story" he also said that the "Eriol-Saga" should be abandoned, although there is no mention of any such matter in the texts of Part One. The only explanation I can see is that the "Eriol-Saga" had been, up to this time, what my father had in mind for the further course of the meetings of the Notion Club, but was now rejecting in favour of "Atlantis."
>
> In the event he did not do so; he found himself drawn back into the ideas that he had sketched for *The Lost Road*.... (*Sauron* 282)

This seems the best explanation for the changes already noted. It is primarily Part Two of the story that takes up the material and ideas Tolkien seems to have felt were of value from *The Lost Road*. The first of these ideas is the primary and central concept of a return to Númenor by modern-day Englishmen with Númenorean identities. In addition, it keeps the same idea of the interconnection of dream and memory and time-travel, although it must be noted that Part One, with its lengthy accounts of Ramer's experiments with consciousness and his dream-experiences also deals with this. But it is clear that Part Two is most closely derived from *The Lost Road* since it uses a similar pattern of names and retains the notion of language as a trigger of ancestral memory. Arundel Lowdham assumes the traveler-dreamer role taken by Alboin Errol in *The Lost Road*, and the same Atlantis dream becomes the focus of the story.

In the event that he did decide, after all, not to abandon the Eriol-Saga, Tolkien might have felt he had only to set up the frame and flesh out the new characters before picking up where he had left off seven years before. But inevitably the new characters made their own demands on the story, not just because they required new backgrounds and histories, but also because they lived in a different time and their personalities, as well as their era, called for new ideas. Thus, though the two stories clearly had the same impetus and used much of the same material, the differences are as important as the similarities. Whatever may have been Tolkien's preliminary scheme, however it may have changed, one thing is clear—the intervening years had changed and darkened the quality of his original time-travel adventure. There is less of faërie and more of the occult in this story's treatment of dreams; the transitions between dream and waking are more hard edged and abrupt— therefore more dramatic—than those of *The Lost Road*. Greater tension and deeper longing pervade this new story.

It was characteristic of Tolkien that he hoped to finish this new book "in a rush" (he had begun *The Lord of the Rings* with similar expectations), and just as typical that he never did. Though obviously some things are easier to finish than others, very little of his scholarly or creative writing ("Leaf by Niggle" is almost the lone exception) came swiftly and fully formed from his pen. The "extraordinary disorderliness" that Constance Hieatt pointed out was plainly in operation here, as Christopher Tolkien's account of drafts

"A" through "F" bears witness. Moreover, the "comparative leisure" mentioned in the letter to Unwin was rare. Other demands
on his time—school examinations, a good deal of academic over-
work, and the well-known second thoughts and extensive revisions—all contributed to prolonged delays. So it was with this newest venture. "Rather silly to mention it," he remarked to Unwin,
"till it is finished." And like *The Lost Road* it never was finished.
After an energetic start the new project was shelved. For many
years the only signs of its existence were the two letters—the one
to his son Christopher, the other to Stanley Unwin—and a brief

mention in the diary of C. S. Lewis's brother Warren Lewis of "a
magnificent myth which is to knit up and concludes [Tolkien's]
Papers of the Notions Club" (194).

The one major effort from that time that Tolkien did, in spite of
delays, carry through to completion was *The Lord of the Rings*. Its
reception is history, and its place among the enduring books of the
twentieth century is assured. We must grant that in the long run
Tolkien's instinct that the *Hobbit* sequel should take priority was
correct. It seems clear in hindsight that even had they been completed, neither *The Lost Road* nor *The Notion Club Papers* was
likely to have matched the quality of *The Lord of the Rings*. Nevertheless, though each of these stories in its turn gave way to *The
Lord of the Rings*, together they have a certain status as unfinished brackets, so to speak, around the larger story—*The Lost Road*
mapped out just before its beginning and *The Notion Club Papers*
emerging when the story was well underway.

Indeed, the very fact that Tolkien never finished either of them
suggests that their ideas and themes still hovered in his mind and
might therefore have carried over into *The Lord of the Rings*. It is
not unreasonable to suppose that their chronological juxtaposi-
tion to that narrative sharpened its awareness of time and perhaps
accented its thematic treatment of time's relativity and variabil-
ity. For these three works are not connected by sequence alone but
at a deeper operating level of the creative mind. In this connection
the rough-worked, unfinished pieces from that period have their
own unfulfilled value, both for the light they shine—up from un-
derneath, as it were—on the finished, polished masterpiece as well
as for what they try to say in themselves. For both stories, and the
single idea behind them, have merit of their own, not just as trial
pieces linked by concept and subject matter, but as increasingly

thoughtful explorations of certain themes, among them the inter-relationship of myth and history, the capacity of the mind/soul to move through time and space independent of the body, and the incarnation of memory.

Both Tolkien's dismissal of *The Lost Road* as "inchoate" and his concomitant preference for *The Notion Club Papers* seem typi-cal of a writer's enthusiasm for current projects over past attempts. But there is something to be said for his judgment. *The Notion Club Papers*, unfinished though it is, conveys a larger sense of ad-venture than its predecessor and in this regard may be seen as an advance over the rather static narrative of *The Lost Road*. Tolkien's notion of "what little" had any value in the earlier story seems to have been the time-travel idea itself, the concept of serial identity as its mechanism and of memory as the vehicle for both. How-ever, the "entirely different frame and setting" and the unexplained "other things beside" brought in much that was new. It replaced the rather retiring Errols with the far more lively and contentious Notion Club (mostly Oxford dons plus a few literate nonacadem-ics, all sharing a love for languages, literature, and argument). It shifted the locale from a quiet cottage on the Cornish coast to col-lege "rooms" and substituted for the time-traveling father and son combination a pair of Oxford scholars. Finally, it delved far more deeply and searchingly into the psychology of time-travel and be-came the context for an important and newly developing language.

The changes were probably all for the better. The simple addi-tion of more individual experience effected through an expanded cast of characters (there are six participants in the opening dia-logue, and more to come) provided a wider forum for ideas, added some psychological complications to the dream structure, and bet-ter explicated the concept behind it. The Oxford setting offered a more likely context for the literary and linguistic debates that in-troduce and undergird the time-travel theme than had the Errols's holiday cottage. Thus the theory and principles of dreaming time-travel, instead of being buried in the dream structure of the narra-tive, as they were in *The Lost Road*, are actively arrived at. They are hammered out, worked through in the give and take of argu-ment among educated, imaginative, opinionated men. The changes enlarge the possibilities and thicken the dramatic texture of *The Notion Club Papers* so that the story itself gains a weight and a substance largely absent from *The Lost Road*.

Either as the result or possibly as the cause of these changes, the narrative shows a decided tilt away from pure fantasy toward science fiction. The dream structure of *The Lost Road* owed something to the romantic nostalgia of *Peter Ibbetson*. The dream mechanism of *The Notion Club Papers*, in contrast, resembles far more the mental journeys into the future of two then-current science fiction novels, *Last and First Men* and *Last Men in London*, by Tolkien's contemporary, Olaf Stapledon. The opening format, on the other hand—a theoretical discussion among a group of friends—is in setting, characters, and dialogue distinctly reminiscent of the opening scene of H. G. Wells's *The Time Machine*.

There is, in addition, what seems a deliberately mysterious, studiedly gothic tone to this story. Its progressively deepening atmosphere of mystery—a carefully orchestrated sequence of psychological aberrations, unknown languages, indecipherable scripts, oppressive weather and cataclysmic storms—creates a tone nearer to Charles Williams's psychic thrillers than to Tolkien's previous fantasies. Indeed, *The Notion Club Papers* has altogether a more contemporary, "mainstream" feel than does any of his other fiction.

All of these elements granted, still the primary instrument of the change is the nature of the new cast of characters. As separate individuals they are not so very different from the two Errols, a bit more argumentative, perhaps, but not notably so. The difference lies in the increased numbers and in the circumstances and the chemistry that brings these particular individuals together, for they are not members of a family but colleagues and friends with wide-ranging interests. The work produced by the Notion Club—from a paper on "Jutland in antiquity" to the book *Imaginary Lands* or a volume of poetic *Experiments in Pterodactylics*—and the vigor of its opinions on these and other subjects inevitably evoke accounts of Inklings evenings as recalled by members. Tolkien was reshaping some of his most immediate personal experience as fiction here, for the collegial camaraderie, the sometimes heated arguments, the badinage and (usually) good-natured insults that mark the exchanges of the Notion Club members are strikingly like the recorded accounts of Inklings meetings.

There can be no doubt that the Notion Club was in the early drafts intended to be a fictive version of the Inklings both in name and in membership. Christopher Tolkien notes that one early draft shows Tolkien playing with specific Inklings identities for characters, writing beneath the name *Ramer* "Self," then striking this out to replace it with first "CSL" and then "To" (for Tolkien) (*Sauron* 150). The name *Latimer* (later changed to Guildford) is then subscribed "T" (certainly also for Tolkien); *Franks* then is assigned "CSL"; *Loudham* (later Lowdham) is "HVD" (Hugo Dyson), and *Dolbear* is "Havard." It seems clear, as Christopher Tolkien has suggested, that Tolkien started out with definite equivalencies between Inklings and members of the Notion Club but later dropped the idea in favor of less definite references. The original subtitle "Out of the Talkative Planet" and the subsequent mention of "Old Solar," together with allusions to "Lewis" and the first two volumes of his space trilogy, make it clear that Tolkien began with an idea of some sort of reply to Lewis's stories of space-travel.

Of the name "Inklings" Tolkien wrote that "in origin it was an undergraduate jest, devised as the name of a literary (or writers') club . . . its procedure was that at each meeting members should read aloud, unpublished compositions [that] . . . might be voted to be worthy of entry in a record book." He added in parentheses "I was the scribe and keeper of the book," a piece of information that will be of some value in identifying at least one of the multiple voices of the Notion Club. Though the undergraduate club soon died, the name survived and was transferred to the circle of friends who met regularly in C. S. Lewis's rooms in Magdalen or in their favorite pubs to drink and talk and read aloud from their work. Tolkien remarked further that the name was "a pleasantly ingenious pun . . . suggesting people with vague or half-formed intimations or ideas plus those who dabble in ink" (*Letters* 388). The name "Notion" agrees pretty well with at least the first half of this description.

Not without some humor—doubtless better appreciated by his contemporaries than the general reader—Tolkien has his fictive editor, "Mr. Howard Green," insert into the manuscript a list of the members together with a brief description and some editorial commentary. Of these members, the most important are Michael Ramer, described as "Professor of Finno-Ugric Philology; but better known as a writer of romances"; Rupert Dolbear, a research chemist with "many other interests, notably philosophy, psychoanalysis, and gardening"; Nicholas Guildford, an archaeologist and the club's recorder, who "appears to have written several novels" and who, as "keeper of the book," may be supposed to speak for Tolkien, at least on the critical level; Alwin Arundel Lowdham, "chiefly interested in Anglo-Saxon, Icelandic, and Comparative Philology"; Philip Frankley, a poet who "suffers from *horror borealis*" and is "intolerant of all things Northern or Germanic"; and Wilfrid Jeremy, who "specializes in Escapism, and has written books on the history and criticism of *Ghost-stories, Time-travel,* and *Imaginary Lands.*"

These are the story's principal actors, and tucked into their descriptions are the clues to Tolkien's intended use of them as characters. The information that Ramer writes romances, that Lowdham's interests are languages and comparative philology, and that Jeremy specializes in escapism and writes on escapist literature should not be lost on the careful reader. Of subsequent importance, too, is Dolbear's interest in philosophy and psychoanalysis. Some minor figures of less importance to theme and action are also listed. These include, with exponential increase in idiosyncrasy, Ranulph Stainer, an expert in banking and economics who writes opera; Sir Gerard Manface, a lawyer who writes children's books; Alexander Cameron, a historian who "plays a pianola"; Dom Jonathan Markison, "a polymath"; and several others, of whom the most memorable is one Colombo Arditi, "Tempestosa Professor of Italian," a basso who collects books and cats and seems never to have attended meetings, or at least not those covered in the story.

Here again, as with *The Lost Road,* the persistent question of elements of autobiography, or at least roman à clef, is bound to arise. How much and how closely did Tolkien want his fictional characters to reflect real personalities? And how much did he intend or expect a reader to recognize? Certainly, individual Inklings—not just Tolkien, but C. S. Lewis, Charles Williams, Owen Barfield—were widely known and read both then and now; and some less-well-known figures such as Humphrey Havard and Hugo Dyson have since had a kind of fame thrust upon them by association. There is undoubtedly the echo of once-heard voices in the dialogue and repartee of the Notion Club. In fictionalizing his Club, Tolkien pretty clearly played with identities, both disguising and revealing them and mixing and matching characteristics. Much of this playfulness, however, was almost certainly for his own and probably the other Inklings' private amusement. Thus while traces of the game remain, and while the knowledgeable reader may feel invited to correlate the fictive characters with what seem to be their real-life counterparts, it would be unwise, however tempting, to become bogged down in a game of Spot-the-Inkling. The story as story would then take second place to the identity hunt, and suspension of disbelief would sag with the inevitable question of how much of what is presented as fiction may really have happened, been said, been thought. We are safest, therefore, if we allow the Notion Club to be typical of the Inklings in spirit without scrutinizing it too closely for one-to-one correspondences.[2]

The specifics of identity aside, Tolkien went to considerable lengths to surround the fantasy aspect of the story, the actual time-travel, with a reportorial framework and a kind of journalistic detail entirely absent from the narrative of *The Lost Road*. He set the new story in what is clearly his own contemporary Oxford and sprinkled it with references to college and university life, Examinations Schools, terms, "vacs"; there is even a local street address. Though the time is advanced from the forties to the eighties, the world has not materially improved—rather the contrary if anything—and the tone is suffused with Tolkien's own postwar pessimism. The "Six Years' War" is over, an atomic explosion has created a black hole in the United States, and, the worst disaster of all to some of the purists in the Notion Club, the fine-tuned expressiveness of the English language has deteriorated into slang.

Having thus grounded his story in place and displaced it in time, Tolkien enclosed it in a multiple frame. The outermost frame surrounds the *Papers* with the mock-scholarly apparatus of a pseudo-editor's Foreword recounting the "history" of their finding, followed by a Note to the "Second Edition" detailing the subsequent controversy between the editor and various experts over the papers' dating and provenance. Within this frame Tolkien nested a second, more dramatic frame, the actual minutes of the Notion Club, and within that second frame he embedded his real story, the journey into past time by some of its members. This sequence is not simply to invest the fantasy with realism, nor is it merely a jeu d'esprit of a writer having a bit of fun with his friends. Rather, the successive framing, the nesting of one story within another within another, has a definite thematic function.

129

*Where the
Dream-fish
Go*

Tolkien's reworking of Part One to fit with draft "F" of Part Two and his note about the Atlantis story, "with Loudham, Jeremy, Guildford and Ramer taking part," suggest that he was envisioning a situation in which certain minds communicating regularly in conscious and present time were to be also and unknowingly in touch with one another in unconscious past time. Ramer's dream research into other worlds and times was to connect with the eruption of ancient memories into the present consciousness of Lowdham and Jeremy. And even Frankley would, by way of his poem of the Voyage of Saint Brendan, sufficiently transcend his horror borealis to find common ground with the others, though he would not fully grasp the implications of his own poetic imagery. The key word in all of this is *Númenor*, and the key concept is of a land overtaken by disaster, an Atlantis. Both of these echo mysteriously (and seemingly quite independently) through the minds of all four. These individual and apparently tangential threads were to have converged as the time-journey continued until all were gathered into one strand leading in one direction.

All this is, sadly, in the realm of what-might-have-been, and, as with so many unfinished works, the power of what might have been plays hide-and-seek with the half-formed images of what is. Added to that, the story itself plays hide-and-seek with the reader in the opening pages of the story. Owing no doubt to the change of direction cited by Christopher Tolkien and the consequent complications attendant on matching Part One with Part Two, the only time-travelers we actually see, Lowdham and Jeremy, are as characters overshadowed at first by the more dominant debaters in the opening dialogue. These are Nicholas Guildford, who as the group's recorder functions also as narrator, and the poet Philip Frankley and, of course, Michael Ramer, the writer of romances whose space-travel story sparks the discussion and whose "ramblings" (accounts of his experiences of dream-travel) provide the psychic and psychological underpinning of the narrative.

Yet another character is the somnolent, seemingly uninvolved Rupert Dolbear, who nods in to the discussion from time to time. He is presented as a sort of hibernating grizzly bear whose habit of apparently sleeping through meetings does not prevent him from keeping a sharp ear on the conversation and a sharp eye on the proceedings. The acuteness of his observation and the timing and perceptiveness of his infrequent comments, plus the fact that one of his interests is listed as psychoanalysis, make him out to be a kind of éminence grise behind the intellectual explorations of the Notion Club and suggest that he might have emerged as a more important figure had the story ever come to completion.

The unfinished state of the story, the fact that all the members of the Club are well known to one another, and the rather reportorial presentation of the text as minutes of meetings make the narrative somewhat short on details of characterization. Dialogue references supply what few clues there are to appearance and personality. Dolbear has a beard, Frankley has a "long nose," and Jeremy (who sits on the floor, apparently in contrast to his fellows) is referred to as "little Jeremy." Tolkien supplies more descriptive detail for Jeremy than for any of his colleagues and is at some pains to give him a specific animal association. He is "as restless as a bird on a twig," and his "black, birdlike eyes" hop from speaker to speaker. He and Lowdham, who is developed more slowly and over a greater period of time, are by far the most carefully drawn characters.

Something of importance seems to reside in the contrast between these two, in the fact that one is unusually small and the other unusually large, that one is birdlike, almost delicate, and the other has a "tall, powerful figure." Jeremy is pictured as rather quiet, while Lowdham is likely to burst unexpectedly into song and is apparently a bit rowdy at times. At one point he rather ruefully refers to his behavior at one meeting as "ragging as usual." As the narrative takes shape, we see him through his colleagues' eyes as "a queer fellow," "a strange mixture"; he is described as wearing "a tortoise-shell, armour-plate," as not talking much about "what he really cares for," and is characterized by the acutely observant Dolbear as one who "walk[s] in disguises."

Lowdham is not the only one who walks in disguises, for, of course, all the characters, all the voices, whoever else they may echo, speak for the internal debates of their author. Behind the near-transparent disguise of the Notion Club, and speaking in the various voices of Guildford, Ramer, Lowdham, and others, Tolkien was free to let his imagination off the leash, free to try out new, sometimes radical ideas, to follow a line of speculation to its farthest reach and see where that took him. This is clear from the very beginning. The second entry (but the first of any length or importance), that for Night 60, begins in midstream with the discussion of Ramer's space-travel story that has apparently just been read to the club by its author. With little or no preliminary, the narrative plunges into a heated discussion of the technical problems of such fiction. The question debated is whether the means of entry into other space or time—be it rocket ship or time machine or similar Heath Robinson contraption—constitutes a mere "frame" around the picture or whether it should be an integral component of the story. Predictably, there is more variety than unanimity among the discussants on this point of principle. Nicholas Guildford, the chief critic of such attempts in general, and of the frame of Ramer's story in particular, states his (and Tolkien's) position: "A picture-frame is not a parallel. An author's way of getting to Mars (say) is part of *his* story of *his* Mars; and of *his* universe, as far as that particular tale goes. It's part of the picture, even if it's only in a marginal position; and it may seriously affect all that's inside" (*Sauron* 163).

In this respect (and this is surely Tolkien's conscious intention) the opening passages of *The Notion Club Papers* are self-reflexive, the best example of their own theory, for the whole frame-embedded discussion of frame is itself a frame. It is designed to present the credentials for *Tolkien's* way of getting to *his* "Mars," that is, to Númenor. His way of getting there, as in *The Lost Road*, is through dreams. His method of introducing this, however, is almost the direct opposite of the sleight-of-hand he practiced in that earlier story. There he eased his readers into dream disguised as waking reality. Here he uses two complementary techniques. The first is dialectical: he methodically leads his characters (and his readers) step by step through a consideration of possible options to have them arrive at last and by elimination at dream as the most believable vehicle for such travel. In true academic fashion (not unexpected from a group of scholars) he sets up the question, dismisses previous attempts, and then produces his own solution. The second technique is dramatic; it shows rather than tells the reader how it works. In this, Tolkien allows the dream state to erupt into, cut across, and momentarily displace the present awareness of his protagonists.

These external authorial devices are paralleled by an internal discussion of fictive authorial devices carried on by the members of the Notion Club. In order to establish and prepare the way for Tolkien's use of dream as vehicle, the general scientific naiveté of other authors and the artificiality and clumsiness of their entry devices are vigorously attacked by the Notion Club, chiefly by Guildford. The discussion is notable for its refusal to accept a too-easy, arbitrary, or unbelievable means of entry into another dimension of time or space. The debaters engage ideas—and one another—with vigor, raising the kinds of questions Tolkien must have raised to himself. How credible ought such entry devices to be? How credible can they be, given the wealth of scientific information and theory that has become more and more available to a general audience?

Although H. G. Wells's format is the model for the opening discussion, his time machine gets low marks, as do the crystal torpedo of David Lindsay's *A Voyage to Arcturus* and C. S. Lewis's crystal "packing-case" in *Perelandra*. Lewis, closer to home than Wells, takes a heavy drubbing in the course of the discussion. Tolkien's original subtitle for the *Papers*, "Out of the Talkative Planet," is an obvious gesture toward Lewis's *Out of the Silent Planet*, published in 1937, and recalls the two men's original agreement back in 1936. Though successive drafts deleted several references to Lewis and softened others, the disparity between Lewis's published space-travel romance and his own long-delayed time-travel story, now in its second incarnation, seemed to be very much in Tolkien's mind when he began again.

In the midst of the debate, Guildford (who seems to be the chief spokesman for Tolkien's own theoretical point of view) gives in a brief sentence what may be the guiding principle of the story and is almost surely the cornerstone of Tolkien's theory of time-travel. This is that "the 'machine' used sets the tone." This dictum arouses protest from other members, notably Ramer, Lowdham, Jeremy, and Frankley, who counter by citing valid precedents—everything from the viability of time machines and gravitation insulators to outright magic to the self-contained enchantment of fairy-stories to the question of whether any device at all is really necessary. Again, it is Guildford who insists on high standards of probability and believability and who most certainly speaks for Tolkien here:

"No! For landing on a new planet, you've got your choice: miracle; magic; or sticking to normal probability, the only known or likely way in which anyone has ever landed on a world."

"Oh! So you've got a private recipe all the time, have you?" said Ramer sharply.

"No, it's not private, though I've used it once."

"Well? Come on! What is it?"

"Incarnation. By being born," said Guildford. (*Sauron* 170)

In the words and voice of Guildford, Tolkien has stated a major credo, one that is both artistic and metaphysical. First of all, the story must be integrated within itself; every element must have what he called the "inner consistency of reality." Corollary to this principle but more metaphysical and certainly far more radical, yet entirely consistent with Tolkien's own beliefs, is that the one believable, scientifically probable, and fictionally credible way of traveling to this and any world or time is by being born into it, by being incarnated.

The word "incarnation," with all its mythic overtones, and its implicit corollary, "reincarnation," with overtones as much mystical as mythic, cannot have been chosen at random. Indeed, Christopher Tolkien notes that "in the original A text (still followed in B) Dolbear, waking up, says with reference to these words of Guildford's: . . . 'Then try reincarnation, or perhaps transcarnation without loss of memory'" (*Sauron* 213). Even though he later omitted Dolbear's line, Tolkien most certainly was aware of all the resonances of the word he put into Guildford's mouth and was using them to foreshadow the modus operandi of his own story. Guildford could simply have said "by being born" and omitted "incarnation" altogether. That he did not, but instead chose to fling it into the conversation almost like a gauntlet, sets up the mode—mystical, mythical, psychological—through which Tolkien is going to establish the credibility of his time-travel narrative. The frame must fit the picture. The machine used will set the tone. Incarnation as a concept, with reincarnation as a kind of ghostly partner, complicates and enriches the corollary concept of dream. It becomes clearer as *The Notion Club Papers* progresses that for Tolkien—at least in terms of his story—incarnation/reincarnation *is* dream. As in *The Lost Road*, the incarnated mind dreams itself, and its reality.

For a practicing Catholic like Tolkien, the idea of reincarnation would have been theologically problematic, although on a purely intellectual basis he seems to have had no trouble with the concept. In answer to an inquiring reader who asked him about the practicality of the Elven concept of reincarnation in Half-elven offspring, he wrote, "I do not see how even in the Primary World any theologian or philosopher, unless very much better informed about the relation of spirit and body than I believe anyone to be, could deny the *possibility* of re-incarnation as a mode of existence prescribed for certain kinds of rational incarnate creatures" (*Letters* 189). Whether he acknowledged the possibility theologically or simply chose to accept it imaginatively, nevertheless, in the limited freedom that comes with being an imaginative world-maker, reincarnation offered him a viable means of entry into his "Mars."

Having thus carefully introduced and integrated his frame, Tolkien proceeds to introduce and to validate his own version of the machine—the dreaming minds of his characters. For like the Duchess of Towers and Peter Ibbetson, like Alboin and Audoin Errol, like Ælfwine-Eriol, like J. W. Dunne, the members of the Notion Club (in particular Ramer, Lowdham, and Jeremy) dream a reality and come to live in it. But these men's investigations into the operations of the dreaming mind, into the world of dreams and the universe of possibilities to which the thoughtful dreamer has access, are of a deeper character than those of their precursors. They are more conscious, more speculative, more analytical, and finally and quite *un*analytically, more concretely experiential than their literary forerunners, even those of Tolkien's own invention. His essays into the operation, the content, and the metaphysics of the dreaming mind comprise some of his most daring and imaginative thought, as well as some of his most vivid description.

Theory evolves into practice through the discussion of Ramer's time-travel story. The general criticism of arbitrary frames, and specifically of Ramer's (though the club quite likes the story it encloses), plus the urging (almost bullying) of Dolbear, who has suspected from the first, lead him to own up. He agrees that his fictive device of "letting an intelligent artist get into a contraption by accident, not knowing what it is," was not only arbitrary and ill matched but was to some degree a "cover" for the story it framed. It could have no organic relationship to the story within it, for that, unlike the frame, was not a fiction of space-travel but an account of Ramer's own dream, his own consciously achieved sense perception of traveling to another world.

Ramer is thus the first to give an account of his dreams, and in his account two interrelated influences emerge. The first of these is plain, for it is specifically cited as an influence, or at least a precedent. From Stapledon's *Last Men in London* (lent him by Jeremy, be it noted) Ramer has gotten the "telepathic notion," the possibility that the mind can travel through space or time independent of the body. But just here the first influence intersects the second in that curious yet predictable coincidence that leads like minds to one another. For in exploring this idea Stapledon himself drew—as did so many before and after him—on J. W. Dunne, whose *An Experiment with Time* was a formative influence on *Last Men in London* and its immediate precursor, *Last and First Men*. Ramer's subsequent statements make it clear that he has read not only Stapledon but Dunne as well, thus getting his time theory at first and second hand. He is really getting it at third hand, however, for this sequence of sources is, of course, Tolkien's own, bestowed on his fictional character and shared through that character with the fictional Notion Club. The semitransparent mask of Ramer enabled Tolkien to explain and explore dream-experience, shielded by another persona and taking advantage of a semipublic forum. The result is some of the most remarkable and vivid writing on the complexity of the experience of dreaming since "Kubla Khan," a poem that Tolkien knew well.[3] Dunne had showed him the door, and Ramer provided the key.

Like Dunne, Ramer has been experimenting with dreams, and his conclusions parallel Dunne's so closely as to be little more than paraphrases of *An Experiment with Time*. His statement that "a pretty good case [has] been made out for the view that in dream, a mind can and sometimes does, move in Time," and his reference to "authenticated modern instances" of such movement are clear allusions to Dunne. A more specific echo of the theory of the mind moving over a field of attention, of Dunne's concept of Time 1 and Observer 1 and Time 2 and Observer 2, can be heard in Ramer's statement that "the mind can be in two places at one time; two or more; once you have made it more than one, the figure is, perhaps, not very important. For I suppose, as far as the mind goes, you can't get nearer to saying where it is than to say *where its attention is*" (emphasis added). Ramer goes on to supply a conscious, waking (and therefore persuasively ordinary, unoccult) illustration of what he means.

"I still associate [he says] a view of a study I no longer possess and a pile of blue-and-yellow-covered exam-scripts (long burnt, I hope) with the opening scene of a book I wrote years ago: a great morain high up in the barren mountains."

"I know," said Jeremy, "the foot of the glacier in *The Stone-eaters*."

The skeptical Notion Club, however, is not about to let Ramer get away with the mystical where the purely psychological will answer.

"I think a connexion could be made out between those two scenes," said Frankley.

"It's very difficult to find any two things that the story-making faculty cannot connect," said Ramer. "But in this case the story-scene came into my head, as it is called, long before the examination reality. The two are connected only because I was re-visualizing, revisiting, the Glacier-foot very strongly that day."

"That doesn't get rid of some connexion other than coinciding in time," said Frankley.

"Well, never mind. They did coincide," said Ramer. "And that is my point at the moment. The mind can be in more than one place at a given time; but it is more properly said to be where its attention is." (*Sauron* 177)

It is the very ordinariness of this example that gives it validity. Any reader with a wandering mind will have had the same experience and can easily identify with Ramer's account. Less readily identifiable, but very much a part of the phenomenon Tolkien is seeking to establish, are the similar experiences in *The Lord of the Rings* of Frodo and Aragorn on the mound of Cerin Amroth, wherein each has a double awareness, a perception of two fields of time.[4] That Ramer's is a spatial and Frodo's and Aragorn's a temporal awareness is a difference in content only. The quality of the experience remains the same.

Unlike the rather cursory exposition of the theory in *The Lost Road*, there is no discussion here of "rule," no queries about "more than habit required?" The questions Tolkien had posed himself in his own reading of Dunne, the questions he translated into the dream-conversation between Alboin and Elendil, are treated as if they have been answered. No rationale is needed. Here is a significant change from the ghostly, ex cathedra declarations of Elendil by which Tolkien had sought to explain the time-travel of *The Lost Road*. Instead of pronouncements, a literary example from the real world (Stapledon's book) triggers Ramer's investigations in the fictive world and leads to his firsthand account of his experience. This account, related to a group of minds imaginative enough and critical enough to both accept and weigh it, becomes the validating evidence. Moreover, the shift from Elendil to Ramer, from a supernatural to a natural authority, invests the concept with credibility just when it is most needed, that is *before* the actual dream-journey is begun and before the reader is asked to accept dream-travel as a given.

Following in Stapledon's footsteps (and those of the uncredited J. W. Dunne), Ramer has been working with Dolbear on the possibilities of harnessing the latent capacities of the dreaming mind, not simply to test a theory of time but to extend his ability to put it into practice. His own efforts at writing space fiction, plus the example provided by Stapledon, have led him to investigate the ability of the mind to operate independent of the body, to cross time and space not merely in thought, but—as we shall see—in actual experience. Related to this is his investigation into the relation between the "story-and-scene-making" ability of the unconscious mind in dreaming dreams and the similar activity of the conscious mind in making fiction. This seems to suggest imagination as a bridge or link between the conscious and unconscious and the imaginative rather than the rational mode as the most conducive to such an experiment.

Another, stranger possibility is that the mind can harness experience other than its own. Ramer has quite consciously attempted to train his mind to enter into and use the awareness and memory of things other than himself. He assumes this awareness to be an innate property of all matter, characterizing it rather inadequately, first as the "memory of the past and the foreshadowing of the future that reside in all things, including what we call 'inanimate matter,'" and then more fully (but no more clearly) as "the causal descent from the past and the causal probability in the present that are implicit in everything." This seems an unnecessary elaboration of the idea of memory and continuity, but it has a purpose that is, in the end, to validate language as the best repository and vehicle for human experience.

As an example, Ramer tells of his first attempt to "get inside" or to empathize with an inanimate object, a meteorite in a park near his boyhood home.[5] The resultant dream-experience is one of immeasurable weight, of interminable passage through space and time, followed by a fiery entry into the earth's atmosphere. But the meteorite's consciousness, though present and accessible, is too alien, and Ramer abandons such efforts, turning his attention instead to trying his own consciousness as the vehicle, penetrating deeper into his own dreams. This has greater success, and he has developed the ability to travel, through his dreams, into other times and places.

Note that this is a far more conscious kind of dream-travel than was presented as the mode in *The Lost Road*. Unlike Alboin Errol, to whom dreams come without his volition, Ramer is actively trying to harness his dream-abilities and is fully aware while he is doing it. There is no seamless transition from one state to the other, no sliding into dream without knowing it. In fact, Ramer describes one particularly sudden dream-experience as a "catastrophe." His description of this makes it a far more marked event than the ordinary drift into sleep:

"It was most like a violent awakening," said Ramer. He was silent for almost a minute, staring at the ceiling as he lay back in his chair.

At last he went on. "Imagine an enormously long, vivid, and absorbing dream being shattered—say, simultaneously by an explosion in the house, a blow on your body, and the sudden flinging back of dark curtains, letting in a dazzling light: with the result that you come back with a rush to your waking life, and have to recapture it and its connexions, feeling for some time a shock and the colour of dream-emotions: like falling out of one world into another where you had once been but had forgotten it. Well, that [is] what it was like *in reverse*; only recapturing the connexions was slower.

"I was awake in bed, and I *fell wide asleep*: as suddenly and violently as the waker in my illustration. I dived slap through several levels and a whirl of shapes and scenes into a connected and remembered sequence." (*Sauron* 184)

Dream experienced as "a violent awakening" in which Ramer "fell wide asleep"—this takes the description beyond metaphor, beyond paradox. The deliberate reversal of language from that usually employed to describe the dream state calls on the only concept capable of conveying the extremity of the experience, neither metaphor nor paradox but outright antinomy, that mind-exploding conflict that demands the simultaneous acceptance of contradictories in order to propel consciousness into a new state. Tolkien and Ramer want to give to dream the very quality the word "dream" conventionally rejects. This is to give to dream an immediacy, a presence and an impact that supersedes not just the "dreamy" quality of the ordinary dream state but the realistic clarity of the ordinary waking state as well.

Ramer is also—and again unlike Alboin Errol, who doesn't talk about them much—willing to describe his dreams, in some of the most striking and pictorial passages in the narrative. They appear to be journeys to utterly strange and altogether *other* worlds, dream-visions of great, albeit inhuman, beauty where crystals and colors grow and forms are perfected with themselves, places with other skies and stars than those of present Earth, places with names that ring strangely in the ear: *Emberü, Ellor Eshúrizel, Minal-zidar*.

It is here that language enters the picture. Unlike the mute consciousness of the meteorite, Ramer's own verbal consciousness responds to these names, and the presence of *name* starts a linguistic and philosophical discussion. His hearers question where Ramer "got" the names, whether he invented them or actually "heard" them within the dream; and if he heard them, whether they were remembered in a strange language by his waking mind or automatically translated into his own. This leads to a discussion of language per se and Ramer's theory that one's "native language" is not necessarily the language of one's birth but may predate present Earth-experience, may be contained, with greater or lesser accessibility, in the deepest parts of one's ancestral, collective memory.

Here again, as in the *Lost Road* conversations of the Errols, Tolkien was calling on his own deepest feelings about language and memory, embedding in the story a more than passing allusion to his own experience of recognizing Anglo-Saxon as something already known. The idea and the experience behind it are at the heart of Tolkien's whole concept of language. It is a formative component of *The Lost Road* and crops up again and again in his essays and lectures. But as a thesis it seems to have got its first full utterance in *The Notion Club Papers:* language is a gateway to memory. Indeed, language *is* memory, containing deep within its vocabulary and syntax the history of its speakers and, on a psycho-mythic level, is itself embedded in the soul-memory of the human organism. As voiced by Ramer, the theory realizes the implications of Guildford's word "incarnation." If the soul can incarnate, there is no particular reason why it cannot reincarnate, and in so doing bring with it the memory of past language.

This represents a considerable advance over *The Lost Road* in the melding of the medium with the message. If time-travel is the genre, and dream the transporting mechanism, language is at once the ignition point, the content, and the theme of *The Notion Club Papers.* However, these multiple functions take some time to develop and come together. They unroll as the story unrolls over the course of several months, building the suspense and introducing a sequence of philological, historical, and quasi-mythical revelations.

Travelers Between the Worlds 6

My soul's desire over the sea-torrents forth bids me fare
—*The Seafarer*

As the narrative of *The Notion Club Papers* moves from Part One to Part Two, the focus shifts from Ramer's account of his dreams and dream-memories to similar accounts by Lowdham. But where Ramer's dreams are primarily visual and scenic, Lowdham's are largely aural and linguistic, not visions that appear to his sight but words and phrases that echo in his mind and only sometimes take shape before his eyes.

It is just here that the entry of an apparently entirely new invented language complicates the picture. The words and phrases dreamed by Lowdham are utterly strange, yet their strangeness is familiar. He describes them as "linguistic ghosts." Many of the words are unconnected, what he calls a "rag-bag" collection. Others—quite a considerable number—he has arranged in two lists. The first he calls language A, which he has named Avallonian, and the second language B, which he calls Adunaic and which seems to have a nonlinguistic but historical relationship to language A. Avallonian is clearly a form of Tolkien's original invented language Quenya, what in *The Lost Road* Alboin Errol had called "Belerian-dic" and what his father, Oswin, had half-jokingly called

"Elven-Latin." Adunaic,[1] which develops into the language of Númenor, makes its entry into the myth together with Lowdham and his dreams.

In addition to Avallonian and Adunaic, these dreams include bits and pieces that Lowdham recognizes as early Anglo-Saxon. One phrase, which he says is "constantly repeated in various forms," from "what looks like ancient Germanic to Old English," is *"westra lage wegas rehtas, wraikwas nu isti,"* or *"westweg wæs rihtweg, wóh is núþa."* His English translation is "a straight way lay westward, now it is bent," clear reference to the end-of-the-world event in Tolkien's mythology in which Númenor is drowned and the straight road to Valinor lost to the Men of Middle-earth. A longer passage that comes to Lowdham is a scrap of Anglo-Saxon verse:

> *Monath módaes lust mith mariflóda*
> *forth ti foeran thaet ic feorr hionan*
> *obaer gaarseggaes grimmae holmas*
> *aelbuuina eard uut gisoecae.*
> *Nis me ti hearpun hygi ni ti hringthegi*
> *ni ti wíbae wyn ni ti weoruldi hyct*
> *ni ymb oowict ellaes nebnae ymb ýtha giwalc.*

> My soul's desire over the sea-torrents
> forth bids me fare, that I afar should seek
> over the ancient water's awful mountains
> Elf-friends' island in the Outer-world.
> For no harp have I heart, no hand for gold,
> in no wife delight, in the world no hope:
> one wish only, for the waves' tumult. (*Sauron* 243–44)

Lowdham recognizes this as being close to some lines from the middle portion of *The Seafarer*, which he describes as "that strange old poem of longing." The version given seems to be a kind of digest of a section of some twenty or so lines from the original poem, but Tolkien has done some shifting and changing to fit his purpose. For one thing, the text is very archaic in form and spelling. For another, the voice is changed from third person to first person, with a consequent shifting of pronouns from *he* to *I*. Moreover, although all the lines are from roughly the same section of *The Seafarer*, they do not have precisely this sequence in the original but have been cobbled together from disparate segments. Indeed, the first line of Lowdham's verse is made up of two half-lines from different portions of the poem.

Lowdham singles out one particular emendation for special notice, a change from the phrase *"elþéodigra eard,"* which he translates "the land of aliens," to *"aelbuinna eard,"* meaning "land of the Ælfwines, the Elven-friends." He goes on to say that he thinks his is "probably the older and better text" (*Sauron* 244). There is some justification for this statement, since most scholars agree that the text of *The Seafarer* is in places distressingly corrupt, though the wording of this particular phrase seems to be largely Lowdham-Tolkien's. Interpretation of the phrase in question has been a matter for some debate among Old English scholars, giving Tolkien license to reconstruct it for his own purpose.[2]

Translated literally the phrase means, just as Lowdham says, "land of aliens," or "land of foreigners." But this is not the only possibility. It has been said of *The Seafarer*, together with its Old English companion piece *The Wanderer*, that they "offer difficulties of interpretation beyond the rest [of Old English poetry], since they exhibit a more richly metaphorical and connotative use of language in accordance with their intellectually complicated themes" (Pope, ed., vii). Thus there is scope for interpretation going well beyond the literal. A legitimate metaphorical interpretation could read the phrase as "the home-land of those who are strangers, or exiles, on earth"—that is to say, the homeland of humankind, exiled from the Garden, but with the hope of Heaven.[3] That Tolkien chooses to replace this phrase with his own "land of the Ælfwines, the Elven-friends," and to go out of his way to call attention to the fact, says much about his concept of and attitude toward the lands in the West.

More important in the immediate context, Lowdham says that the lines sound to him "almost like my own father speaking across grey seas of world and time" (*Sauron* 244). It can be no accident that he then goes on to cite what he calls "echoes of some older lines that are not found at all among the preserved fragments of the oldest English verses."

Þus cwæð Ælfwine Wídlást Éadwines sunu:
    Fela bið on Westwegum werum uncúðra,
    wundra and wihta, wlitescéne land,
    eardgeard ælfa and ésa bliss.
    Lýt ænig wát hwylc his langoð síe
    þám þe eftsíðes eldo getwǽfeð

Thus spake Ælfwine the Fartravelled son of Éadwine:
    There is many a thing in the west of the world unknown
    to men; marvels and strange beings, [a land lovely to
    look on,] the dwelling place of the Elves and the bliss
    of the Gods. Little doth any man know what longing is
    his whom old age cutteth off from return. (244)

This should immediately be recognized as the same verse re-membered by Alboin Errol from his dream and quoted with some chagrin to his father, Oswin. Clearly, Tolkien intended to retain the motif from his earlier story, not as then, from a son to a father, but now from a far-distant father to his son. Here, however, the verse is more directly related to present company. "My father's name was Edwin," Lowdham tells the Notion Club, and a notable change in this version of the poem from the one in *The Lost Road* is the addition to the first line of the phrase *Éadwines sunu*, "son of Éadwine." While in the poem this clearly refers to Ælfwine the Fartravelled, it can hardly be accident that Alwyn Lowdham also is "Éadwines sunu." Indeed, he calls attention to the fact: "I think my father went before Eld should cut him off. But what of Éadwine's son?" (244).

Both the similarity to and the change from *The Lost Road* are significant. Though he may well have desired to, Alboin Errol's father, Oswin, declared to his son that "we can't go back," whereas Edwin Lowdham's son, as we learn, is convinced that his father has done just that, has attempted to voyage from one world and time to another. The replication of the verse, the similarity in situ-ation of sons speaking either to or of their fathers, reintroduces the "father-son affinity" that was to have been the structural "thread" of *The Lost Road*. For although the relation in the earlier story begins with father Oswin and son Alboin and then shifts to father Alboin and son Audoin, the pair composed of father Edwin and son Alwin in *The Notion Club Papers* keeps the concept and simply reverses the names. In a later dream sequence in which he appears as Ælfwine in the Anglo-Saxon time-travel episode, Lowdham-Ælfwine refers to "my father, old Éadwine Oswin's son." This inevitably recalls Oswin Errol and suggests the possibility that Tolkien was still considering some version of the father-son pattern he had projected for *The Lost Road*. To add to the evidence— and further to complicate the matter—Christopher Tolkien notes that in the initial drafts Lowdham's father was called Oswin Ellendel "(a modernisation of Elendil)," and Lowdham himself was Alboin Arundel (*Sauron* 284). If, as seems likely, the father-son thread was a significant feature of what Christopher Tolkien has called "the Eriol-Saga," this jumble of names suggests that the element was not, finally, abandoned in the shift to the Atlantis story.

In addition to the significance of his name, or names, what we have of the story as well hints that Edwin Lowdham was to be a more important figure than his *Lost Road* counterpart, Oswin Errol. Though he never speaks in his own voice, and though (or perhaps because) he is behind the narrative rather than in it, he is a far more powerful presence than the rather colorless Oswin. "An odd sort of man," as his son describes him. "Large, tall, powerful, dark. Don't stare at me," he protests. "I'm a reduced copy." Nearly fifty when his son was born and thus already far removed from him in time, Edwin Lowdham was a man in love with the sea, a mariner who disappeared with his ship, *The Éarendel*, when his son was a boy of nine. According to Lowdham, his father's disappearance was "a strange story. No storm. His ship just vanished in the Atlantic," leaving, as his son says, "No signals. No trace. No news" (*Sauron* 234). Lowdham's account points to the possibility of some later revelation or discovery about his father. But the narrative never got that far. Thus Edwin Lowdham is doubly lost, once at sea and again by an author who never finished his story, and so his mystery remains forever unsolved. Even though Edwin does not appear in the surviving text, he works as a brooding presence behind the unfolding revelations of dream and language. For it was by exploring his lost father's books and papers that Alwin Lowdham first became interested in languages. Furthermore, a manuscript page in mysterious and indecipherable script from Edwin's diary makes a portentous appearance late in the narrative. Within the story this becomes a kind of visual corollary of the relationship between Lowdham's languages and a "real" language, for it is a passage of Anglo-Saxon done into Tolkien's Elvish script, tengwar. Translated for the Notion Club by "old Rashbold at Pembroke," the passage and the mystery of its transcription become significant clues to the source of Lowdham's languages and the history behind them.

There is as well the motif of time-travel, which connects the voyages of old Edwin Lowdham—especially the last one—with the name of his ship, *The Éarendel*, and with the names he gave his son. His choices were *Ælfwine Éarendel*, altered "out of deference to prudence and my mother," says Lowdham, to *Alwin Arundel*. "I modernized 'em," admits old Edwin "to save trouble. But my ship bears the truer name. It does not look to Sussex, but to shores a great deal further off. Very far away indeed now" (234). This is a hint worth attending to, for it points directly to Valinor and suggests that Edwin Lowdham's role might have been intended as a later development of one of Tolkien's projected *Lost Road* episodes, "the man who got onto the Straight Road." In addition, the "truer name" of old Edwin's ship, *The Éarendel*, connects him—and by the gift of name his son—with one of the most significant references in all of Tolkien's work.

No one familiar with Tolkien's mythos could mistake the importance of the name Earendel or miss its pervasive presence deep in the fabric of his cosmology. From his earliest glimpse of it in the Anglo-Saxon *Crist*, this name awoke in Tolkien echoes of some half-known meaning, a forgotten but familiar dream.

*Éala Éarendel, engla beorhtost
ofer middangeard monnum sended!*

Hail Earendel brightest of angels
above the middle-earth sent unto men!

"When I came across that citation in the dictionary I felt a curious thrill, as if something had stirred in me, half wakened from sleep. There was something very remote and strange and beautiful behind those words, if I could grasp it, far beyond ancient English" (*Sauron* 236). Tolkien gives these words to Lowdham, but they could easily be his own. Indeed, when he came to write Tolkien's biography, Humphrey Carpenter appropriated most of them and gave the words to Tolkien (64). The fictive character who grew out of

Tolkien's response to them, Earendel (or Eärendil), became one of the earliest, oftest mentioned, yet least explicable figures in his mythology. Earendel is, of course, the half-Elf half-Man savior figure from *The Silmarillion* who sailed his ship to Valinor in order to plead with the Valar for the rescue of Elves and Men. The resonance of the figure developed over time and underwent considerable change, yet he stands out as the closest thing to a Christfigure in all of Tolkien's fiction. But why the name itself was so important and what precisely it meant to Tolkien has never been made clear, perhaps even to him.

The significance of these references in *The Notion Club Papers* becomes clearer when we turn again to *The Lost Road* and "The Song of Ælfwine." Christopher Tolkien's assignment of the first version of that poem to the time of *The Lost Road* is not surprising and fits reasonably well with the overarching Elendil-Ælfwine consciousness that lies behind that work. His guess that the second version might be associated with *The Notion Club Papers* is more provocative, for the poem describes the disappearance of Ælfwine under circumstances that seem to match the disappearance of Edwin Lowdham. The prose note cited by Christopher Tolkien gives the story:

> Ælfwine (Elf-friend) was a seaman of England of old, who, being driven out to sea from the coast of Erin, passed into the deep waters of the West, and according to legend by some strange chance or grace found the "straight road" of the Elvenfolk and came at last to the Isle of Eressëa in Elvenhome . . . . Of no other man is it reported that he ever beheld Eressëa the fair. Ælfwine was never again able to rest for long on land, and sailed the western seas until his death. Some say that his ship was wrecked upon the West shores of Erin and there his body lies; others say that at the end of his life he went forth alone into the deeps again and never returned. It is reported that before he set out on his last voyage he spoke these verses:

> Fela bið on Westwegum werum uncúðra
> wundra und wihta, wlitescýne lond,
> eardigeard Ylfa and Ésa bliss.
> Lýt ænig wát hwylc his longað sý
> þám þe eftsíðes yldu getwǽfeð. (*Lost Road* 103)

The insertion of this same verse into *The Notion Club Papers*, together with old Edwin Lowdham's last reference to "shores a great deal further off" than Sussex, plus the similarity between his disappearance and that of Ælfwine, offers evidence that Tolkien had carried the figure of Elendil-Ælfwine forward from *The Lost Road* and had at least considered the possibility of making Edwin Lowdham an avatar of Ælfwine in *The Notion Club Papers*.

But a discrepancy arises here, for in the *Papers*, while Edwin is the mariner and the bearer of the sea-longing that is Ælfwine's most characteristic feature, it is the son, not the father, who is named Ælfwine. As if to underscore the significance of the name, an earlier comment by Dolbear referring to Alwin Lowdham as "your little Elf-friend" makes it clear that it is Lowdham himself, and not his father, who is to carry all the Ælfwine associations. Though the weight of the father's presence behind the action is more powerful here than in *The Lost Road*, it is still the son, Alwin-Ælfwine, who is to be the principal dreamer in *The Notion Club Papers*, just as was Alboin-Ælfwine in *The Lost Road*. Indeed, he seems to be dreaming the same dreams, or some version thereof.

But here the narrative scheme takes a sharp departure from the plan of *The Lost Road*. There is no ghostly dream-visitor to ask Lowdham if he wants to make the journey, or to explain to him that it is possible. Simply, his waking experience begins to be bizarrely punctuated by sudden flashbacks into the past, moments when he invokes, or seems to see, as did Alboin Errol, the Eagles of the Lords of the West. Lowdham, however, enters into these moments more deeply than Alboin was ever shown to do, for he is emotionally entangled in the dream-past to a much greater degree. As well as invoking the Eagles, he cries out on several occasions against a mysterious figure named *Zigūr*, yet moments later has no recollection of his outburst and no recognition of the name.

Such an unpremeditated outburst, a flashback without warning to a forgotten earlier state, is a recognized phenomenon involving the involuntary eruption into present consciousness of some memory—usually repressed and often violent—whose return is triggered by a present event. Scent can be a trigger, as can sound or, though less often, touch. It is not so much a remembering as a re-experiencing of the past, of any moment too powerful to be initially absorbed by the receiving psyche. Most often used as a cinematic or literary technique to increase the scope of a narrative, it is in actual experience normally viewed as a psychological phenomenon and, if properly followed up, can be a road back into locked-off areas of the mind. In Tolkien's use, it is not so much a literary, or even a psychological, technique as it is a psychic gateway into locked-off areas of the soul. He has extended the concept from reconnection with past memories to include reconnection with past lives.

It is just here that the story takes on its gothic tinge. It becomes in this respect strongly reminiscent of the spiritual thrillers of Tolkien's fellow Inkling Charles Williams, who had no hesitation in moving his characters in and out of alternative realities. It is reminiscent as well of another book that shows Williams's influence, C. S. Lewis's *That Hideous Strength*. This is a new departure for Tolkien, not previously noted for creating or even liking the sort of psychic frisson that such past-life flashbacks can imply. Lowdham is increasingly—and apparently involuntarily—dipping into some inner, hitherto unrecognized repository of memory. Or, as ultimately becomes apparent, moving in and out of a previous identity that gains increasing power until, in a climactic scene of storm and memory, it takes him over altogether and sweeps him into another time.

In its handling of this transition from present to past, *The Notion Club Papers* is considerably more skillful in its use of dramatic tension than was its precursor. Whereas the Errols were to move into the past as Alboin fell quietly asleep in his chair and Audoin stepped "into sudden darkness," the comparable episode in *The Notion Club Papers* has the past come storming directly into the present in a night of philological and meteorological tumult. All this comes to a head in the meeting of Night 67. The Club has gathered in Ramer's rooms, all present except Lowdham, who arrives late, crying "Syntax at last!" and waving a sheaf of papers at the Club. He has been dreaming intensively and is afire with fresh information—not just individual words but actual texts recovered from his dreams. These are in the two languages, Avallonian and Adunaic, and seem to be paired accounts—indeed laments—concerning the destruction in storm, earthquake and flood, of some mighty kingdom, of *Atalante,* the Downfallen.

The weather keeps pace with the mood of the texts, and the discussion proceeds in a thunder-sultry atmosphere of growing oppressiveness. The exploration of these texts somehow increases the intensity and duration of Lowdham's sudden flashbacks into the past. I have described these eruptions of memory that with increasing force overtake Lowdham as "flashbacks," but they might as well be called "flashforwards" or, better still, co-incidents in the most literal sense. For they are neither backward nor forward but concurrent, both apparent directions simply choices in the static field of time over which the attending consciousness can move.

A new manifestation of this phenomenon is that the power of these eruptive memories begins more and more to engulf Jeremy as well as Lowdham, until suddenly, and to the total bewilderment of the other Club members, the two undergo a complete regression into past identity. While still fully present in body, Lowdham and Jeremy pass mentally and emotionally out of their present-day Oxford into another time-consciousness, wherein they begin to address each other as *Nimruzīr* and *Abrazān*.[4] Familiar to one another in that time frame as they are in this one, they apparently share not only a history but common knowledge of some anticipated and impending catastrophe.

Bizarre as the scene is, however, the groundwork for it has already been laid in a previous meeting's discussion of the interconnection of myth and history that had led Jeremy to suggest that "if one could go back, one would find not myth dissolving into history, but rather the reverse: real history becoming more mythical—more shapely, simple, discernibly significant, even seen at close quarters." Frankley, skeptical of such a process, questioned for example the reality of the myth/history of the Arthurian romances, even though there was a historical Arthur at their center. Jeremy, for whom the spiritual and philosophical truth of myth, rather than its factual reality, is the central importance, defended the power of myth itself, especially of "the major kind that has acquired a secondary life of its own and passes *from mind to mind*" (emphasis added). Ramer agreed, citing "the daimonic force that the great myths and legends have" and comparing them to "an explosive: it may slowly yield a steady warmth to living minds, but if suddenly detonated, it might go off with a crash: yes: might produce a disturbance in the real primary world" (*Sauron* 228).

This is precisely what happens on Night 67. As the members of the Notion Club become more and more absorbed in Lowdham's transcriptions of the Downfall, the daimonic force of the Atlantis-

Númenor myth is detonated. It does indeed "go off with a crash" and produces a cataclysmic disturbance in the real primary world. Mentally and emotionally separated from their colleagues, together with one another in their past world, Lowdham and Jeremy stand at Ramer's window staring into the storm and speaking apprehensively to one another of Zigūr and Nimruzīr, of the Lords of the West, of Eru and the Valar, as dark clouds come up over Oxford and "blackness [crawls] slowly onward from the West." The two worlds and the two times collide, with Lowdham and Jeremy at the point of collision.

A significant detail here is Guildford's irresistible visual impression as they stand at the window, of "two people hanging over the side of a ship," which conveys in one phrase the obvious but important fact that, swept into another time, they are also in another place. The impression of a ship is no accident, for that other place is Elendil's ship riding out the cataclysm that drowns Númenor. Whether intentionally or not, the scene also evokes the wreck of *The Éarendel* and Lowdham's father lost at sea. Suddenly the two men fall to their knees and cover their eyes and cry out to one another of "glory fallen into the deep waters," of wind like "the end of the world," of huge waves "like mountains moving." Together they stumble out of the room toward some unknown destination. As the gathering storm sweeps over Oxford, inundating Ramer's rooms, soaking and scaring the daylights out of the hapless Notion Club, so it also and in another time frame sweeps Lowdham and Jeremy into the destruction of Númenor.

It seems clear that the storm was intended to be the structural and psychological centerpiece of the action as well as the bridge between the two worlds. To "structural and psychological" we might safely add "historical" and "metaphysical" as well, for it is a storm out of another time, summoned up by the psychic energy of Lowdham's and Jeremy's memories and the power of their dreams. It is important to note that this is not a simple case of the past coming into the present or of the present's return to the past, but a kind of psychic simultaneity in which past and present merge in a single event. As Lowdham and Jeremy regress into the past, the storm they both evoke and experience comes blowing into the present. For a little space the two times are superimposed, and the storm is a synchronous event in both worlds. It is an extraordinarily vivid piece of writing, conveying with immense skill what is both technically and temporally a complex event.

This storm had a central place in Tolkien's time-travel vision, and his subsequent account of it suggests that it was to have been the means of linking Númenor to still another body of myth, the Celtic. The Norse and Germanic elements in Tolkien's myth have been widely acknowledged and thoroughly discussed, but less attention has been paid to his knowledge and use of Celtic myth. There are a few exceptions. One is Tolkien's lay of "Aotrou and Itroun," inspired by the Celtic legends of Brittany, for which the earliest manuscript copy is 1930 and which was published some years later in the *Welsh Review* (Carpenter 168). This is discussed at some length by Jessica Yates in her essay on "The Source of the Lay of Aotrou and Itroun." In *The Road to Middle-Earth* Shippey cites the knowledge of Celtic myth evident in Tolkien's essay "The Name 'Nodens,'" which appeared as an appendix to the *Report on the Excavation of the Prehistoric, Roman, and Post-Roman Site in Lydney Park, Gloucestershire*. Shippey describes the essay as an exploration of the descent of Nodens "from god to Irish hero (*Núadu Argat-lam*, 'Silverhand'), then to Welsh hero (*Llud Llaw Ereint*, also 'Silverhand'), finally to Shakespearean hero—King Lear" (28). Shippey also cites—and connects to Númenor—Tolkien's poem "Imram" (a Celtic term meaning roughly "voyaging about"), a retelling of the voyage of St. Brendan (212). Tolkien inserted a version of this into *The Notion Club Papers*, where its authorship is assigned to Philip Frankley.

Other references connect *The Notion Club Papers* to Celtic myth and legend. Perhaps the first is Lowdham's remark that his family lived in Pembrokeshire. Pembrokeshire, in the southwest of Wales, was the medieval Welsh *cantref* of Dyfed, which, in a typically Celtic mix of history and myth, was both a political and a mythic reality. In the third century A.D. Dyfed was settled by Irish immigrants. The *Inndarba inna nDési*, "The Expulsion of the Dési," is the Irish account of Eochaid Mac Artcharp and his followers, expelled from Ireland by Cormac Mac Art circa A.D. 254–277. According to historian Peter Berresford Ellis, "The Irish kingdom of Demetia (Dyfed) prospered and was accepted by the British Celts. Eventually it became absorbed into a British Celtic cultural ethos" (Ellis 56) but seems to have retained its Irish identity for many centuries.

Dyfed is also the setting for "Pwyll, Prince of Dyfed," the First Branch, or story of *The Mabinogion*, the medieval Welsh myth in which the hero Pwyll, out hunting in the forest, suddenly discovers himself to be simultaneously in a clearing in a wood in Dyfed and in Annwfn, the Welsh Otherworld. It seems more than possible that Tolkien, who certainly knew *The Mabinogi*, intended his Pembrokeshire-Dyfed to have the same Otherworld overlap. But even without this specific connection, Lowdham's Pembrokeshire would be rich in mythic associations, for Wales, like Cornwall and Somerset and parts of Scotland, is King Arthur country. Here too is a possible connection with the *Papers'* Night 65 discussion, in which Arthurian myth is cited as one of the great, "explosive" myths of Western culture.

Thus in the possible Otherworld overlap between Dyfed and Pembrokeshire, Tolkien may have intended an Irish as well as a Welsh reference. There is a recognizable Irish strain in Tolkien's work, often overlooked in the search for sources and influences. We should not forget the knowledge of Irish myth shown by the mention in his *Lost Road* outline of a "Tuatha-de-Dánaan or Tír-nan-Og" episode and the reference to Fintann, "the oldest man in the world," supposed to have been a survivor of the Flood who came to Ireland. Christopher Tolkien cites an "isolated note" among his father's *Lost Road* papers that reads "See Lit. Celt. p. 137," a reference to Magnus MacLean's 1906 *Literature of the Celts*. The passage is then quoted in full (*Lost Road* 82).

The explicit Irish references In *The Notion Club Papers* become more frequent toward the end of the surviving text. They emerge in a lengthy discussion of *immrama*, the legendary Irish voyages of discovery, in Frankley's poem on the voyage of St. Brendan, whose "bones in Ireland lie." They are brought in more directly in the adventures of Lowdham and Jeremy, who try as best they can to bring the bemused, confused Notion Club up to date on where they have been and why, after their return from the journey they began on the night of the storm. Following where their dreams lead them, they have journeyed up and down the western coasts of England, Scotland, and Ireland. "A good many dreams came," Jeremy reports, "*especially in Ireland,* but they were very slippery; we couldn't catch them. Arry got whole lists of ghost-words, and I had some fleeting pictures, but they seldom fitted together" (*Sauron* 268; emphasis added). This difficulty notwithstanding, the dreams and flashbacks in Ireland are more vivid than anywhere else, evidence of the more and more specifically Celtic flavor that Tolkien was adding to his story. Jeremy continues:

> The great storm had left more traces there than anywhere. We both heard many tales of the huge waves "high as hills" coming in on the Black Night. And curiously enough, many of the tale-tellers agreed that the greatest waves were like phantoms, or only half-real: "like shadows of mountains of dark black wicked water." Some rolled far inland and yet did little damage before, well, disappearing, melting away. We were told of one that had rolled clean over the Aran Isles. (268)

The motif of the drowned land is pervasive in Celtic myth and legend. The best-known example is probably the Arthurian-related lost land of Lyonesse, supposed to lie sunk between the coast of Cornwall and the Scilly Isles. There is as well the parallel Breton story of the overwhelming of the city of Ys. And there is an Irish version. Recurring accounts in Irish legend tell of a storm or a wave that roared in off the Atlantic and rolled far inland, inundating the land, sweeping away a good part of it and drowning the rest. This drowned land, of which the Aran Islands are said to be the last remnant, is by some equated with the Atlantis myth and is here linked by Jeremy with it and with Númenor. One Irish incident remembered by Jeremy specifically links the present both with Ireland and with the past of Tolkien's own legendarium:

> And we came across one old man, a queer old fellow whose English was hardly intelligible, on the road not far from Loughrea. He was wild and ragged, but tall and rather impressive. He kept pointing westward and saying, as far as we could gather: "It was out of the Sea they came, as they came in the days before the days." He said that he had seen a tall black ship high on the crest of the great wave, with its masts down and the rags of black and yellow sails flapping on the deck, and great tall men standing on the high poop and wailing, like the ghosts they were; and they were borne far inland, and came, well, not a soul knows where they came. (267)

It is worth recalling that Tolkien (if only in a note) wrecked his mariner Ælfwine "on the West shores of Erin" and that his outline for further *Lost Road* dream adventures had included two Irish episodes, one of the Tuatha de Danaan and one of Finntan, the oldest man in Ireland. These references make it clear that Tolkien intended to establish a specifically Irish connection for his own Atlantis and for the participation of Lowdham and Jeremy in its demise.

It is not, however, until they return to the west of England, to Porlock—the scene, as Christopher Tolkien points out (*Lost Road* 80–81), of an historic battle—that like Alboin and Audoin, like Peter Ibbetson and the Duchess of Towers, the two men's dreams coincide, and they begin to dream together. "I began to *see* as well as to hear," reports Lowdham. "Tréowine, that is Wilfrid Trewin Jeremy, and I seemed to have got into the same dream together, even before we were asleep" (*Sauron* 268). What they dream is the "Anglo-Saxon" episode with the story of King Sheave, brought forward from *The Lost Road* and for the first time formally woven into the narrative as a story told by Lowdham. It is unclear how Tolkien had planned to incorporate the later time-travel sequences into *The Lost Road*, but here in *The Notion Club Papers* this first adventure comes simply and plainly, as a remembered dream narrated by the dreamer to his audience. Tolkien sustains the dream quality throughout the narration, for when Lowdham finishes his story "with a sudden change of tone and voice," his listeners startle, "like men waked suddenly from a dream." They have seen the Hall, and the firelight, and heard "the wind rushing above all the words" (276). As they come back with a start to the present, Lowdham promises that "after that we shall flit more quickly, for we shall pass further and further from what Stainer would call History—in which old Ælfwine really walked, at least for the most part, I guess" (277).

The Club agrees to meet again in a week, to hear further tales of "Ælfwine and Tréowine." But there were to be no further tales, for there, at the end of Night 69, the typescript and the story came to a halt, never to be taken up again. The next heading, for "Night 70. Thursday, 2 October, 1987," is followed by a frustratingly blank page. The reader's expectations, by now raised as high as the Notion Club's, must, like theirs, perforce remain unfulfilled. We will never know for sure what was to have happened next. Yet we can follow Tolkien's thought a little way, for as with *The Lost Road,* he left some sketched-out notes that give an indication of his intentions.

A Question
of Time

Further Off Than Sussex

West, west away, the round sun is falling.
Grey ship, grey ship, do you hear them calling,
The voices of my people that have gone before me?
—Legolas Greenleaf

Two brief texts by Tolkien suggest that *The Notion Club Papers* was to have continued with Lowdham and Jeremy—that is, with Ælfwine and Tréowine—voyaging into the West and finding the straight road. There is mention of "later fleeting visions" (presumably dream-visions like the one already completed) that hint of other, never-developed episodes, perhaps similar to those Tolkien had roughed out for *The Lost Road*.

At one point Tolkien's notes refer to "descendants of Elendil and Voronwë (=Tréowine)" (*Sauron* 278). Jeremy, whose full name is Wilfrid Trewin Jeremy, is clearly Tréowine, and Tolkien's equation of this character with Voronwë implies a parallel equation of Lowdham-Ælfwine with Elendil. This last makes explicit what has never really been in question since the decision to "Do the Atlantis story," the fact that this narrative, like *The Lost Road*, was intended to culminate in the presence of its heroes at the downfall of Númenor. Moreover, the reappearance of Elendil is evidence that Tolkien had carried forward—again from *The Lost Road*—the concept of an ancestral consciousness that was to be the link among all the time-travelers. The heated and technical opening debate by the Notion Club underscores the importance to Tolkien's whole theory of time-travel of a believable device, not just a "machine" by which to get there but an effective link between the worlds, and specifically between his mythological world and the so-called real world, the world of everyday, of his own England.

As described by Guildford and hinted at by Dolbear, Tolkien's device—both a "machine" and a psychological and spiritual link—was the incarnate traveler himself, whose consciousness and memory bridge the worlds. Consequently, the notion of travel, and of a far-traveled character, at first only an essential device, became over time a theme in itself, developed out of the seminal concept of the figure of Eriol-Ælfwine, the traveler who "dreams alone" and who comes to the Cottage of Lost Play and there hears the tales of Melko and the Valar. From the very beginning in *The Book of Lost Tales*, this figure was to have been the connecting link, his presence the frame to the stories. Time was his road and the Book of Stories, the Book of Lost Tales, was the record of his journey.

In this respect the several mentions in Tolkien's notes of a "Book of Stories" connected with one or the other of the two time-travelers are worthy of special attention. In one of his notes Ælfwine is said to get a "view" of this book, while in another the book is specifically said to be written by Elendil, whose descendants then "get glimpses" of it. It is safe to assume that, as was the case in *The Lost Road*, Elendil is to be understood as the Númenorean identity of "Ælfwine, also called Eriol." This is the "Elf-friend" figure whose descendants are all the Alboin-Alwin-Ælfwine personalities whom Tolkien intended to make participants in the overarching perceiving consciousness. Given this connection, it is tempting to associate this Book of Stories with the fragmentary texts, both dreamed and actual, which play such an important part in *The Notion Club Papers* and of which Alwin-Ælfwine Lowdham does get glimpses. Much is made in that narrative of Lowdham's fascination with his father's papers, and there are hints that Edwin Lowdham himself got a glimpse, and perhaps more than a glimpse, of some ancient history that may be Elendil's Book of Stories. If this is the case, then Tolkien may have intended this book to be the source for the mysterious page of Númenorean history transcribed into Old English that Lowdham finds among his father's papers and that Ramer describes as "evidently made up of excerpts from a longish book or chronicle."

It is not the purpose of the present study to explore the complexities, the shifts and changes, in Tolkien's treatment of Eriol-Ælfwine, for his visions and revisions, especially in the early stages, produced a tangled skein whose unraveling only reveals further confusion in what is an already incoherent picture. The best and most informed disentangling of the threads is Christopher Tolkien's discussion and commentary on "The History of Eriol or Ælfwine" in *The Book of Lost Tales, Part II*. But however complicated and various Tolkien's efforts were to incorporate this figure into his mythos, its centrality to his developing vision should not be underestimated. Its importance is made clear in Christopher Tolkien's declaration that "From the beginning of this history the story of the Englishman Ælfwine, called also Eriol, who links by his strange voyage the vanished world of the Elves with the lives of later men, has constantly appeared" (*Sauron* 279).

The figure transcends the history per se and is part of a fluid, shifting conception that over the course of writing penetrated the whole body of Tolkien's fiction, a conception that is present to some degree in all of his major works and appears in many of his lesser stories and poems as well. His likeness appears everywhere, and however it varies from narrative to narrative, however it is named, the figure never changes in his essential aspects. He is often a dreamer, always a traveler, always a likeness of Ælfwine the Fartravelled, whose journey, initially conceived as a journey through space, develops over the course of Tolkien's writing into a journey through time as well. The recurrence of this far-traveled figure gives a thematic unity far deeper than the more obvious motifs of light and dark, good and evil, innocence and experience that critics have noted and explored. The figure and the theme, though both were part of Tolkien's thought from early in the history, developed at least in part out of the voice of the Anglo-Saxon poem *The Seafarer*, the poem that Tolkien deliberately paraphrased and cited by name in *The Notion Club Papers* to emphasize his theme and to underscore Lowdham's longing to follow his father.

Lowdham's description of *The Seafarer* as "that strange old poem of longing" (*Sauron* 244) very likely takes its cue from the poem's line 47, "*ac a hafað langunge seð on lagu fundað*," "but ever he feels longing who fares out to sea." However, while the sense of longing is powerfully conveyed, its object is less clear. Apparently it is not the sea itself, for the poem graphically pictures the hardships and trials of seafaring and contrasts the bitter cold of dark waves and icy seas and the lonely cry of gulls with the warmth and fellowship of the meadhall. But neither is it longing for the lands of men, but rather, in Lowdham's paraphrase, *"lust mith meriflóda forth ti foeran"* (243), the seafarer's "desire to fare forth over the sea-torrents." We must then ask "fare forth" toward what? What is the longed-for destination? The answer may lie in the controversial phrase cited in the last chapter, *"elþéodigra eard,"* and Tolkien's emendation of it to *"aelbuuina eard."* If the Seafarer's "land of the aliens" can legitimately be read as "land of the exiles," then we can take the next step and read Tolkien's "land of the Ælfwines, the Elven-friends" as Númenor and his "exiles" as those who survived the Downfall.

Here we must refer back to the mysterious page of Old English in Elven script found among Edwin Lowdham's papers, for it has a direct connection to *The Seafarer* and to Tolkien's emendation. We may safely assume that it is intended to be a page or a transcription of a page from Elendil's Book of Stories and agree with Ramer's comment, "I don't doubt that the actual penman was old Edwin." Rashbold's translation gives an opening line remarkably close to the mood of *The Seafarer:* "All the seas of the world they sailed, seeking they knew not what." The body of the text then clearly describes the downfall of Númenor in cataclysmic detail and the fate of the survivors, in which "black winds arose and drove away Ælfwine's seven ships" (*Sauron* 258). The page, and indeed the whole history of which it is a part, thus becomes Tolkien's extended continuation into his own fantasy of the historical tradition of Old English seafaring in general and of the literary tradition of *The Seafarer* in particular. In connection with the mention of Ælfwine, two phrases in old Edwin's final, summary paragraph are of particular significance, and their relationship to the mood and even the language of *The Seafarer* is unmistakable. "Now we sit in the land of exile" and "longing is on us."

It is this longing that engenders the wanderlust of all of Tolkien's far-traveled characters, of whom there are many. Yet however the particular story is conceived, whoever the particular character is, in whatever work he occurs, the destination of every such traveler is always some version of another world, whether it lies beyond Bree or in Númenor or in the Uttermost West. Writ large, the destination is Faërie, the world for which Tolkien longed all his life, the realm of imagination in which his vital creative life was lived. Whoever he is, the traveler is one who not only travels far but who—in one way or another—travels away from the world of ordinary humanity, the land of those (himself among them) whom Tolkien saw as exiles.

The first was Eriol/Ælfwine himself, who is sometimes called Ælfwine Wídlást, Fartravelled, and who in one early version took the by-name of Wæfre, Old English for "restless, wandering." But there were to be many more. There was Eärendil, whose ship ceaselessly traveled the sky, and Bilbo Baggins, who took off for parts unknown and ended up in the Elven refuge of Rivendell. There was Edwin Lowdham, whose voyage very likely took him to a similar destination, at least to shores a good deal further off than Sussex. And there are the followers: Frodo, whose longing to follow Bilbo is (at least at first) one motive for his journey; and Arry Lowdham, whose longing to follow his father is a near match. There are Alboin and Audoin, and, as we will see, several of Tolkien's lesser venturers into Faërie, all belonging to that line of far-traveled figures whose procession marks a clearly discernible trail through his fiction.

Some travel overland, like Bilbo, or, like the hero of Tolkien's last story, *Smith of Wootton Major,* wander in and out of the Perilous Realm almost at will—for a while. Many go over the sea, victims of that special unrest, that sea-longing with which Tolkien infected even his Wood-elf Legolas, who grew up in a forest but, near the end of *The Lord of the Rings,* acknowledges the powerful attraction of the sea and goes down the hill singing:

To the Sea, to the Sea! The white gulls are crying,
The wind is blowing, and the white foam is flying.
West, west away, the round sun is falling.
Grey ship, grey ship, do you hear them calling,
The voices of my people that have gone before me?
(*Return of the King* 234)

That same sea-longing haunts the Shire-bound Frodo when he has as yet no idea of how far he will travel. And it haunts the nameless voyager of Tolkien's early poem "The Sea-bell," whose surrender to that longing brings him no joy and who (alone of all the procession) suffers bitterly for his presumption.

These figures tend to be dreamers as well. Some dream of travel, some travel through their dreams, some realize their dreams by way of their travel. Most pertinent to the present discussion are the figures of Alboin Errol, Alwin Arundel Lowdham, and Frodo Baggins. Alboin and Lowdham travel through their dream-identities, Frodo through his actual journey, which may have more to do with dream than at first appears. Though he is certainly moved by other forces as well, Frodo, like Alboin, like Lowdham, is one for whom dream becomes reality, one who is, whether he knows it or not, motivated by his dreams, guided by them and impelled to follow where they lead him.

As has already been observed, both Frodo and Lowdham have been given the epithet "Elf-friend." Lowdham, in addition, has the name Alwin, which is also "Elf-friend." His *Lost Road* counterpart, Alboin, has the Lombardic equivalent as well as the surname Errol (*Eriol*, "One who dreams alone"). They seem an oddly assorted threesome. A surface resemblance between Frodo and Alboin is easy enough to see. Both appear to be quiet, contemplative fellows. Both have a not-so-buried streak of adventurer in them. Each has a father or older father-figure who shares his interests and whose presence is deeply missed when he is gone. For Alboin it is his father, Oswin; for Frodo it is Bilbo. In contrast, Lowdham and Frodo seem at first about as different as two characters invented by the same author can be—the one tall and powerful, "ragging as usual," the other quiet and retiring, initially self-effacing and ultimately self-sacrificing. It is a detail worth remembering, however, that Lowdham also was profoundly influenced by a father-figure and missed him terribly as a boy, and though too young to share in Edwin's interests, he explored them after Edwin was gone.

This is not to suggest that these characters' relationship to Ælfwine or their similarities to one another were part of some grand, preconceived design. This would endanger the autonomy of all three characters and their stories. But they are part of a continuing theme that grew and put out shoots as Tolkien continued to work with it. The tale grows in the telling, as Tolkien knew. As the concept of Eriol-Ælfwine grew from its beginnings in the *Lost Tales* to what I am suggesting was its ultimate development as Dunne's presiding consciousness, so too it spilled over into and colored other of Tolkien's characters who most readily offered themselves to its scope. These are the travelers, and most obviously these are the dreamers, those "who dream alone" and who travel in, and see in, their dreams with a freedom they cannot command in real life.

As with the character and function of Eriol-Ælfwine, the concept of dream arose early in the construction of Tolkien's fictive world and by its nature as he defined it associated itself easily with the idea of travel to other realities. It is not always easy, in assessing the development of an author's work, to mark with complete accuracy just how or when over the course of that development an idea or concept arose or how and when it assumed its final significance. This is especially difficult with Tolkien, who complicated the question of origins by late comments on and revision of earlier material, by retroactive creation of fictive rationales for already-created things or ideas (such as the Ring, Wizards, Gollum, Galadriel, and the Cats of Queen Berúthiel). So it is with the idea of dream in Tolkien's fiction. However, the evidence suggests that dream as a phenomenon, a concept, and a theme was already important in his earliest figurations of his fictive world and came more and more to be a structural element as his world and its mythology developed and changed.

Dream as both word and concept occurs early, and in contexts of some significance. The name *Eriol,* meaning "One who dreams alone," first appears in the High School Exercise Book into which, in 1917, Tolkien's wife Edith copied out the first version of *The Cottage of Lost Play* (*Lost Tales I* 13, 14). Contemporary with this are two small books containing the earliest lexicons of the Elvish languages, cited by Christopher Tolkien in his appendix to Part 1 of *The Book of Lost Tales*. Here we find listed the word *Fanturi,* with a root FANA and derivatives referring to "visions, dreams, falling asleep" (253). Here also is the word *Lórien,* a derivative of the root LORO, "slumber," with variants *olm, oloth, olor,* meaning "dream, apparition, vision" (259). We can safely assume this to be the earliest appearance of the concept in both story and language, however much earlier Tolkien may have had the idea. A very late (1954) essay refines this concept but does not materially change it. The essay, prepared for an index of names to be included in *The Lord of the Rings,* gives Olórin as an Elven name for Gandalf and cites *Olor* as "a word often translated 'dream,' but that does not refer to (most) human 'dreams,' certainly not the dreams of sleep. To the Eldar it included the vivid contents of their *memory,* as of their *imagination:* it referred in fact to *clear vision,* in the mind, of things not physically present at the body's situation. But not only to an idea, but to a full clothing of this in particular form and detail" (*Unfinished Tales* 396). Christopher Tolkien cites "an isolated etymological note" that gives a similar explanation of meaning: "*olo-s:* vision, 'phantasy': Common Elvish name for 'construction of the mind' not actually (pre)existing in Eä apart from the construction, but by the Eldar capable of being by Art *(Karmë)* made visible and sensible. *Olos* is usually applied to *fair* constructions having solely an artistic object (i.e. not having the object of deception, or of acquiring power)." He goes on to say that "Words deriving from this root are cited: Quenya *olos* 'dream, vision,' plural *olozi/olori;* *ōla-* (impersonal) 'to dream'; *olosta* 'dreamy.' A reference is then made to *Olofantur,* which was the earlier 'true' name of Lórien, the Vala who was 'master of visions and dreams'" (*Unfinished Tales* 396–97).

It would seem clear from this evidence that dream as both word and concept was prominent and important in Tolkien's world from its earliest conceiving, that neither as word nor as concept did it change materially over time, and that Tolkien was fully aware of all the psychic and psychological possibilities inherent in the idea. We may suppose, then, that in any of his works in which it may appear his use of dream with all its implications was conscious and deliberate, that its effects were intended, and that any reworking or amplification of the idea would almost surely have been in the direction of further enhancing the significance of dream in the world of Middle-earth.

Dream is the reality of *The Lost Road,* by means of which its heroes travel between worlds. Dreams are both the frame and the vehicle for *The Notion Club Papers,* whose heroes do much the same thing. Dreams and dreaming have a similar function in *The Lord of the Rings,* where they are equally important as theme and structure. Dreams are embedded in its structure, they are thematic parallels to its action, and they are a key to its treatment of time. Tolkien's continuing immersion in the mode of dream-vision as he worked on all three stories would only have increased his awareness of its possibilities and enlarged his ability to use them. As a corollary of their similar handling of time, these three works— *The Lost Road, The Lord of the Rings,* and *The Notion Club Pa-*

pers—are reciprocal in their handling of dream. In all three, dreams function as both personal and extrapersonal manifestations, as the upwelling out of the unconscious and also as the operation of some outside force.

In particular, Tolkien's treatment of dreams in *The Lord of the Rings* has a direct bearing on their very similar treatment in *The Notion Club Papers*. He has carefully situated Frodo's dreams throughout the narrative like one laying a trail. And in a very real sense they are a trail, one that, if carefully followed, will lead to some inescapable conclusions about the consciousness of the story's central character. The dreams of Eriol-Ælfwine, of Alboin and Herendil, and of Lowdham and Jeremy are echoed in and through Frodo's less singly focused but no less portentous dream-visions at Crickhollow, in the house of Tom Bombadil, in the Prancing Pony at Bree, and in a myriad half-remembered or forgotten dreams along the road to the Cracks of Doom. And though he does not dream so often or so intensely as Alboin or Lowdham, Frodo travels in his dreams deeper and farther than any of the others was ever allowed to go: to Orthanc, to a tall tower at the edge of the Sea, and finally out of Middle-earth altogether. He takes the Straight Road across that Sea to whatever fate awaits him, all the way to the Uttermost West. In so dreaming, he becomes more deeply connected than might at first appear to other, similar figures whose dreamlike adventures take them into other worlds and other aspects of reality.

Some, it is clear, can go farther than others, and this may well have to do with the nature of the journey. We have seen that in both of Tolkien's projected time-travel stories the conception became more and more complicated, and in each case the project was ultimately abandoned. Whatever may await him at the end of the voyage, Frodo finishes his journey. He makes it all the way. The more explicit time-travelers, Alboin and Audoin and Jeremy and Lowdham, do not. Instead of the "further tales of Ælfwine and Tréowine" we are promised, and of which jotted notes are the only evidence, we are left to make what we can of the one tale we have, left with a jumble of unsolved puzzles and a trail of clues without connections. A note on the recurrent question of reincarnation shows that Tolkien was still working out the rationale behind his treatment: "The theory is that the sight and memory goes on with *descendants* of Elendil and Voronwë (=Tréowine) but *not* reincarnation; they are different people even if they still resemble one another in some ways even after a lapse of many generations" (*Sauron* 78).

This seems to suggest, despite Dolbear's earlier interjection of the term, that Tolkien was uneasy with the implications of outright reincarnation and considered substituting the more psychologically acceptable idea of ancestral memory and collective unconscious for the perhaps theologically too-radical concept of the rebirth of the individual soul. This question, like so many others, must remain unsolved. The loose ends, the unaddressed questions include not just the possible succession of identities or the further adventures of Ælfwine and Tréowine but the more practical considerations of how these were to be fitted in with "The Ramblings of Ramer," with the explicitly noted dreams of the other members of the Notion Club, and with the apparently unconscious interconnections among them. All these were clearly meant somehow to play a part in the unfolding of a complex of ideas that was becoming an increasingly complicated story.

Yet in spite of this complexity, or perhaps paradoxically because of it, the unfinished *The Notion Club Papers* is a more satisfying, if also more frustrating, narrative than *The Lost Road*. There the pattern, though uncompleted, was plain in outline. Here, the text as we have it seems made up largely of puzzles without solutions. What was to be the relationship among the dreamers? It seems clear that there was to be a further role for Ramer, since he also dreams of the Wave and since he discloses, apropos of Lowdham's use of the word *Númenor* in his first outburst about the Eagles of the Lords of the West, that Númenor is *his* (that is, Ramer's) name for Atlantis. And what about Dolbear? What part was he to play in the time-traveling? Were the quiet power of his presence and his observation, his "work" with Ramer and later with Lowdham and Jeremy simply facilitators for the mind-explorations of his colleagues, or was he to reenter the action at some later point?

On the basis of Tolkien's note to himself to do the Atlantis story "with Loudham, Jeremy, Guildford and Ramer taking part," it is tempting to speculate whether Tolkien might have found a precedent or perhaps an inspiration for his overall design—if, indeed, he had one—in the plot of an early Algernon Blackwood novel, *Julius le Vallon*, in which a group of men agree, at a time in the historical past, to meet again in the narrative present (which is, of course, their future) in order to further or complete some sort of action. Such a design would fit the available evidence, and the putative culmination seems a plausible one; but the question, like all the others, must remain moot. In the absence of any comprehensive outlines, such as those Tolkien had sketched for *The Lost Road*, the subsequent course of the narrative can only be a matter of conjecture.

There are other questions as well, about the many elements provocatively introduced and provokingly unexplained concerning such puzzles as the unaccountable disappearance of *The Éarendel*; the jumble of languages that the narrative interrelates, Avallonian, Adunaic, and Anglo-Saxon; the intended meaning of the mysterious page of Anglo-Saxon done into Elvish script. Most of all, mystery surrounds the elusive, beckoning figure of the double father Edwin-Éadwine, on whom much of the mystery seems to focus. Thus a central consideration in Tolkien's transfer of elements from *The Lost Road* to *The Notion Club Papers* is how—or perhaps whether—he meant to fit the old father-son "thread" to the new design in which a non-father-and-son pair, Lowdham and Jeremy, appear to be the main strands. "Do the Atlantis story and abandon Eriol-Saga." The tone of this note is unequivocal, but is contradicted by the clear evidence that Tolkien had intended to weave into the pattern a search for, or reunion with, a lost father-figure. But of how that would have fit with the Notion Club itself, with the final Númenorean destination of the time-travel, and with the Downfall of Atalantë there is little indication.

And perhaps all these elements would not have fit, perhaps even could not have fit comfortably, workably with one another. Perhaps *The Notion Club Papers* had simply accumulated too much baggage to allow the story to move easily. Christopher Tolkien's discussion of the *Papers* strongly suggests that the story was abandoned not just because his father was determined to finish first *The Lord of the Rings*, as stated in the letter to Unwin, but because the entire project had become too complicated. The whole conception, he says,

has now developed a disturbing complexity: the Downfall of Númenor, the Straight Road into the West, the ancient histories in unknown language and unknown script preserved in Eressëa, the mysterious voyage of Edwin Lowdham in his ship

The *Éarendel* and the single preserved page of his book in Anglo-Saxon, the "re-emergence" in his son Arundel (Éarendel) and his friend Wilfrid Trewin Jeremy of "the sight and memory" of their forebears in distant ages communicated in dreams, and the violent irruption of the Númenórean legend into the late twentieth century—all framed within an elaborate foreseeing of the future (not without comic and ironic elements). (*Sauron* 280–81)

His commentary on his father's note about the Atlantis story and

the Eriol-Saga offers a solution.

The only explanation that I can see [he says] is that the "Eriol-Saga" had been, up to this time, what my father had in mind for the further course of the meetings of the Notion Club, but was now rejecting in favour of "Atlantis."

In the event he did not do so; he found himself drawn back into the ideas that he had sketched for *The Lost Road* (see V. 77–8), but now in a conception so intricate that one need perhaps look no further for an answer to the question, why were *The Notion Club Papers* abandoned? (*Sauron* 282)

Whatever the answer, there can be no question as to the value of the story and its overall concept—whether it worked or not—as a step forward from *The Lost Road*. In its very intricacy, in the promise implicit in the loose ends of a more complex and rewarding pattern, *The Notion Club Papers* represents a sizable technical advance. Its initial sketching out of the complexities of narrative, its development of theme, its delineation of character, and (albeit only potentially) its handling of plot are all at a greater level of sophistication. Lowdham and Jeremy, the imaginative Ramer and the Boreal-phobic Frankley, as well as the reticent but influential Dolbear, are more completely realized individuals than ever the Errols were, and their intellectual abilities to move among the theories of time, space, and fiction were developed well beyond those of the Errols. The developing situation is at once more credible and more richly fantastic, with believability gradually established through the experience and argument of the rumbustious, debative members of the Notion Club.

The treatment of time, too, is bolder and more sophisticated than in *The Lost Road*, as if Tolkien had developed the courage of his imaginative convictions. Time here is more than a field, more than a road, more than an enveloping circumstance. Time has energy in *The Notion Club Papers*, almost a life of its own, independent of the individuals who play with it and whose lives it shapes. It is as though Tolkien had taken Einstein's $E=mc^2$ and reshaped it to his own use, so that Ramer and Lowdham and Jeremy and Dolbear are playing not just with time but with fire. The members of the Notion Club, rummaging around in the potentialities inherent in the concept of space-time, tinkering with the hidden reaches of the unconscious mind—"each mind," as Ramer observes, "an engine of obscured but unmeasured energy" (*Sauron* 228)—detonate forces beyond their control, forces that, when unleashed by their collective investigations, explode into and sweep away their present lives.

Several elements contribute to this difference in treatment of time between *The Lost Road* and *The Notion Club Papers*. One of these elements was the actual passage of "real" time, which, like any sequence of days and years, inevitably brought changes, in this case a particular event that occurred in and shaped that particular time. Seven years of war had been brought to an end by the detonation over Hiroshima, an event that Owen Barfield most disturbingly—and I think quite accurately—ascribed to the explosive forces of the human unconscious. Much more than an event, it is a persistent presence, a continuing explosion in the minds of the very generation that brought it into being. Evidence that it had a powerful effect on Tolkien is given in a letter to Christopher, dated August 9, 1945: "The news today about 'Atomic bombs' is so horrifying one is stunned. The utter folly of these lunatic physicists to consent to do such a work for war-purposes: calmly plotting the destruction of the world! Such explosives in men's hands, while their moral and intellectual status is declining, is about as useful as giving out firearms to all inmates of a gaol and then saying that you hope 'this will ensure peace'" (*Letters* 116).

This impassioned denunciation of what was clearly shocking news, coming at a time when the "new *Hobbit*" had been in the works for nearly a decade, should put paid once and for all to the notion that *The Lord of the Rings* and its central artifact were meant to have a direct correlation to world events. The Ring is not the Bomb. It embodies power, raw, total, ultimately corrupting, and it is as a corruptor, not as a weapon, that its power is most visible. On the other hand, no author writing fact or fiction at the time of Hiroshima could conceivably have kept awareness of this world-changing event out of his work. Nor is any direct reference necessary in order for an audience to hear its reverberant echo throughout the stories generated in and by its time.

But for direct evidence of such awareness, *The Notion Club Papers* is a better source than *The Lord of the Rings*. In December 1945, just four months after the news of the bomb was announced to the world, Tolkien was at work on a story in which a character ascribes "explosive power" to myth and legend and suggests that through the operation of the conscious or unconscious mind such power may be "suddenly detonated," may "go off with a crash." It does not take much imagination to speculate that the detonations over Hiroshima and Nagasaki might have been the source (perhaps at an unconscious level) of such figures of speech. Even if they were not, there were plenty of conventional bombs exploding throughout World War II. The London Blitz, the bombings of Coventry and Dresden, the persistent reminders of these and other explosions in newspapers and newsreels would have been more than enough to make their impression. It is worth noting as well that the particular legend about which Tolkien's character was speaking was that of Arthur and the destruction of Camelot, the story of the downfall of a civilization and its overthrow in a devastating cataclysm.

On a quieter note, there is as well the actual physical act of writing, which can let loose its own power, can explode the mind into new ideas and expand it in unsuspected directions. The experience Tolkien gained in the writing of the "new *Hobbit*" and the ideas that developed as part of its ever-expanding plot and cast of characters brought their own energy to bear on the creative process. There can be little question that Tolkien's work on *The Lord of the Rings* directed and disciplined his creative energies and increased his range. He had jumped from *The Lost Road* to *The Lord of the Rings* and from thence to *The Notion Club Papers* and back again. It seems reasonable, therefore, to evaluate both *The Lost Road* and *The Notion Club Papers* in the light of the "new *Hobbit*" as works having an extrinsic significance greater than themselves.

They are not just stories that never got finished, but sidelights—angle shots, as it were—throwing light on, bringing into sharper focus some hitherto overlooked aspects of *The Lord of the Rings*, aspects that in turn enlarge their own significance. For the creative imagination is not a self-enclosed container but a continual sifter of material, or perhaps a permeable membrane through which elements pass in both directions. There cannot but have been an exchange of ideas, of influence both forward and backward and overlapping among these three works. Indeed, the whole concept of Númenor, and all that it brings to the background of the War of the Ring and the Return of the King, derives, as Christopher Tolkien points out, from *The Lost Road:*

> I conclude therefore that "Númenor" (as a distinct and formalised conception, whatever "Atlantis-haunting," as my father called it, lay behind) arose in the actual context of his discussions with C. S. Lewis in (as seems probable) 1936. A passage in the 1964 letter can be taken to say precisely that: "I began an abortive book of time-travel of which the end was to be the presence of my hero in the drowning of Atlantis. *This was to be called Númenor, the Land in the West.*" Moreover, "Númenor" was from the outset conceived in full association with "The Silmarillion" . . . (*Lost Road* 9–10)

But there are deeper thematic connections. There are, for example, the strikingly similar instances of a double field of attention experienced by Ramer in his study and by Frodo and Aragorn in Lórien. If nothing else, these two episodes surely derive from the same idea, the same Field 2–Observer 2 concept Dunne proposed. Certainly they contribute to the same theme. Having tried and abandoned as too complex the idea of explicit time-travel in *The Lost Road* and *The Notion Club Papers*, Tolkien found a way to weave the same idea less explicitly though no less significantly into his ever-deepening concept of *The Lord of the Rings*. To be sure, everybody travels in that story; its form is the journey and its variations simply the individual versions experienced by the members of the Fellowship. These circumstances notwithstanding, some journeys are explicitly and deliberately made to occur on several different levels of meaning—literal, psychological, and spiritual. Frodo, of all the travelers, is the character whom Tolkien is most likely to have operate on all these planes. It is Frodo who most clearly moves through various levels and most explicitly and consciously travels through time. We have seen already the trouble Tolkien took over the question of time in Lórien and the special awareness of time with which he invested Frodo both on his arrival and on his departure from the Elven land. An inadvertent traveler between worlds, Frodo steps over a bridge of time as he enters Lórien and reluctantly returns to the time that flows through mortal lands as he sets out on the waters of the Great River. His last sight is of Galadriel, whom he perceives as if floating away from him, preceding him into the past, very much as in Tolkien's illustrations of space-time expressions in English.

Time-travel, then, is a mode of journeying accessible to Frodo on all levels, literal, psychological, and spiritual. The last and perhaps the deepest level unites all these into one journey, though the implications of this level are buried deep within the narrative and are surrounded by other more overt incidents. One has to look closely to recognize this as time-travel at all. But on this level Frodo, like Alboin and Lowdham, like Peter Ibbetson and the Duchess of Towers, like J. W. Dunne, though less overtly than all of these, travels through his dreams.

Frodo's Dreams 8

Our life is no dream,
but it ought to become one and perhaps will.
—Novalis

Dream as a way of accessing consciousness in time is realized in its fullest potential in *The Lord of the Rings*. While the chief traveler and dreamer in *The Lord of the Rings* is Frodo, it is the actual concept of dream itself in all its potential, mystery, and variousness that in this work gathers the threads from *The Lost Road* and *The Notion Club Papers* and reweaves them. Perhaps because he had (or perhaps because he took) the time, but most certainly because he took the space, Tolkien's interweaving of dream and time and his exploration of their interconnected possibilities are richer and more varied in *The Lord of the Rings* than in any of his other work, even *The Lost Road* and *The Notion Club Papers*, where dream is the very substance of the plot. Here dreams are not so much a part of the action as correlative to it. They correlate the waking and the sleeping worlds, they parallel or contrast conscious with unconscious experience, and they act as chronological markers. Free in a way the rest of the narrative is not to move beyond the confines of conscious experience, the dreams in *The Lord of the Rings* reach into unsuspected regions of the mind, bridge time and space, and so demonstrate the interrelationship between dreaming and waking that the two states of being can be seen as parts of a greater whole.

Some dreams are touched so lightly that they are barely remembered even by the dreamers themselves, as when Merry, overcome by the Black Rider at Bree, has "an ugly dream, which [he] can't remember" (*Fellowship* 186), or when, in Ithilien, the exhausted Frodo wakes from "another gentle, unrecoverable dream of peace" (*Two Towers* 263). Or yet again in the passage of the Dead Marshes, when the narrative tells us that Frodo "had been dreaming. The dark shadow had passed, and a fair vision had visited him in this land of disease. Nothing of it remained in his memory, yet because of it he felt glad and lighter of heart" (*Two Towers* 242). Here, as often in real life, it is the act of dreaming that is remembered, rather than the dream itself. The substance vanishes with the waking but leaves some essence of itself behind. In these cases it is not the content but simply the presence of the dream that the narrative calls to our attention. In other cases the dream-substance is of definite, though not always immediately relevant, importance, and the subject matter warrants a close look.

But even with those dreams whose contents are described, it would be unwise to assume a predetermined pattern behind them or to claim an equal significance for all of them. Tolkien did not set out to write a book about dreams; rather, he discovered in dream an effective vehicle by which to convey his theme, a way to deepen and strengthen the book he was already writing. In addition, though as a man of the twentieth century he was undoubtedly aware of the dream theories of Freud and Jung, he was by nature more psychic than psychological, and more medieval than either. Thus his treatment tends more toward that of the Middle Ages, toward Chaucer's dream visions rather than Freud's, and responds best to a literary analysis compatible with his imagination. His fictive dreams are to be understood as hidden (or not so hidden) messages, and more often than not are messages from a spectrum of external reality wider than the dreamer's own unconscious. For the principle behind his use of dream Tolkien drew on Dunne's theory; for the dreams themselves he trusted his personal experience, added to that the examples of his literary precursors, and heightened both with his own powers of invention and discrimination.

Some dreams are plainly used for atmosphere and to emphasize the quality of the adventure. They comment on the action but do not add to it. Typical of this kind is Pippin's dream in the house of Tom Bombadil, wherein he reexperiences his all-too-recent sojourn in the interior of Willow Man. Here Pippin's dream-consciousness recreates as vividly for the reader as it does for him the sensation he has just escaped, that of being caught inside the willow. A similar experience is tacked on, so to speak, to the very end of Frodo's dream that same night, when just before waking he dreams so vividly of the galloping hooves of pursuing Black Riders that he expects to see hoofprints under the window in the morning. It is no accident that this sensation comes to Frodo just before waking, a point in the continuum of sleep when the conscious mind is re-emerging, beginning to reassert its awareness and its authority. In the case of each dream, a terrifying waking experience is relived in sleep, as if its power could not be shaken off by the unconscious mind on which it left its deepest impress. This is familiar terror, the common stuff of nightmare.

Tolkien had no hesitation in pushing such dreams and their nightmare sensations past the limits of common experience and mere atmosphere, however. Thus some dreams have a significance beyond the dreamer and imply far more than their slight impress on the narrative would suggest. An example of this is one of the book's most bizarre dream sequences, as vivid as it is brief and unexplained. This comes in the moment on the Barrow Downs when Merry, newly awakened from his captivity in the barrow, relives an experience out of another time—indeed out of another life—than the one he is presently in. While held unconscious in the barrow, he and Pippin had been arrayed in "thin white rags, crowned and belted with pale gold." Now, though they are conscious and out and free, Merry is still half-captive in the dream state. "'What in the name of wonder?' began Merry, feeling the golden circlet that had slipped over one eye. Then he stopped and a shadow came over his face and he closed his eyes. 'Of course, I remember!' he said. 'The men of Carn Dûm came on us at night, and we were worsted. Ah! the spear in my heart!' He clutched at his breast. 'No! No!' he said, opening his eyes. 'What am I saying? I have been dreaming'" (*Fellowship* 154).

He may have been dreaming, but what he dreamed was not his own experience. However much they may distort reality, ordinary dreams reflect their dreamers, and this extraordinary dream or memory is no part of Merry's present reality. The language is archaic, not the typical "hobbit speech." Moreover, the phrase about "the spear in my heart" and the instinctive action that goes with it can only be the recollection or the reexperience of a death blow, while Merry, though he has narrowly escaped from death, is very much alive. It may be, as Shippey suggests, that Merry has taken on the personality of the body in the barrow (84–85); but whether that is the case or not, whoever the speaker is or was, it is not Meriadoc Brandybuck of the Shire. That this is the case is clearer in the published text than in Tolkien's earlier draft of the episode, in which, after Merry's "What in the name of wonder?" the text continues in a slightly different direction. "Then he stopped," it reads, "and a shadow came over his face. 'I begin to remember,' he said. 'I thought I was dead—but don't let us speak of it'" (*Return of the Shadow* 128). In this version Merry seems to be speaking in his own voice and referring not to some memory of violent death but to his unconsciousness in the barrow. No mention is made of the men of Carn Dûm or of "the spear in my heart," and there is no reason to suppose that a transfer of identity or any kind of transpersonal memory is part of the experience. In making the change to the text as published, Tolkien clearly saw a chance to introduce, however briefly, some much deeper, more psychic concept.

Both the episode and the change from draft to final text are worth noting, since the first version was written before he wrote *The Notion Club Papers* and the second, altered version was developed after, and possibly in the light of, Lowdham's similar flashbacks. The published text of Merry's outburst inevitably recalls, even replicates—in form if not in content—Lowdham's talk of Zigūr, or the Eagles of the Lord of the West. It seems plain that Merry, like Lowdham, is having some kind of eruption into his conscious life of another life and time. A crucial difference is that unlike Merry's single episode, Lowdham's flashbacks are repeated and cumulative, developed over time as integral elements of the narrative. They are in that story the clues to the action both for the inquisitive Notion Club and for the reader and were intended to arouse and ultimately to satisfy curiosity.

The rather unsettling implications of Merry's outburst, on the other hand, are not followed up. No past is explored, no other identity is invoked, no particular point is made of the little scene. Indeed, not only does no one (including Tolkien) take any special notice of the incident, but the hobbits almost immediately take up their normal lives again—if being rescued from death and running about naked on the grass can be described as normal. Wherever his dream has taken him, Merry forgets it utterly once he is fully awake. This brief brush with the occult is introduced only to be dropped, and by the time we get to the next dream, at Bree, so many more immediate things have intervened that we have forgotten about it. But we have witnessed the interaction of the past with the present and have seen the overlapping of two time schemes. We will see these again.

Other equally occult but more carefully seated dreams are also important, and one—dreamed not by a hobbit but by a man—is essential not just to the theme but to the movement of the plot. That is the very important dream of the cryptic verse that sends Boromir from Gondor to Rivendell seeking an interpretation. This pivotal dream is directly responsible for Boromir's inclusion in the Company and thus leads directly to his crucial role in the breaking of the Fellowship at the Falls of Rauros. Among all the dreams included in the narrative it is unique in two respects. First, it is the only dream that is both shared and recurrent; Boromir recounts that it "came to my brother in a troubled sleep; and afterwards a like dream came oft to him again, and once to me" (*Fellowship* 259). This inevitably recalls Tolkien's recurrent dream of the Great Wave that was shared by his son. Second, this alone among the dream experiences of the book is unmistakably oracular, containing both admonitions—"Seek for the Sword that was broken"— and predictions—"Doom is near at hand" and "the Halfling forth shall stand." Thus it works more emphatically than Merry's dream to imbue the narrative with strongly psychic overtones.

As ought properly to be the case for the central character, by far the most thematically important dreams are Frodo's. It should be noted immediately that one of Tolkien's main concerns throughout his many painstaking revisions was the positioning of those dreams and their contents *in time* and the establishment of their temporal relationship not just to the dreamer but to other surrounding events. This involved a continuing exploration of significance and ramification and often led to the restructuring of content, the shifting of whole sequences from one dream to another, and, in at least two cases, the belated discovery by the author of what he was really writing about. Following this lead, let us look with some care at the placement, the content, and the function in the narrative of Frodo's dreams as they develop from Tolkien's endlessly revised rough drafts to the published text. Most of these relate, among other things, directly to Dunne's theory of time. Like Merry's dream, these take the dreamer beyond his temporal frame, across actual fields of time and space and into situations inaccessible to the waking mind. Unlike Merry's, they are described at length, and their implications are fully explored.

It is this sort of dream Frodo has while in the house of Tom Bombadil; he dreams of seeing Gandalf at Orthanc. This is also the sort of vision that comes to Frodo (also in Tom's house) of the grey rain-curtain and the far green country, though when he dreams it no one including Frodo can know what it is. This last is a prevision of his arrival in the Undying Lands, though not until the very end of the book is the connection made, when, "as in his dream in the house of Bombadil, the grey rain-curtain turned all to silver glass and was rolled back, and he beheld white shores and beyond them a far green country under a swift sunrise" (*Return of the King* 310). By then the reader has come to accept and even to expect prevision, time- and space-travel, and out-of-body experience as part of the dream process. The dreams have added up, and we can appreciate their cumulative effect and appreciate also that Tolkien has brought us a long way from the first dream to this the last.

The first dream treated at any length is also Frodo's first dream, which Tolkien christened the Dream of the Tower. It comes to Frodo on September 25, during the one night the hobbits spend at Crickhollow before setting off into the Old Forest. This dream in particular has a significance beyond itself, a meaning having as much to do with its placement in the narrative as with its contents:

> Eventually he fell into a vague dream, in which he seemed to be looking out of a high window over a dark sea of tangled trees. Down below among the roots there was the sound of creatures crawling and snuffling. He felt sure they would smell him out sooner or later.
>
> Then he heard a noise in the distance. At first he thought it was a great wind coming over the leaves of the forest. Then he knew that it was not leaves, but the sound of the Sea far-off; a

sound he had never heard in waking life, though it had often troubled his dreams. Suddenly he found he was out in the open. There were no trees after all. He was on a dark heath, and there was a strange salt smell in the air. Looking up he saw before him a tall white tower, standing alone on a high ridge. A great desire came over him to climb the tower and see the Sea. He started to struggle up the ridge towards the tower: but suddenly a light came in the sky, and there was a noise of thunder" (*Fellowship* 118–19).

The images thus pictured—as with those of any dream, real or imagined—are obviously open to a psychological interpretation, Freudian or Jungian or what you will, that might hope to uncover something about Frodo's psychology, his childhood, his sexuality, or his buried fears. Such an interpretation could see in the snuffling, crawling figures among the roots of the trees repressed anxieties, might make the tall tower into a phallic symbol, might interpret the sea as the depths of the unconscious, and so on. But while this may be valid criticism of its kind, it is not to the present purpose, which is to explore Tolkien's intended use of dream as a part of his understructure of time.

Avoiding, then, the obvious psychoanalytical reading, let us look at the revisions Tolkien made in the content of the dream and the changes of placement he tried out within the narrative, for both content and placement underwent a number of alterations before the dream came finally to rest at Crickhollow. Although Christopher Tolkien has provided a long note on this particular dream in his continuing discussion of the many phases of Tolkien's revisions, it will be necessary here to go over some of the same ground, for the shifts and revisions of this dream show Tolkien trying out— much as he did with time in the Lórien chapters—several different strategies in order to create a particular and desired effect.

The first section, with the crawling, snuffling figures at the roots of the trees, appears in embryo in an early draft of the chapter at Crickhollow, in which Bingo (Frodo) "fell asleep into a vague dream, in which he seemed to be lying under a window that looked out into a sea of tangled trees: outside there was a snuffling" (*Return of the Shadow* 104–5). At this point this is all there is to it; the dream is simply a vague vision without action or movement, a dream-impression. The snuffling clearly derives from Frodo's memories of pursuit by the sniffing Black Riders and refers only to immediate past experience. The rest of the dream, which, though somewhat different in content is the basis of the "Tower" portion, was initially placed later in the narrative, in the episode at Bree when Trotter and the hobbits wait out the night attack of the Black Riders on the Prancing Pony. Christopher Tolkien cites "two preparatory drafts and a finished manuscript" of this episode, with few significant differences among them. Here is the passage at Bree as it appears in the finished manuscript, beginning directly after Frodo wakes to see Trotter still keeping watch and then falls asleep again:

Frodo soon went to sleep again; but now he passed at once into a dream. He found himself on a dark heath. Looking up he saw before him a tall white tower, standing alone upon a high ridge. Beyond it the sky was pale, and far off there came a murmur like the voices of the Great Sea which he had never heard nor beheld, save in other dreams. In the topmost chamber of the tower there shone dimly a blue light.

Suddenly he found that he had drawn near and the tower loomed high above him. About its feet there was a wall of faintly shining stones, and outside the wall sat silent watchers: black-robed figures on black horses, gazing at the gate of the tower without moving, as if they had sat there for ever.

There came at last the soft fall of hoofs, climbing up the hill. The watchers all stirred and turned slowly towards the sound. They were looking towards Frodo. He did not dare to turn, but he knew that behind him another dark figure, taller and more terrible, had appeared: it beckoned, and called out in a strange tongue. The horsemen leaped to life. They raised their dark heads towards the lofty chamber, and their mocking laughter rang out cruel and cold; then they turned from the white wall and rode down the hill like the wind. The blue light went out.

It seemed to Frodo that the riders came straight towards him; but even as they passed over him and beat him to the ground, he thought in his heart: "I am not here; they cannot hurt me. There is something I must see." He lifted his head and saw a white horse leap the wall and stride towards him. On it rode a grey-mantled figure: his white hair was streaming, and his cloak flew like wings behind him. As the grey rider bore down upon him he strove to see his face. The light grew in the sky, and suddenly there was a noise of thunder. (*Treason* 33–34)

As it stands in relation to the draft Tolkien was working on at the time, this is no ordinary dream, but a full-fledged dream-vision, for it refers directly to an episode in Tolkien's projected outline in which he had planned for Gandalf to be pursued by the Riders and to flee to the Elf-towers (*Treason* 34). Thus it widens the dreaming Frodo's field of attention beyond the scope of his waking mind to a scene that could only be witnessed by means of Field 2–Observer 2 awareness. Tolkien devoted much time and energy to setting the chronology of Gandalf's movements in this part of the narrative, and while this relates most directly to the overall shape of the story, it has a bearing as well on the placement and significance of Frodo's dreams. Noting that his father worked out four different chronologies of Gandalf's movements, Christopher Tolkien labels these for convenience "A," "B," "C," and "D." In relating the chronology to the Dream of the Tower, he writes that "In A and B the date of Gandalf's escape from the Tower was first given as 24 September, the night that Frodo and his companions passed with the Elves in the Woody End, and in B there is a suggestion, struck out, that Frodo 'dreamt his dream at night with the Elves'; as is seen from the other schemes, he dreamed of Gandalf in the Western Tower" (*Treason* 11).

The struck-out phrase appears to have been Tolkien's first, tentative try at making the dream and the event it refers to contemporaneous and at expanding Frodo's field of vision to include a wider dreaming consciousness. But he then evidently changed his mind, for, as Christopher Tolkien continues, "In C it is said that Frodo dreamt of the Tower when 'with the Elves near Woodhall,' but against this my father wrote: 'No—at Crickhollow'; . . . . In D the placing of Frodo's 'vision of Gandalf' or 'Dream of the Tower' hesitates between the night he spent with the Elves, the night at Crickhollow, and the first night at Bombadil's house" (11).

In a subsequent outline, although the final dates were changed from this rough scheme, it can be seen that the various placements Tolkien tried out for the dream had to do at least in part with whether or not it was to coincide with the actual event. As Christopher Tolkien sets out the final chronology of this "third phase" scheme, Tolkien settled on having Gandalf escape on September 25 (*Treason* 12). But having initially placed Frodo's dream on September 24, making it coincident with the first date given for Gandalf's escape, Tolkien then moved it to the 25th, the day after the escape, when Frodo was at Crickhollow. But he did not leave it there, as Christopher Tolkien notes: "For some reason, however, my father decided to place [the dream] after the event, on the night of the 29th, when Frodo was at Bree and Gandalf was at Crickhollow" (33).

For the dream's final placement in the "fourth phase," Tolkien moved it back to Buckland and "A Conspiracy Unmasked," putting the hobbits rather than Gandalf at Crickhollow and rewriting the ending. Frodo's original dream of the snuffling is retained, but now the Dream of the Tower, shifted back from Bree, is added to it. This reestablishes the coincidence of the dream with the escape, for now, as Christopher Tolkien notes, "Frodo has the vision of Gandalf's escape from the Western Tower on the night of the event itself, the 25th of September."

> Eventually he fell into a vague dream, in which he seemed to be looking out of a high window over a dark sea of tangled trees. Down below among the roots there was the sound of creatures crawling and snuffling. He felt sure they would smell him out sooner or later.
>
> Then he heard a noise in the distance. At first he thought it was a great wind coming over the leaves of the forest. Then he knew that it was not leaves, but the sound of the Sea far-off: a sound he had never heard in waking life, though it had often troubled other dreams. Suddenly he found he was out in the open. There were no trees after all. He was on a dark heath, and there was a strange salt smell in the air. Looking up he saw before him a tall white tower, standing alone on a high ridge. In the topmost chamber a blue light shone dimly.
>
> As he drew near the tower loomed high above him. About its feet there was a wall of faintly gleaming stones, and outside the wall sat silent watchers: there seemed to be four black-robed figures seated on black horses, gazing at the tower without moving, as if they had been there forever.
>
> He heard the soft fall of hoofs climbing up the hill behind him. The watchers all stirred . . . (*Treason* 35)

The rest of the vision follows the previous draft, and ends in the same way, with the light in the sky and the noise of thunder. Had composition in this phase stopped there, the dream would have remained as evidence of dreaming space-travel in the mode of J. W. Dunne, which Tolkien—at this point at any rate—clearly intended. But he was still revising and rethinking, and later, when the story changed and Gandalf's escape was moved from the Western Tower to his imprisonment by Saruman at Orthanc, though the dream sequence as such was kept in place, much of the description of the tower and the waiting Riders was struck out. The opening was retained, however, as far as the sight of the tower on the ridge, and a variant ending that altered the focus was attached: "A great desire came over him to climb the tower and see the Sea. He started to struggle up the ridge towards the tower; but suddenly a light came in the sky, and there was a noise of thunder" (*Treason* 36).

And so for all the placements and replacements, the visions and revisions, Tolkien's final decision was to keep this dream as a mood piece rather than as an actual incident of clairvoyance or travel through the field of space and time, to have it foreshadow but not predict or parallel any actual occurrence. And in this he was successful, for as it stands the dream combines surreal dream quality with extraordinary tension and manages to sustain a remarkable mixture of apprehension, ominousness, and hope without any reference to specific events.

The relationship of dream to actual event became retrospective when Tolkien moved Gandalf's escape from the Western Tower to Orthanc, for the actual escape occurred on September 18, before Frodo left Bag End, but did not enter Frodo's dreams until September 26, the hobbits' first night in the house of Tom Bombadil. Frodo is thus traveling back in time, but to visit an event of which he could have had no prior awareness. Here is the dream as published:

In the dead night Frodo lay in a dream without light. Then he saw a young moon rising; under its thin light there loomed before him a black wall of rock, pierced by a dark arch like a great gate. It seemed to Frodo that he was lifted up, and passing over he saw that the rock-wall was a circle of hills, and that within it was a plain, and in the midst of the plain stood a pinnacle of stone, like a vast tower but not made by hands. On its top stood the figure of a man. The moon as it rose seemed to hang for a moment above his head and glistened in his white hair as the wind stirred it. Up from the dark plain below came the crying of fell voices, and the howling of many wolves. Suddenly a shadow, like the shape of great wings passed across the moon. The figure lifted his arms and a light flashed from the staff that he wielded. A mighty eagle swept down and bore him away. The voices wailed and the wolves yammered. There was a noise like a strong wind blowing, and on it borne the sound of hoofs, galloping, galloping, galloping from the East. "Black Riders!" thought Frodo as he wakened, with the sound of hoofs still echoing in his mind. He wondered if he would ever again have the courage to leave the safety of these stone walls. He lay motionless, still listening, but all was now silent, and at last he turned and fell asleep again, or wandered into some other unremembered dreams. (*Fellowship* 138)

Pippin and Merry also dream on this same night, Pippin of being caught inside the willow, and Merry of water falling into his sleep and drowning him. Sam, sleeping like a contented log, has no memory of any dream. The contrast here is plain and quite clearly purposeful. Pippin and Merry have the kind of predictable bad dream one might expect after so nightmare an experience as their encounter with Old Man Willow. Their dreams have something of the memory quality of the first part of Frodo's Dream of the Tower at Crickhollow, the "tip-tap, squeak" of the willow and the sound of gurgling water haunting them with recent experience, just as the snuffling in Frodo's dream recalled the sniffing Black Riders. Frodo's dream, while it ends with the sound of galloping and thus recalls what he knows of Black Riders, has otherwise a very different quality and content. He is not a participant in the dream but the witness of its events. Where the others' dreams are vague aural sensations, Frodo's is both concrete and visual; he *watches* rather than experiences the events of the dream. Moreover, aside from the galloping, this dream, unlike the others, has no recognizable relationship to his past experience, immediate or distant.

But this dream, too, changed significantly from the early drafts. The first narrative of the hobbits' stay in the house of Tom Bombadil tells it very differently:

In the dead night Bingo [Frodo] woke and heard noises: a sudden fear came over him [?so that] he did not speak but lay listening breathless. He heard a sound like a strong wind curling round the house and shaking it, and down the wind came a galloping, a galloping, a galloping: hooves seemed to come charging down the hillside from the east, up to the walls and round and round, hooves thudding and wind blowing, and then dying away back up the hill and into the darkness.

"Black Riders," thought Bingo. "Black Riders, a black host of riders," and he wondered if he would ever again have the courage even in the morning to leave the safety of these good stone walls. He lay and listened for a while, but all had become quiet again, and after a while he fell asleep. (*Return of the Shadow* 118)

The dreams of the two other hobbits call for no comment, since they are substantially the same as in the published version, though here the dreamers are called Odo and Frodo. The first thing to be noted, as Christopher Tolkien has observed, is that what in the published version is a dream is in this early draft a waking experience (*Return of the Shadow* 118). The Frodo character (here called Bingo) explicitly *wakes up* to hear noises and then falls asleep "after a while," and so there is every reason to suppose that what he hears is the noise of actual hooves galloping round and round the house. This apparently did not change until Tolkien came to the full story of what had happened to Gandalf just before he began the fifth version of "The Council of Elrond." It is here that the earlier conception of the Western Tower as Frodo first saw it in his dream—in which Gandalf stood guarded by Black Riders—changes to Orthanc. And the change of Frodo's dream apparently comes as a direct result of what Tolkien wrote in this "fourth phase" account of Gandalf. As Gandalf narrates the story of his imprisonment, Frodo breaks in with a question:

"Who sent the eagles?" said Frodo eagerly, for suddenly the strange dream that he had came back to him.

Gandalf looked at him in surprise. "I thought you asked what had happened to me," he said. "But you seem to know, and don't need . . . the telling of my tale . . ."

"Your words have recalled a dream," said Frodo, "that I thought only a dream and had forgotten."

"Well," said Gandalf, "your dream was true." (*Treason* 134)

Christopher Tolkien's comment on this passage throws a revealing light on the sometimes unexpected and unplanned aspects of Tolkien's creative process:

> Before writing this passage about Frodo's dream ("'Who sent the eagles?' . . .") my father first put "'And how did you get away?' said Frodo." It was thus probably at this very point that he decided to introduce Frodo's vision of Gandalf on the pinnacle of Orthanc into his dream in the house of Tom Bombadil . . . . His vision of Gandalf imprisoned in the Western Tower had also of course to be removed. (*Treason* 139)

Thus the final discovery, as it were, of what had happened to Gandalf introduced changes in previously written and seemingly "set" material and repositioned the alignment of dream and event. Frodo's Crickhollow dream of the Western Tower, as it was first drafted, was powerful, but what its effect would have been had it been retained in the narrative is difficult to judge. Familiarity with the dream of Orthanc as published overpowers appreciation of how it might otherwise have been. Nevertheless, to have introduced such an explicitly occult experience into the consciousness of so unremarkable a figure as Frodo seems to be *after* establishing dreams and dreaming as ordinary occurrences seems a wise judgment on Tolkien's part. By now we are, as we will be in the as-yet-unwritten *Notion Club Papers*, comfortable with dreams as a part of life and of the story. What Frodo had at Crickhollow (however prescient it was to begin with) was simply a dream of vague anxiety (the snuffling, crawling figures) that led him, as dreams will, to other impressions—the sound of the sea, a vision of a tower, and a final, ominous combination of thunder and light in the sky. Vivid, memorable, strange (but only in the way that any dream is "strange"), this dream is yet a credible experience for the person we know Frodo so far to be, in reference to the adventures we know him so far to have had. It is in character.

His next dream takes the jump from psychological to psychic. When in the house of Tom Bombadil he has the vision of Gandalf at Orthanc, it is a full-fledged dream-vision, an out-of-body experience in which the dreamer travels to another place and there witnesses an actual event that he could not possibly see in real life. But at this point the reader does not know this, and neither does Frodo. This dream is followed in quick succession by the more "normal" dreams of Pippin and Merry, dreams of immediate past experiences with which we are already familiar. And Sam, the log, does not dream at all. The occult is surrounded and in a sense masked by the everyday, and, so far as we know, we are still safely in the realm of the real and the realistic.

As with Frodo's "fair vision" in the house of Tom Bombadil, which Tolkien did not reveal to have been true prevision until the end of the book, it is not until the narrative is well into the Council of Elrond, and Gandalf well-launched on the story of his imprisonment, that (remembering Christopher Tolkien's comment) the reader, Frodo, and Tolkien all discover together that Frodo has had a clairvoyant dream. The function of this discovery is twofold. First, it singles out Frodo as an ordinary person to whom extraordinary things can happen and thus assists his gradual transformation from unremarkable hobbit to exceptional—indeed in some sense "chosen"—individual. Second, and thematically as significant, it begins the process of establishing for Frodo and thus for the reader a wider field of attention than the waking mind is alert to and so prepares the way for the dual time-scheme introduced through the differing perceptions of Elves and Men that we are to meet in the episodes in Lórien.

Dream piles on dream in the Bombadil sequence. Three hobbits dream four dreams, and out of the four the two dreamed by Frodo are greater than the sum of their parts. This is especially true of his last and happiest dream. On his last night in Tom's house Frodo has a dream-vision, a journey not backwards into the recent or far past, nor sideways into another aspect of the present, but forward into his own future, though it will not be revealed as such until the very end of the book. Again we are in the presence of the occult without knowing it, and when at last and finally the vision is revealed for what it truly is, the reader and Frodo have suffered through so much together that its first appearance now seems to have been not occult but heaven-sent, an epiphany, a promise of the best that could happen—the antidote, if we had but known it, to all that was yet to come.

Falling
Asleep Again 9

Imagine an enormously long, vivid, and absorbing dream
being shattered—say simultaneously by an explosion in the
house, a blow on your body, and the sudden flinging back of
dark curtains, letting in a dazzling light: with the result that
you come back with a rush to your waking life, and have to
recapture it and its connections, feeling for some time a shock
and the colour of dream-emotions: like falling out of one world
into another where you had once been but had forgotten it.
—Philip Frankley

Most of the dreams in *The Lord of the Rings*, whether they are
nightmares, prophetic visions, or remnants of past-life experience,
are presented quite explicitly as dreams. We experience them as
they happen to the dreamers, accept them as the dreamers accept
them, and come to realize what Tolkien already knew, that "in
dreams strange powers of the mind may be unlocked." But there
are times, as there were in *The Lost Road*, when the narrative action and the dream are so intertangled that we find ourselves par-
ticipating in a kind of waking dream or a dream-memory without
knowing which is which, when or how we got there. In such a case
we are never told that we are in a dream, but a close inspection reveals the clues. Predictably, these are most apparent in regard to
Lórien. There are hints suggesting that the whole of the Lórien episode, as well as taking place outside ordinary time, also takes place
somehow outside ordinary consciousness. "In Rivendell," says the
narrative, "there was memory of ancient things; in Lórien the ancient things still lived on in the waking world." The waking world
is the conscious world, the world of Observer 1 and that observer's

limited field of attention. But perhaps beyond it, in Lórien, the ancient things live on at some deep subconscious level of memory, for it is in Lórien if anywhere, that the inhabitants of the waking world can be in touch with memory and dream.

It is notable that none of the Fellowship is described as having dreams in Lórien—in fact, at one point the narrative comments that "no sound or dream disturbed their slumber." Rather, it would seem that the experience of being there is itself the dream. Treebeard translates Lothlórien as "Dreamflower" and comments to Merry and Pippin that its inhabitants are "falling behind the world." There may be more to this deliberate association of Lórien with dream than meets—or was intended to meet—the eye. The etymological evidence cited in chapter 7 suggests this. Recall that *olo-s* meant "vision, phantasy," and that one of its derivatives was *Olofantur*, "the earlier 'true' name of Lórien, the Vala who was *'master of visions and dreams'*" (*Unfinished Tales* 396–97; emphasis added). From the early stages of Tolkien's mythology, *Lórien* was the name of the God of Dreams. The replication of the name, the fact that *Lothlórien* the place is called the Dreamflower,[1] the circumstance that none of the Company dreams while they are there, cannot be unrelated. I suggest, then, that Lórien itself is in a very real sense a dream sent or dreamed by the God of Dreams and that the Company in Lórien is, in one sense at least, inside that dream. If this seems like forcing the evidence, or appears to be a too highly wrought interpretation of the phenomenon, consider what Tolkien had to say in "On Fairy-Stories" about the relationship between dream and Elven Art:

> Now "Faërian Drama"—those plays which according to abundant records the elves have often presented to men—can produce Fantasy with a realism and immediacy beyond the compass of any human mechanism. As a result their usual effect (upon a man) is to go beyond Secondary Belief. If you are present at a Faërian drama you yourself are, or think that you are, bodily inside its Secondary world. The experience may be very similar to dreaming and has (it would seem) sometimes (by men) been confounded with it. But in Faërian drama you are in a dream that some other mind is weaving, and the knowledge of that alarming fact may slip from your grasp. (142)

"You are in a dream that some other mind is weaving." When they are in Lórien the Fellowship is in truth "bodily inside a Secondary World," as the difference in time so deliberately suggested but carefully did not state. Here in the critical essay Tolkien has allowed himself the explicitness that he carefully kept out of his narrative. He kept it out with good reason. If he had made it plain he would have had to make it explainable, and to do so would have been laborious and cumbersome—and utterly unconvincing. "But how?" the reader might well have asked. "How can they be inside someone else's dream unless Lórien has no actuality at all? And in that case how did they get there?" The story would dissolve into a Looking-glass puzzle with Frodo, Sam, and all the rest, like Alice, part of the Red King's dream. When Sam, in Lórien, says he feels as if he is "inside a song," we take as a metaphor what Tolkien means as a hidden reality. Sam is in truth inside a song, inside an artistic creation, a "Faërien Drama" woven by some other mind. Lothlórien is indeed a Dreamflower, a dream woven, a song sung by some other mind than those of the Company who are inside this dream. It is no wonder they don't dream in Lórien; their whole experience is on one plane at least a part of a larger dream.

We have already examined the evidence that Lórien time is different from "outside" time through the Company's discussion of the differences between the two, after they are back out in the world and going down the river. There is evidence inside Lórien as well to suggest within it the presence of a different and wider field of time, not unlike that accessible to the dreaming mind. Suppose the dreaming mind to be that of Lórien, the God of Dreams. He, if anyone, would be the "observer at infinity," and Tolkien has found a way to give the reader access to that observer's field of attention. Situated in Lórien (and it would be unlikely to be anywhere else) is the Mirror of Galadriel, as wide a window onto the field of time as is Dunne's window of dreams, of which it more and more seems to be a reflection. Galadriel's mirror encompasses the same field of attention as that of Dunne's observer at infinity; it can manifest all time to those who look into it. "It shows," as Galadriel tells Frodo and Sam, "things that were, and things that are, and things that yet may be. But which it is that he sees, even the wisest cannot always tell" (*Fellowship* 377).

Sam's vision shows him two out of the three, more than enough for him. First looking (though he does not know it) ahead in time and space to Cirith Ungol, he sees "Frodo with a pale face lying fast asleep under a great dark cliff" and himself "going along a dim passage, and climbing an endless stair." Then, "like a dream," the vision shifts and he sees the apparently simultaneous present— the ruination of the Shire, with trees crashing to the ground, a new red-brick building being erected where the Old Mill had been, the Gaffer turned out of his home—events distant in space but, as Sam interprets them, events going on right now and all he needs to spur him into action.

His impulse to return home immediately and put everything right is stalled by Galadriel, who reminds him of the Quest and tells him that not everything shown in the Mirror has yet come to pass. She follows this with the statement that "some things never come to be, unless those that behold the visions turn aside from their path to prevent them. The Mirror is dangerous as a guide of deeds." This is perplexing. The events that Sam has seen (though he does *not* turn aside to prevent them) are already coming to pass, as Sam discovers when he returns to the Shire. Just what Tolkien intended Galadriel's caution to mean, and how it fits into his cosmology, is an open question. It appears to address itself to the conflict between desire and duty and seems also to imply a distinction between prevision and predestination; what the Mirror shows is foreseen but not intended. From a purely psychological perspective this is pretty solid ground; the irony that what you fear you also create is as old as Sophocles and as new as Freud. But Sam is not Œdipus, and the mechanics of how such events could be brought about by the effort to prevent them are not explained, either by Galadriel or by Tolkien.

Frodo's look in the Mirror is less provocative, and, on the surface at least, less philosophically complicated. Concomitant with the wider consciousness developed by his wounding in the attack on Weathertop and by his possession of the Ring, he sees in the Mirror a predictably wider vision than Sam's. First, he sees an old man on a road and (assuming Gandalf to have been lost in Moria) cannot tell if he is seeing a vision of Gandalf as he was in the past or of Saruman as he is in the present. Next, Frodo sees Bilbo "walking restlessly about his room." The table is littered with papers, and rain beats on the window. Unlike the vision of the old man, there is no reason to suppose that this is not a vision of the actual present; Frodo in Lórien is in fact seeing Bilbo in Rivendell. And then, in the widest attention field of all, the mirror shows "many swift scenes" that Frodo knows in some way to be "parts of a great history in which he had become involved." They are indeed, but could only be recognized as such by a reader familiar with *The Silmarillion* as well as with *The Lord of the Rings*, for they come out of both stories.

> The mist cleared and he saw a sight which he had never seen before but knew at once: the Sea. Darkness fell. The sea rose and raged in a great storm. Then he saw against the Sun, sinking blood-red into a wrack of clouds, the black outline of a tall ship with torn sails riding up out of the West. Then a wide river flowing through a populous city. Then a white fortress with seven towers. And then again a ship with black sails, but now it was morning again, and the water rippled with light, and a banner bearing the emblem of a white tree shone in the sun. A smoke as of fire and battle arose, and again the sun went down in a burning red that faded into a grey mist; and into the mist a small ship passed away, twinkling with lights. (*Fellowship* 379)

The events that Frodo sees in the Mirror are indeed "parts of a great history"; they are scenes spanning a great stretch of time that begins far back in the history of Middle-earth. Of special interest to the present discussion are the three ships. The first vision, that of the storm at sea and the tall ship, is probably not, as many early readers might have supposed (unless they had read carefully Appendix A to *The Lord of the Rings*), Aragorn's ship but is more likely to be the ship of Elendil riding out the downfall of Númenor. The vision as shown seems very like that in the account of the Great Storm given by the old man in Ireland to Lowdham and Jeremy. His description of "a tall black ship high on the crest of the great wave, with its masts down and the rags of black and yellow sails flapping on the deck" seems of a piece with Frodo's vision, and the two visions together suggest the power and presence (both in the theatrical and temporal senses) of this event in Tolkien's imagination.

From the past the vision then shifts to the near future. The next ship to be seen, the black-sailed ship with the white banner, is unmistakably Aragorn's fleet sailing up the Anduin to Minas Tirith from the South and thus occurs many hundreds of years in the future after the first ship and some several months after Frodo's vision of it. The last vision looks even farther ahead. Not until his part in the history is finished will the last ship, small, twinkling with the light of Eärendil's star caught in the Phial of Galadriel, carry Frodo—like Ælfwine, like Éadwine, like old Edwin Lowdham—by the Straight Road to the Undying Lands, to Valinor.

Though the elements of this scene were arranged and rearranged, the scene itself and the concept behind it were a part of the story from its very early drafts. In Tolkien's preliminary outline it was "King Galdaran's mirror" (Galadriel not having yet fully emerged as a character), and the vision of the despoiled Shire was given to Frodo, Sam not being added to the scene until a later writing. The Gandalf-Saruman figure, the city with the seven towers, and— clearly of great importance—a vision "breathtaking and strange and yet known at once: a stony shore, and a dark sea into which a blood red sun was sinking among black clouds, a ship darkly outlined against the sun" all were part of the vision from its earliest inception (*Treason* 251–53). The vision of the stormy sky and the ship against the sun was one of the most persistent elements, and it seems clear that Tolkien fully intended to bring in, or at least gesture toward, the Fall of Númenor. Laid aside as in *The Lost Road*, not yet envisioned as part of *The Notion Club Papers*, the ghost of Atlantis and the Great Wave haunts *The Lord of the Rings*.

The importance to Tolkien of this picture of all time as *verthandi*, as always "happening" and always in some sense "present," cannot be doubted. The episode of the Mirror has an obvious technical function in that it recapitulates key events in the history of Middle-earth and uses these to foreshadow important moments in the story to come. But it has a thematic function as well, resting on the hidden dream-activity of Lórien, "master of visions and dreams," and both using and illustrating the widened field of time that is central to Tolkien's fictive vision.

The deepest dream, and the longest, may well be one that does not appear to be a dream at all until nearly the end of the story. When the War of the Ring has ended, and all the rejoicings and celebrations that follow it are finally over, the ride back to Hobbiton of Frodo, Sam, Merry, and Pippin has something of a dying fall, an end-of-the-party quality, that mellow time when one by one the guests depart and the remaining few congregate in the kitchen for

196

A Question
of Time

quiet talk. "Well here we are just the four of us that started out together," says Merry. "We have left all the rest behind, one after another. It seems almost like a dream that has slowly faded." "Not to me," says Frodo. "To me it feels more like falling asleep again" (*Return of the King* 276). If we take this statement seriously, it seems to suggest that what for Merry has had the quality of a dream has been for Frodo his waking reality, that the sometimes nightmarish experience of the journey and the rigors of the quest are more vivid, more real to him than all the rest of his life, and that his quiet existence before and after these experiences is the dream. Like David Lindsay's Nightspore, Frodo has awakened from the dreamy peace of the Shire into the active center of his life, the dangerous journey and the encounter with the dark that are at the heart of human experience. Returning to the old life would be for Frodo, as it was for Nightspore, a falling asleep, a reentry of the soul into its old body and habitat, to make the journey once again. The difference is that for Frodo it is not a true return. His life back in the Shire can never again be for him "the old life," and his next journey will take him out of it altogether.

We have met this concept before, though not so explicitly. This reversal of ordinary norms, which suggests dream as real experience and dismisses waking life as a dream, resonates with the interconnected dream-reality of Alboin Errol, which, as we saw, comprised the whole narrative of *The Lost Road*. The Errols dreamed themselves into a past more real, more active, more awake than their rather somnolent present. The active dreamers of the Notion Club, too, as the story progresses, find their present reality less "real" than the dreams in which they become more and more involved. The idea is not new to Tolkien, only the quiet unobtrusiveness with which the paradoxical reversal is introduced. It is, of course, a fundamental tenet of Eastern philosophy, found in both Hindu and Buddhist belief, that what is perceived as reality is only *maya*, "illusion," a dream from which the soul will awake.

But Tolkien need not have gone East for the idea that reality is only a dream and dream the true reality. Two of his great predecessors in the dream-vision mode, George MacDonald and David Lindsay, both used the concept. It is the informing principle of MacDonald's *At the Back of the North Wind*, where his boy-hero, Diamond, "wakes into a dream" that is more real to him than his waking life. So skillfully does MacDonald manage the reversal that when Diamond dies at the end of the book the reader has no difficulty in understanding that his apparent death is an awakening into another life. And it is, as we have seen, the informing principle of Lindsay's *Voyage to Arcturus,* that ultimate in dream-journeys, where the death of the body (Maskull) brings to waking consciousness the soul (Nightspore). Barring the ultimate death of both MacDonald's and Lindsay's characters, this reversal is replicated concept for concept, if not quite word for word, in the experience of Ramer in *The Notion Club Papers,* who "fell wide asleep" into a dream more real to him than waking reality. It is replicated more profoundly in the experience of Frodo, who feels at the end of his adventure that he is "falling asleep again."

While the end of what I shall call Frodo's waking dream is fairly well marked (if his own statement about falling asleep again is to be credited), no such explicit description marks the beginning. Certainly no experience as abrupt, violent, and shocking as the one that Ramer described wakes Frodo into the deeper reality of his great adventure. Instead, there is a series of small clues that taken together suggest such a transition, widely separated phrases hardly to be noticed and acquiring their larger meaning only in retrospect, in the context of Frodo's answer to Merry. As the Bucklebury Ferry takes Sam across the Brandywine to Crickhollow, he feels that "his old life lay behind in the mists, dark adventure lay in front" (*Fellowship* 109). Crossing a body of water is a standard literary marker for a profound change of state. Sam is surely not alone in this feeling. If we equate Sam's "old life" with the sleep state Frodo's later statement to Merry implies that he left behind in the Shire, then the "dark adventure" that lies in front will be the waking dream for Frodo as well as Sam. Other suggestions of a change of state abound in this and the following sequence. When he first enters the house at Crickhollow, Frodo finds himself "wishing that he was really coming here to settle down in quiet retirement" (*Fellowship* 110–11). The fact is, however, that he is not going into retirement; he is coming out of it. A life of quiet hibernation such as he has lived at Bag End is just what he is waking up from. Instead of digging in at Crickhollow, he will "fall wide asleep" onto the world stage and into the middle of great events.

Those events are not long in coming. The Crickhollow chapter ends with Frodo's first dream, which comes to him that same night and mixes his all-too-recent memory of Black Riders with a fore-taste of the Sea he will cross at the end of his story. The next day and the next chapter open with the terse sentence "Frodo woke suddenly." This is, of course, literally the case, since he has been asleep and is wakened by Merry banging on his door. But it is also metaphorically the case if his old life, like last night's sleep, lies behind him, and dark adventure most certainly lies ahead. He is waking up to a new reality. As the four hobbits pass through the tunnel and approach the Old Forest, the ominous clang of the gate closing behind them announces that they are outside the Shire and into their adventure. All the details so far noted—crossing water, coming out of retirement, waking suddenly, coming out on the other side of a tunnel—indicate a profound, life-and-mind-expanding change of state.

In order to understand Frodo's adventures from this point in terms of the dream/reality reversal implied by his own words to Merry, that reversal described by Ramer in *The Notion Club Papers* or experienced by the boy Diamond in MacDonald's *At the Back of the North Wind*, we must take a fresh look at the whole center of the book. We must re-view the whole of Frodo's journey from Crickhollow to the Cracks of Doom as if he has fallen wide asleep into a dream so vivid that ordinary waking life takes on the evanescent quality of a dream in comparison. Once he and his three companions are outside the Shire, they enter a world in which waking experience becomes the stuff of dreams, often of night-mares, and in which their dreams cross over into waking experience. They are from now until the end of the journey in a world far removed from ordinary daylight experience. Its first shadowy region is the Old Forest, the next the storied, haunted Barrow-downs, both already the raw material for nightmare. In quick succession the hobbits encounter Willow Man, Tom Bombadil, and the Barrow-wight, "creatures of night brought to light." Each of these, the merry Bombadil included, has a pronounced dreamlike quality, though unlike the other two, Tom has all the qualities of a good dream.

The first, and the most explicitly associated with dream-conditions, is Willow Man. He is a figure out of a child's nightmare, a gnarled and twisted Arthur Rackham tree with wrinkled bark skin, knothole eyes, grasping roots, and groping twig-fingers, the very personification of the unhuman, peopled forest that comes awake to haunt your sleep. Indeed, *sleep* is the operative word in the Willow Man sequence. The hobbits feel sleepiness "creeping out of the ground"; Frodo feels "sleep overwhelming him" as, "half in a dream," he sits with his feet in the water and his back against the willow. "Hark at it singing about sleep now!" exclaims Sam, the only one to fight successfully the uncanny drowsiness. And when Frodo tells of being thrown into the water and half-drowned by the willow, he remarks, "You were dreaming, I expect, Mr. Frodo" (*Fellowship* 128). If coming back to the Shire feels to Frodo like falling asleep again, then his enchanted sleep in the Withywindle Valley must be a dream within a waking dream, an ironic variation on the whole dream of his adventure.

Though the sleep-associations for the next episode are not so strong nor so explicit, the Barrow-wight, too, is the stuff bad dreams are made of. The wight is a dark presence out of a dream lost on waking, a vague, ominous, faceless memory on the edge of awareness, sensation without shape or substance. Deeper, darker sleep than that sent by Willow Man, a sleep bordering on true unconsciousness, is the central concept in this far more frightening sequence, and here, as in the Old Forest, dreaming and waking are interwoven. After their unplanned, unexpected nap by the standing stone, the hobbits *wake* "suddenly and uncomfortably from a sleep they had never meant to take" (148–49), only to lose themselves in a cold mist. Later, in the stony dark of the barrow, they lie unconscious, and only Frodo wakes in the green light to hear the wight's song, like a ghastly lullaby, "a cold murmur, rising and falling." Here night and dream are at their worst, a Poe illustration by Harry Clarke. Here is the night "railing against the morning of which it was bereaved," chanting the hobbits' sleep into their deaths, chanting "cold be sleep under stone," chanting them a dreadful incantation "nevermore to wake on stony bed" (152).

Tom's rescue lets in the light of day, and by it Merry, Pippin, and Sam look now "as if they were very deeply asleep." They are brought out into the sunlight and laid on the green grass. "Wake now, my merry lads!" commands Tom, and only as they wake and rub their eyes do we realize how deeply they have been asleep. Only when we are witness to Merry's waking confusion about the men of Carn Dûm, when we hear his cry at the spear in his heart, do we know just how far into dream they have gone. They run about on the sunwarmed grass like suddenly happy children, and their joy in their recovery is that of "people that, after being long ill and bedridden, wake one day to find that they are unexpectedly well and the day is again full of promise" (154–55).

Tom has brought them, as he says, "out of deep water." But even Tom Bombadil, stamping, chanting, crashing through the underbrush with his blue feather and his yellow boots, is not your ordinary, everyday kind of fellow. Tom is not less substantial than the waking world but more so. His vivid ultrareality makes the world around him seem pale and insubstantial in comparison. As a realistic character Tom is problematic, and in some ways it is easier to accept the dark barrow-wight than bright Tom. Tolkien himself observed that not everyone liked the character, noting in a letter to a reader that "many have found him an odd or indeed discordant ingredient" (*Letters* 192). Both those who like him and those who find him "discordant" may be responding in their separate ways to the same thing: the child's-drawing quality, the crayon colors, the absence of shading or depth that seem to characterize this episode. It can appear simplistic, it certainly seems one-dimensional. This is precisely what gives it the quality of dream. The Bombadil chapters have all the cheerful, bright aspect of a happy dream, one in which we can be assured, as we never wholly can in real life, that the dark fears are banished, the lights are on, and we are home and safe. Everything is all right.

There is more to it, of course, and not all is light. The crayon colors stand out in contrast to the dark background of the Forest, and the apparently one-dimensional Tom shows unexpected depths of memory and perception. It is apparent that there is far more to him than a hopping, singing, flower-gathering nature spirit. The hobbits' first sight of Tom's house, with the path winding up the grassy hillside and the river leaping down beside it, the twinkling lights, the open door with the yellow beam of light shining out, has all the concrete beauty and hard-edged enchantment of a Bilibin illustration to a Russian fairy-tale, as does the wonderful first sight of Goldberry, surrounded with water-lilies and lighted by candles.

But once the hobbits are inside, the experience takes on other dimensions. Tom knows the dark, and the Forest, and his stories bring the hobbits uncomfortably close to fears they would rather avoid, to Willow Man behind them and the Barrow-downs ahead. Tom's tales take them "into strange regions beyond their memory and beyond their *waking* thought" (*Fellowship* 142; emphasis added). Tom takes them from the heart of the Forest to the shadowed Barrows, to the long-ago wars of little kingdoms (one of which could be Carn Dûm, a fortress of the witch-kingdom of Angmar) and the deaths of forgotten kings and queens, and so on and back "into times when the world was wider, and the seas flowed straight to the western Shore" (142). A history of Middle-earth comes to life through the spell of Tom's words. Moreover, the phrase "waking thought" suggests that somehow, in this dreaming wakefulness that the hobbits are in, Tom has given them access to the whole field of time.

This is borne out by the implication of the opening sentence of the next paragraph: "Whether the morning and evening of one day or of many days had passed Frodo could not tell" (142). As we have already noted, this same blurring of time perception will occur in Lórien, where it is impossible for the hobbits to tell how many days have passed. And again, as with Lórien, Tolkien reworked the text to move it from a more to a less specific presentation of the experience. In his discussion of the Bombadil chapter, Christopher Tolkien notes that "A detail worth remarking is the sentence in the old version: 'Whether the morning and evening of one day or of many days had passed Bingo [Frodo] could not tell (nor did he ever discover for certain).' The bracketed words were soon to be removed, when the dating of the journey to Bree became precise; the hobbits stayed with Bombadil on the 26th and 27th of September, and left on the morning of the 28th" (*Return of the Shadow* 121).

The "bracketed" words "nor did he ever discover for certain" appear to have had the purpose of reinforcing the ambiguity of time in the house of Tom Bombadil, much as does the inconclusive discussion among Frodo, Sam, Aragorn, and Legolas after the Company leaves Lórien. As with his final decision to remove much of the specificity from the Lórien discussion, the demands of an external calendar of events and a manageable sequence of days and weeks and seasons forced Tolkien to delete the bracketed comment here and to keep such observation subjective, within the shifting realm of human perception. With the narrative comment removed, there is only Frodo's impression of the passage of time. But the fact that such an impression comes in Tom's house, and at a moment when the hobbits and Tom have been ranging over the whole field of time, strongly suggests that here dream and waking are interconnected, that in their experience in Tom's house the hobbits, and especially Frodo, are waking up to a reality more real than anything in their previous experience.

This being the case, it is probably not an accident that Frodo's most vivid and significant dreams come to him in Tom's house, nor that they transcend his usual waking or sleeping states. His first dream in Tom's house gives him access to something his ordinary waking self could not possibly know: the sight of Gandalf on the tower. We have seen how Tolkien worked and reworked that dream to get the most out of it, shaping it for maximum effect and discovering, finally, that, properly situated, it could carry Frodo and the story across space-time, across the barriers of the conscious mind. As already noted, this use of the dream seems not to have arisen until Tolkien's narrative had arrived at Gandalf's account of his captivity at Orthanc. At this point it became a vehicle for thematic development of Dunne's theory, but it also served to emphasize the ultrareality of certain kinds of dream experience.

Frodo's second dream in Tom's house, his vision of the rain-curtain and the far green country, is, in terms of his own history and because of the significance of its reappearance, arguably the most important dream in the book. In the Bombadil sequence it is called a "vision" and is not described as a dream until the reality it foretells appears to Frodo at the end of the story. In its first context, then, this was not prevision but simply vision, an idyllic alternative to the terror of pursuit that Frodo was already experiencing and the burden of obligation he was carrying. But its significance as a foreshadowing, and its reappearance at the end of the book, was foreseen by Tolkien in his sketch of Book Five in a letter of November 29, 1944, to Christopher Tolkien: "the final scene will be the passage of Bilbo and Elrond and Galadriel through the woods of the Shire on their way to the Grey Havens. Frodo will join them and pass over the Sea (linking with the vision he had of a far green country in the house of Tom Bombadil)" (*War of the Ring* 219).

Notwithstanding this forecast, when Tolkien finally came to write it, the first text of "The Grey Havens"—the "A" text—did not at first include any mention of the far green country or indeed any further mention of Frodo after he kissed Merry and Pippin and Sam and went aboard the ship. Christopher Tolkien notes, however, that though absent from the text, the final sight of the green country "was roughed in marginally" and was subsequently included in the emended "B" text. A close look at the two published accounts, the first as dream, the second as reality, shows how carefully Tolkien located the first in the shifting terrain between sleep and waking. The first account opens Chapter 8, "Fog on the Barrow-Downs":

> That night they [the four hobbits] heard no noises. But either in his dreams or out of them, he could not tell which, Frodo heard a sweet singing running in his mind: a song that seemed to come like a pale light behind a grey rain-curtain, and growing stronger to turn the veil all to glass and silver, until at last it was rolled back, and a far green country opened before him under a swift sunrise.
> The vision melted into waking . . . . (*Fellowship* 146)

A song that comes like light. "In his dreams or out of them." "Running in his mind." A vision that *melts* into waking. All is ephemeral, undefined; neither Frodo nor the reader knows exactly what is happening. Sound is presented as light, the line between dream and waking is blurred, the vision softens into waking experience. If nothing else, this is a lyrical and evocative passage, a simple but utterly desirable composition of rain, green country, and sunrise described in the simplest possible language. But it has another purpose, for aside from its beauty, its very ambiguity makes it a solid reinforcement of the premise that some kinds of dream transcend, rather than replace, waking experience.

The second vision, this one no dream nor half-dream but true, waking reality, necessarily occurs so far from the first, so removed from it in fictive time and actual space (nearly a thousand pages) and with so many other things between, that some effort is required to connect the two. Not a few readers encountering the second vision have to turn back to the Bombadil sequence to be reminded of the first one. The act of conscious comprehension this requires serves to reinforce the reader's impression of the whole time-and-space complex that Tolkien has been so carefully building. The visions are reciprocal and therefore doubly effective. They bridge the heart of the book and encompass nearly the whole of Frodo's waking dream. Here, unlike his experience in the house of Bombadil, there is no question of dream or waking. We are told that the ship went out into the High Sea and passed on into the West, until at last on a night of rain Frodo smelled a sweet fragrance on the air and heard the sound of singing that came over the water. And then it seemed to him that as in his dream in the house of Bombadil, the grey rain-curtain turned all to silver glass and was rolled back, and he beheld white shores and beyond them a far green country under a swift sunrise.

But to Sam the evening deepened to darkness as he stood at the Haven; and as he looked at the grey sea he saw only a shadow on the waters that was soon lost in the West. (*Return of the King* 310–11)

Here for the first time the vision in the house of Tom Bombadil is called a dream, but only because it pales in comparison with the reality of this present experience. Morning and evening are contrasted in the disparate experiences of Frodo and Sam. Sam's day is ending; he is going back into that same Shire that has been night and dream for Frodo. Frodo's night is over, and his sunrise brings daylight and waking, a real awakening this time, in which what was dream is now the true reality.

So treated, so reinvoked, this realization of Frodo's dream stretches to the outer limit of the book—and therefore to the extent of the fictive experience—the field of time over which the consciousness of Observer 2, the observer at infinity, can range. Like the figure of Eriol-Ælfwine, of whom Elendil became the earliest incarnation, Frodo has become the overarching consciousness, the observer at infinity for whom the field of time is spread open like a book whose story may be read and reread, ranged over at liberty, or focused on any point. And at this point it is the reader, even more than Frodo, who is the observer at this widened field of time, this fictive infinity. Anyone reading the book again (and most readers repeat the experience not once but many times) will inevitably assume the position of Dunne's Observer 2, able to see two fields of attention at once, one field limited to the immediate moment and another encompassing the entire experience.

This is true to some extent of the second reading of any book, but it is especially true of a book like Tolkien's, in which time and the shifting boundaries of perception play a more than usually important part. Anyone reading *The Lord of the Rings* not just again but also in the context of the larger history of which it is a part will become an observer not just doubled but squared, cubed, carried to the nth power as the field of attention widens and the vision expands. The reader will know the limits of mortal time and the long count of Elven time, will experience memory and nostalgia in Lórien and vision and prevision in the house of Tom Bombadil, and will come awake with Frodo as his dreams carry him beyond his old reality. Thus Tolkien's medium becomes its own message, and through our reading experience we learn what Tolkien created the whole of *The Lord of the Rings* in order to show us, and himself.

A Dream of 10
Light and Dark

Never will my ear that bell hear,
never my feet that shore tread
—"The Sea-bell"

Lesser narratives, Tolkien's minor works both early and late dealing with "other" time, with journey and return, remain to be considered. These are less like the conventional time-travel treatment that Tolkien gave *The Lost Road* and *The Notion Club Papers* and closer to the treatment he adopted for Frodo in the Lórien chapters of *The Lord of the Rings*. Nonetheless, they have something to say about dream and time and Faërie.

The first is the story of a voyage to the Otherworld narrated by the nameless wanderer in Tolkien's early poem, "The Sea-bell," the most explicit treatment of the faërien time warp that Tolkien made. The poem tells of a voyager who takes a magical boat to an enchanted land. Although the land seems deserted, the signs of its inhabitants are everywhere, the echo of their song, the sound of their footfalls, the linger of their music in the air. But wherever the voyager comes, the fairy folk have vanished; nor will they answer when he calls. In the midst of his solitary progress, and utterly without warning, the ambient beauty darkens, the air turns chill; he is suddenly old. Passing in a moment from joyous summer to bleak winter, he passes also from eager youth to disappointed age. At last, bereft of his vision of beauty, estranged and alone in a cold, unpeopled world, he returns home in the same boat, only to find that he is estranged from his own world as well.

"The Sea-bell" is one in a collection of minor poems published in 1962 as *The Adventures of Tom Bombadil and Other Verses from the Red Book* that Tolkien called "old, half-forgotten things" (*Letters* 309). Old they are, though just how forgotten might be open to question. Many of them, and "The Sea-bell" in particular, rehearse themes and ideas that appear throughout Tolkien's work. An earlier version of "The Sea-bell," with the less evocative but more explicit title "Looney," was published in *The Oxford Magazine* on January 18, 1934. Worthy of note is the fact that less than a month later, another early poem, "The Adventures of Tom Bombadil," also appeared in *The Oxford Magazine*, this one in the issue for February 15, 1934.[1] This poem, revised, also reappeared in the later collection, and gave its title to the whole.

Although "Looney" was published close to the time when Tolkien was reading J. W. Dunne, the actual writing of the poem probably preceded his encounter with *An Experiment with Time* by a year or so. Christopher Tolkien puts the date of the poem's composition "pretty confidently (though without any possibility of proof)" at 1932 or 1933.[2] We may suppose, however, that Tolkien's mind was already tending in a direction that would make him receptive to the theory when he encountered Dunne's book. The notion of time as a field, and the possibility that, as in Faërie, it is a field wherein one can lose the way, could as easily derive from Tolkien's familiarity with fairy lore as from any particular theory. When the mind is ready, the idea appears.

Nearly three decades after "Looney" was published, it was rewritten as "The Sea-bell" for inclusion in *The Adventures of Tom Bombadil*. This intent notwithstanding, Tolkien's letters display a confusion of attitudes toward the poem. Some of the letters, written while he was in the process of organizing the collection, come close to apologizing for it. Others (specifically one to W. H. Auden) manifest a quite justifiable pride in it. Some of this mix of attitudes has clearly to do with Tolkien's difficulty in getting "The Sea-bell" to harmonize with the other poems in the book. He clearly felt that the collection as a whole should have some overall ethos or consistency at least of tone and wrote about this to Rayner Unwin in April 1962. "I have done a good deal of work trying to make them [the poems] fit better" (*Letters* 315). Nevertheless, a letter of about the same time to Pauline Baynes, who was to illustrate the collection, suggested that he somehow felt that "The Sea-bell" did not fit, that it was out of keeping with the rest. He called it "the poorest and not one that I shd. really wish to include, at least not with the others" (*Letters* 312).

Several factors make this rather severe judgment difficult to understand. For one thing, he did, after all, include it with the others. For another, it fits rather well with the dark undertone of, for example, "The Mewlips" or the ironic implications underlying "The Hoard." Moreover, not only is it very far from being the poorest, it can lay claim to being one of the best in the collection, as Tolkien must have known. He certainly didn't protest when a letter from W. H. Auden called it "wonderful." On the contrary, he allowed himself to be pleased and wrote to Auden in reply: "I was greatly cheered . . . by your praise . . . of *Frodo's Dreme* ["The Sea-bell"] . . . . That really made me wag my tail" (*Letters* 379).

But that his feelings about the poem were, at the least, mixed is shown in another of his comments to Pauline Baynes, this that, "with the exception of 'The Sea-bell,'" the poems were conceived as "a series of very definite, clear and precise, pictures—fantastical, or nonsensical perhaps, but not dreamlike!" (*Letters* 312). The addition of the "Dreme" title and Tolkien's exception of "The Sea-bell" from the other, emphatically "not dreamlike," poems suggests that, unlike the rest, this one *was* intended to be dreamlike. And indeed it is a dream—or nightmare—from beginning to end. It is not a dream-vision, for there is no frame. The whole of the poem is to be experienced as a dream. Moreover, the fact that it is *Frodo's* dream is a clear signal that the mood and content are now to be a continuation of the dream motif associated with Frodo in *The Lord of the Rings*. No longer "Looney," the poem is now to be associated with an already-familiar character whose tragic history can then become its context. It is the addition of Frodo that makes the difference.

It is not the purpose of the present study to attempt a close reading of either poem or to make an extended comparison of the early and late versions. This has been done with care and sensitivity by T. A. Shippey. Among other things, Shippey finds in the revision from one version to the other an expansion of the element of menace, an "increasing darkness," and a sense, absent from

"Looney," of the guilt of the speaker, who seems in "The Sea-bell" himself to have provoked or somehow brought on the darkness that overwhelms him. Shippey's final reading of the poem suggests that it comes out of Tolkien's doubt about the "legitimacy of his own mental wanderings" (211). A distinction should be made here between tone and content. While Shippey's term "legitimacy" rather overstates the case—Tolkien would not have spent a lifetime in the exercise of his imagination if he had entertained serious doubts about its legitimacy—his association of the voice with Tolkien's own is, in terms of the overall tone of the poem, both pertinent and persuasive.

Aspects of both poems are worth exploring. First of all, and simply in terms of quality apart from context, "The Sea-bell" is much the better poem. It is twice as long as "Looney," and this extra length affords a deeper exploration of both the speaker and the perilous world of Faërie into which he ventures. The poem's voice is clearer, its air colder and purer, its beauties more sharply incised. Tolkien's revisions intensified but did not change the overall mood. Rather, they enhanced its dreamlike quality. The mood of eager expectancy changing into despair, the shift from unearthly beauty to deathly desolation, are intensified in the rewritten version.

Secondly, "The Sea-bell" is an infinitely lonelier poem. One small but significant change materially alters the situation and contributes to that tone of increasing darkness that Shippey finds in the revised "Sea-bell." The early "Looney" begins in the style of Coleridge's "The Rime of the Ancient Mariner" with a nameless questioner inquiring of an undescribed someone: "Where have you been; what have you seen / Walking in rags down the street?" The reply, "I come from a land, where cold was the strand / Where no men were me to greet" (*Oxford Magazine* 340), launches the poem, the story of a voyage to and return from an enchanted land which tells the invisible auditor where the speaker has been and what he has seen. No motive for the voyage is given, and the reasons for the return are unclear. Once home, however, the narrator finds himself lonely and alone, and the concluding couplet, "Ragged I walk. To myself I must talk / for seldom they speak, men that I meet," brings the poem round to the opening question again. It is worthy of note, as well, that this opening question, and the situation it sets up, effectively prevent the poem from being understood as a dream.

The revision of "Looney" into "The Sea-bell" omits the opening question, eliminating any vestige of human contact. There is no introduction. Instead, the poem begins straightaway with the solitary voice of the voyager. The change from conversation to monologue is significant. First, it allows the poem to be a dream, which "Looney" does not. Second, it immediately sets up a situation in which there is no one to hear, no one to care. The speaker, the dreamer, is talking to himself. This alters the ethos of the poem from that of someone asked to share his story to that of someone utterly cut off from other beings, both from the fairy folk who reject him and the human community to which he no longer belongs. An equally significant change in the concluding couplet drives home the point. "Ragged I walk. To myself I talk / *for still they speak not*, men that I meet" (emphasis added). Just as in "Looney," the poem comes round to its beginning again, but with a difference. Here we are still in the dream, pinned in a kind of ghostly deathlessness. Moreover, the shift from "seldom they speak" to "still they speak not" sharpens the outcome, pointing up the utter isolation of the speaker.

Purified in tone and concept by the removal of the introductory situation, "The Sea-bell" becomes a painful reverie, a remembered dream that turns unexpectedly to nightmare.

A Dream
of Light
and Dark

> I walked by the sea, and there came to me,
> > as a star-beam on the wet sand
> a white shell like a sea-bell:
> > trembling it lay in my wet hand.
> In my fingers shaken I heard waken
> > a ding within, by a harbour bar
> a buoy swinging, a call ringing
> > over endless seas, faint now and far. (*Adventures* 57)

Not only is the style smoother (eliminating the awkward diction of such phrases as "were me to greet"), but the voice is now solitary and fully aware of it, and because of that awareness the situation is at once heightened and distilled.

Furthermore, in this version there is a specific reason for the journey, a reason that links it to the new title, "The Sea-bell." It is now the sea itself, sounding in the sea-shell, that calls to the voyager—the sea and the land beyond it "over endless seas." This new sea-longing then becomes a link between the poem and its annotation, "Frodos Dreme," for it is a longing typical of Frodo, and common as well to a number of Tolkien's characters. It recalls Frodo's first dream at Crickhollow, which ends with his desire to climb the tower and see the sea, whose far-off sound has "often troubled his dreams."

It also recalls Edwin Lowdham's "shores a great deal further off" and, like *The Notion Club Papers* and *The Lord of the Rings*, uses once again the device of the fictive editor. The preface was not only meant to add veracity but to confer on the whole collection the only real unity it could possess. Beyond that, and in specific reference to "The Sea-bell," it enabled Tolkien to add in the voice of the pseudo-editor the significant comment that "a hand has scrawled at its head *Frodos Dreme*." In addition to the title, Tolkien has the pseudo-editor add an extended commentary that enlarges and makes more specific the context in which the poem is to be understood. He says:

> though the piece is unlikely to have been written by Frodo himself, the title shows that it was associated with the dark and despairing dreams which visited him in March and October during his last three years. But there were certainly other traditions concerning Hobbits that were taken by the "wandering-madness," and if they ever returned, were afterwards queer and uncommunicable. The thought of the Sea was ever-present in the background of hobbit imagination; but fear of it and distrust of all Elvish lore, was the prevailing mood in the Shire at the end of the Third Age, and that mood was certainly not entirely dispelled by the events and changes with which that Age ended. (*Adventures* 9)

This "wandering-madness" is a species of the same wanderlust that possesses so many of Tolkien's characters from Ælfwine to Bilbo to Edwin Lowdham. Its importance both in the note and in the present discussion lies not just in the fact that it is a recurrent motif but also because it suggests an additional link with Frodo. It seems reasonable to suppose that this late and deliberate association of "The Sea-bell" with Frodo was meant to deepen the significance of both the poem and the character. Certainly it gives the poem a greater resonance, a context beyond itself. In addition, the added title and the fictive editor's commentary assimilating the poem into the larger mythos of Middle-earth make the dream nature of the poem clear.

Not only does the poem thus acquire another dimension, but so, too, does Frodo, however tenuous his relation to the poem. In this respect, and because it is a replication with variation of some of the same motifs, "The Sea-bell" could easily be read as the companion and partner of Frodo's other dreams. Specifically, it is the dark brother of his dream or vision in the house of Tom Bombadil of the end of his voyage to the Undying Lands, of the lifting rain-curtain and the far green country. Both dreams are about the same subject matter, the voyage to the Otherworld, whether it be called the Undying Lands, the Fortunate Isles, Tir nan Og, or Faërie. But, again, with a difference. The one is a joyful vision that comes true; the other is a nightmare with no waking. The special dreadfulness of the nightmare lies in the suggestion that it may be the dark continuation of the vision, which ends with sight of the shore but no landing. "The Sea-bell" takes up the thread where the vision left off but turns its promise into fairy gold.

Indeed, the whole vision has the ephemerality of fairy gold, which disappears in the light of everyday. It has another resonance as well, for the evanescent, ungraspable beauty that the speaker in "The Sea-bell" can feel but cannot contact inevitably recalls Tolkien's animadversions against the treatment of Faërie in Barrie's *Mary Rose*. One of the most haunting aspects of Tolkien's poem is the Barrie-like invisibility of the faërie inhabitants of the enchanted land. Their echoes are everywhere, but they will not show themselves to the traveler. Yet though the situation in "The Sea-bell" is superficially like the situation in *Mary Rose*, it goes beyond that play to make another, deeper point.

His chief criticism of *Mary Rose* was that "no fairies were seen," that, in his words, "the fairies do not matter, except as being inhuman or malicious; no explanations are given, there are none." While in "The Sea-bell" no explanations are given and no fairies are seen, here this absence becomes the focus, not the periphery, of the poem. It is precisely the fairies' absence that makes the speaker (and the reader) conscious of their presence. They are all the more apparent for being unseen. Barrie passed over the fairies; Tolkien withholds them but makes his protagonist and his reader vividly aware of them. It is that very awareness that causes the longing and the consequent suffering of the human visitor. The fairies do "matter"; they matter terribly.

In *Mary Rose* the central incident—that is, her encounter with the fairies—takes place offstage, and only the results are shown. In "The Sea-bell" it is the encounter itself that is aborted, but that is the center of the action. The isolated traveler is always in view, and what he wants is not offstage but at the edge of vision. No voice answers his call, though the voices are heard.

> But wherever I came it was ever the same:
>   the feet fled, and all was still;
> never a greeting, only the fleeting
>   pipes, voices, horns on the hill. (*Adventures* 58)

His efforts to make contact with the elusive inhabitants are unavailing, leaving him solitary, desolate, and ultimately disenchanted. The beautiful otherworld evades his grasp with the evanescence of a receding dream.

> proudly I cried: "Why do you hide?
>   Why do none speak, wherever I go?
> Here now I stand, king of this land,
>   with gladdon-sword and reed-mace.
> Answer my call! Come forth all!
>   Speak to me words! Show me a face!" (59)

When still no answer comes, the voice, and with it the tone, changes abruptly from challenge to despair; as suddenly and without warning, faërie-time catches up with the traveler, and age and darkness fall upon him. Bereft of the vision, lost and solitary, "queer and uncommunicable," he speaks for all those wanderers whom Tolkien—again citing Barrie and *Mary Rose*—described as "entangled in Faerie, pinned in a kind of ghostly deathlessness." It is as if Faërie has two faces, and only one of them is bright.

The traveler's account of his experience is as bleak a vision as poetry has produced, recalling the bitter landscapes and nightmare experience of parts of Eliot's "Waste Land," or—even bleaker—the bizarre topography traversed by Browning's Childe Roland on his solitary way to the Dark Tower.

> Black came a cloud as a night-shroud.
> Like a dark mole groping I went,
> to the ground falling, on my hands crawling
> with eyes blind and my back bent
> I crept to a wood: silent it stood
> in its dead leaves; bare were its boughs.
> There must I sit, wandering in wit,
> while owls snored in their hollow house.
> For a year and a day there must I stay:
> beetles were tapping in the rotten trees,
> spiders were weaving, in the mould heaving
> puffballs loomed about my knees.
>
> At last there came light in my long night,
> and I saw my hair hanging grey.
> Bent though I be, I must find the sea!
> I have lost myself, and know not the way . . . (59)

At last he must come back to what was home. After a year and a day, the traditional span of fairy time, the traveler returns, sailing past "old hulls clustered with gulls / and great ships laden with light" to a haven "dark as a raven / silent as snow, deep in the night" (60). Here "The Sea-bell" follows "Looney" almost word for word, but the newly conferred context invests it with a deeper desolation. It proposes an alternative dream for Frodo, as if the sick and wounded hobbit were to find no refuge, no healing in the Undying Lands, as if the dream in the house of Tom Bombadil was never to be made a reality. Moreover, the dream of return brings no recognition and no more welcome than was to be found in fairyland, for here as well there is a withdrawal, though whether it is of others or of the speaker himself is unclear:

> Houses were shuttered, wind round them muttered,
> roads were empty. I sat by a door,
> and where drizzling rain poured down a drain
> I cast away all that I bore:

in my clutching hand some grains of sand,
    and a sea-shell silent and dead.
Never will my ear that bell hear,
    never my feet that shore tread,
never again, as in sad lane,
    in blind alley and in long street
ragged I walk. To myself I talk;
    for still they speak not, men that [I] meet. (60)

As in the opening of "Looney," although now more bitterly, "The Sea-bell" echoes "The Rime of the Ancient Mariner." Not Coleridge's nightmare Life-in-Death who thicks men's blood with cold, but Tolkien's equally hideous Death-in-Life becomes the speaker's fate. He is changed forever, taken out of his time, lost from the otherworld and estranged from his own, very much as Frodo was after his return from Mordor to the Shire, not just "falling asleep again" but caught in a nightmare from which he cannot awaken.

The two widely disparate titles of "Looney" and *Frodos Dreme*, then, are more related than at first appears. The second title comes out of the first as well as out of *The Lord of the Rings*, and together they emphasize in their separate ways distinct but complementary aspects of the poem. There is more than a hint of madness in the speaker's state of mind at the end of "The Sea-bell," while its pronounced dreamlike quality takes on added poignance if the speaker and dreamer is thought to be the Frodo of the last "dark and despairing" dreams in the Shire. Whatever the final context assigned to the poem, whether it is called "Looney" or "The Sea-bell" or *Frodos Dreme*, the picture it presents of the journey to the otherworld is unchangingly and unrelievedly bleak. Desolation verging on despair may be the fate of the visitor who would rashly venture into Faërie.

The theme is one that Tolkien began exploring early on in his writing career, and he returned to it again and again. As early as the middle twenties, while they were on the faculty of Leeds University, Tolkien and E. V. Gordon had amused themselves and their students by writing verses, mostly comic, in the languages of their linguistic study, chiefly Anglo-Saxon, though Tolkien contributed one in Gothic. These were part nonsense, part linguistic exercise, part satire. The poems were later privately published as *Songs for the Philologists.* Tolkien's contributions were substantial—thirteen poems in all—and while most were made for fun, a few were more serious and gave hints of even more serious things to come.

One of these, *Ides Ælfscýne,* "Elf-Fair Lady," is of a type that Shippey calls "trapped mortal" poems, made on the ballad model of "Tam Lin" and "Thomas Rhymer." It tells of a youth who is beguiled by an elf-maiden into leaving his home. She lures him onto a boat that carries them *"on fyrlenum londe, on silfrenum stronde / þær darode dweorg under beorgum,"* to a "far-off land, on the silver strand, where the dwarf lurked under the mountains." At last, tired of his exile he prays to God, *"be dimmun ond dréorigum wǽgum / Þær sunne ne scán,"* "by the dim and dreary waves, where the sun did not shine," but fifty years pass before he returns, *"wǽdla ond wund,"* "poor and hurt," *"wániʒe ána,"* to "dwindle, grey and alone." His youth is gone, and *"on moldan wæs nú se ðe cúðe me iú,"* the one who had known him before "was now in the mould." The seeds of "Looney" are plain to see, not just in the theme of the poem, but in the details—the sudden journey by boat, the far-off land, the silver strand, the dim and dreary waves. The motif of exile from Faërie was present in Tolkien's mind and work before "Looney."

The sentiment is expressed just as sharply and only slightly less poetically in "On Fairy-Stories," in which Tolkien restated in prose his awareness of the dark face of Faërie, wherein are "pitfalls for the unwary and dungeons for the overbold" and where "its very richness and strangeness tie the tongue of a traveller who would report them. And while he is there it is dangerous for him to ask too many questions, lest the gates should be shut and the keys be lost" (109). It is safe to assume that he was speaking from experience and thus to conclude that he felt some kinship with the speaker in "The Sea-bell," who returns from his voyage unable to communicate his experience. And his fate is precisely the one that Tolkien describes in the essay.

This is the danger not only of Tolkien's particular world of Faërie but of any world of the creative imagination, any enchanted secondary world into which the far-traveling mind can enter, but in which it is all too easy to become lost. And lost or not, the wanderer finds a world whose beauty and terror can never be truly communicated to those who have not been there. The traveler is tongue-tied, he comes back to the primary, "real" world "queer and uncommunicable," unable to express to those about him the *otherness* of where he has been or the strange beauty of the sights he has seen. The deepest pitfall for the unwary, the real madness of "wandering-madness," lies as much in the return as in the wandering. It is a pitfall experienced not by the Shire hobbits alone, but by many wanderers in Faërie. Ramer had trouble trying to tell the Notion Club about the wonders of Emberü and Ellor Eshúrizel. And the creator of all of these people and places knew as much about the pain of return as did his characters. Though his wandering was a voyage of the imagination rather than of the body, the worlds that Tolkien saw or dreamed were just as real, just as magical, and just as evanescent as Emberü, or Faërie, or those "shores a great deal further off" than Edwin Lowdham's Sussex.

And so in "Looney," even more in "The Sea-bell," and still more if it is understood as "Frodos Dreme," Tolkien shows the reader those pitfalls that he knows so well, where the unwary visitor may fall and bruise his imagination on harsh reality. He takes a hard look at the dark side, at the true nature of those dungeons for the overbold. They are barred against the wanderer, and the overbold venturer may find that they lock him out, not in. This might be the greater punishment, and a yet-greater one might be never to find the way in again. Perhaps this is finally the most truly lost of all the lost roads—the road to fairyland. And as bitter as it would be to lose the keys to Faërie, it would be bitterer still to find that they were never yours to begin with, to realize that the beauty that you dreamed really was just a dream, lost upon waking. For the time of dream, the time of Faërie, is not like the time of mortal men, and the real dungeon—as Tolkien said in "On Fairy-Stories"—is in the grim and smoky "waking" world on the other side of the gate. This is the down side of dream, of Faërie, of nostalgia, of time-travel. It shows what seems to be the futility of trying to go back, to have any real connection with the past, or to hold onto beauty and enchantment. It is the loss of Lórien without the promise of the far green country. It is what might have happened to Frodo, what might have happened to Tolkien, what might happen to anyone.

Ironically, this bereavement has—and had especially for Tolkien's generation—a dark and bitter counterpart in the real world. The poems, diaries, and memoirs of the men who came back from the battlefields of World War I provide a kind of skewed corollary to the feelings of loss and estrangement that Tolkien has so vividly pictured. Granted, the nature of the experience itself is different. The incommunicability is not of beauty but of horror; the lost world is not Faërie but a curious mixture of the world they left to go to war and the world of mud and death and destruction they found at the front. Nonetheless, the quality of the feelings produced by that experience are strikingly like those Tolkien has expressed, both in the essay and in the poem.

Tolkien's statement in "On Fairy-Stories" that "Faërie cannot be caught in a net of words; for it is one of its qualities to be indescribable, though not imperceptible" (114), sounds strikingly like Paul Fussell's account of the war's impact on the sensibility of those who survived to try to write about it. "The problem for the writer trying to describe elements of the Great War," says Fussell, "was its utter incredibility, and thus its incommunicability in its own terms" (139).

Whatever the cause, the presumed inadequacy of language itself to convey the facts about trench warfare is one of the motifs of all who wrote about the war. . . . Even to a man destined to become a professional writer, the fact of the constant artillery thunder audible on the line seemed quite incommunicable. Robert Graves says in an interview:

The funny thing was you went home on leave for six weeks, or six days, but the idea of being and staying at home was awful because you were with people who didn't understand what this was all about.
SMITH: Didn't you want to tell them?
GRAVES: You couldn't: you can't communicate noise. Noise never stopped for one moment—ever. (170)

The literature of the postwar period in which Tolkien, like many others, began to write, spoke with the voice of the "lost generation" trying to come to terms with incommunicable experience. Robert Graves, Erich Maria Remarque, Wilfred Owen, Siegfried Sassoon, Eric Blunden, Julian Grenfell, Guillaume Apollinaire, Ernest Hemingway—each tried to communicate his experience of the Great War during the long slide into the next war. More than any other war in history, the Great War was characterized by horror and poetry, the one giving immediate, almost galvanic impetus to the other. It was a war that gave to literature and the academy the very term "war poet." It was a war that forced scholars who had been reading glorious Homer all their lives to take another look at what is really going on in *The Iliad*. Of all that generation, nobody talked about it more poignantly than Erich Maria Remarque, speaking to the victors and vanquished alike in the voice of Paul Bäumer, the German schoolboy-soldier narrator of *All Quiet on the Western Front*. "I believe we are lost," says Paul, whose life is uprooted and obliterated by the war before it kills him. "If we go back we will be weary, broken, burnt out, rootless, and without hope. We will not be able to find our way anymore" (127, 295).

Not only do Paul's words sound disturbingly like Looney, but they are a striking parallel to Tolkien's own description of those who return from Faërie, "pinned in a kind of ghostly deathlessness." In light of this, it is notable that Tolkien, though he was already thinking of himself as a poet at the time he went to war in 1916, seems never to have written any war poetry, either then or, like so many of his peers, in bitter memory afterward. By his own accounts of his time in the trenches (in his letters and the little essay "A Secret Vice"), any noncombatant energy he had was bent toward the creation of invented languages. Yet memory can find more than one way to express itself. More than three decades after *All Quiet on the Western Front*, the lonely voyager of "The Seabell" was to say "I have lost myself, and I know not the way," and the parallel between this statement and Paul Bäumer's despairing words, if indeed it is mere coincidence, is (and perhaps for that reason) all the more remarkable.

While Tolkien did not write anything that could be specifically termed war poetry, he did, nevertheless, publish a collection of poems—not his own—written chiefly during the war. In June 1918, just two years after his own return from France and only a few months before the war was ended, he brought out a small book entitled *A Spring Harvest*, a gathering of poems by Geoffrey Bache Smith, who was killed in France in 1916. Both Smith and Tolkien had been members of the T.C.B.S., Tolkien's first fellowship and the forerunner of the Inklings, and the two in particular had much in common—not only their shared Oxford experience, but the fact that Smith was, as Carpenter has pointed out, "a practicing poet of some competence" (47). His friendship and his example did much to foster Tolkien's own early inclinations toward poetry. Smith encouraged him to read more widely in English poetry (not just Anglo-Saxon and Middle English) and recommended Browne, Sidney, and Bacon. He recommended as well the "moderns," some of their own contemporaries, among them the poet-soldier Rupert Brooke, who, because of his wartime death as well as his talent, was to become an emblem and embodiment of his brief time, "a symbol," as Modris Eksteins observes, "of the spiritual confusion and yearning of his generation" (26).

The four schoolboys who met to study, talk, and read poetry to one another maintained their fellowship after King Edward's, when Tolkien and Smith were both at Oxford and Gilson and Wiseman at Cambridge. Too soon they found themselves in the midst of war. Three of the fellowship—Tolkien, Smith, and Rob Gilson— were called into the army and sent to France in 1916. The fourth, Christopher Wiseman, was serving in the navy. All three young men (like so many in that war, they were hardly more than boys) were in the trenches and were part of the disastrous Allied offensives of the ruinous second summer of the war. Amid the turmoil and disruption of their lives, and certainly because of it, they were intensely mindful of their fellowship and determined to keep it alive. They corresponded as much as the exigencies of war would allow, and Tolkien kept the letters all his life. In a letter dated February 3, 1916, Smith wrote to Tolkien urging and encouraging him to get his work into print.

> I am a wild and wholehearted admirer, and my chief consolation is that if I am scuppered tonight . . . there will still be a member of the great T.C.B.S. to voice what I dreamed and what we all agreed upon. . . . Death can make us loathsome and helpless as individuals, but it cannot put an end to the immortal four! . . . Yes, publish. You, I am sure, are chosen, like Saul among the children of Israel. . . . May God bless you, my dear John Ronald, and may you say the things I have tried to say long after I am not there to say them, if such be my lot. (*J. R. R. Tolkien* 31)

But the continuance of the fellowship was doomed, like so many hopes in that nightmare time. Rob Gilson was one of the twenty thousand Allied troops killed at La Boiselle on July 1, 1916, the first day of the Somme offensive. Smith's letter to Tolkien of July

15, 1916, is a moving testament to the loss: "I saw in the paper this morning that Rob has been killed. I am safe, but what does that matter? Do please stick to me, you and Christopher. I am very tired and most frightfully depressed at this worst of news. Now one realizes in despair what the T.C.B.S. really was. O my dear John Ronald what ever are we going to do?" (*J. R. R. Tolkien* 33). Four months later, on December 3, Smith was injured by bursting shells. He died of his wounds within a few days. Two of the "immortal four" were gone.

In the end, the only one to voice the dream, the only one to carry on what they had all agreed upon, was John Ronald. G. B. Smith and Rob Gilson were lost in 1916, and Christopher Wiseman, though he survived that war and the next one and the difficult peace that succeeded each of them, did not write. What Tolkien wrote, the world knows, but it should be recognized that at least one of its roots lies deep in the soil of his war and its aftermath. Many years after that war and the one that followed, Tolkien wrote in the Foreword to the second edition of *The Lord of the Rings* that "to be caught in youth by 1914 was no less hideous an experience than to be involved in 1939 and the following years," and followed this with the stark and simple statement that "By 1918 all but one of my close friends were dead" (*Fellowship* 7).

There can be no doubt that the memory of the T.C.B.S., the warmth of its fellowship, the sense of promise untimely cut off, and the poignance of its loss stayed with Tolkien throughout his life. It was certainly echoed in his need for the other, more mature but essentially similar "school" fellowships that it foreshadowed, most notably the Inklings. And while his posthumous publication of Geoffrey Smith's poems may well have been Tolkien's effort to carry out his friend's wishes and voice what his friend had dreamed, it would scarcely be surprising, as Humphrey Carpenter has observed, if he also envisioned his own future work as another way of doing it, of saying in his own voice some of the things that Smith had tried to say, long after he was not there to say them.

Carpenter's observation was made with specific reference to the Silmarillion, the great invented mythology on which Tolkien was shortly to begin the work that would occupy him for much of the rest of his life. But it might also be applied to some of his lesser work. What Smith had tried to say, as manifest within the small compass of *A Spring Harvest*, has more than a passing likeness to some of Tolkien's own early efforts—hardly surprising in two friends close in age, education, and experience. But out of the slim collection of Smith's poems that Tolkien put together in memoriam, one particular lyric, called "The House of Eld," stands out as deserving of special notice in the context of the present discussion of "The Sea-bell." I give it in full.

Now the old winds are wild about the house,
And the old ghosts cry to me from the air
Of a far isle set in the western sea,
And of the evening sunlight lingering there.
Ah! I am bound here, bound and fettered,
The dark house crumbles, and the woods decay,
I was too fain of life, that bound me here;
Away, old long-loved ghosts, away away! (Smith 41)

Though it is hardly more than a fragment compared to "The Sea-bell," and though its emphasis is on mood rather than on narrative, the similarity between the two, both in ethos and in tone, is unmistakable. No reader setting the two poems side by side could fail to see the likeness or, having read "The House of Eld," could fail to hear its echoes in "The Sea-bell." The wild winds, the old ghosts, the far isle in the western sea, the crumbling house and decaying woods, the despairing cry of the bound and fettered first-person voice "too fain of life" are brother images to those of "Looney" and "The Sea-bell." Whether "The House of Eld" is strictly speaking a war poem or not, its author's death in France and the circumstances of its publication as a memorial make it next to impossible that Tolkien could have thought of it or remembered it in any context that did not include war. Moreover, its more-than-passing resemblance to the voice, the setting, and the situation of "Looney" and "The Sea-bell" suggests that both its memory and Geoffrey Smith's last request of him were buried deep in Tolkien's mind, to surface in another context—when the poet was ready.

And so, though unlike most of his contemporaries, Tolkien chose the fantastic mode rather than the realistic as the vehicle for his imagination, he said in his own way as much about war as did any of them. "A real taste for fairy stories," he wrote of himself, "was wakened by philology on the threshold of manhood, and quickened to full life by war" (135). There is more to this statement than meets the eye. The first part of it is obvious and historical. The pairing of philology and fairy-stories was established by Jacob Grimm, whose collection and investigation of Germanic *Kinder und Hausmärchen* were impelled by his conviction that folk language was the repository of a culture's myth. Tolkien explored this at length in "On Fairy-Stories."

The pairing of fairy-stories and war is more complex, for they would seem to be opposites. The easy, surface reading builds on the opposition, inferring from Tolkien's words a purely escapist impulse, a retreat from the horror and boredom of the trenches into the magical world of Faërie. Beneath the surface, however, his words suggest a deep but unmanifest connection between these apparently unlike things. In the way that extremes can sometimes meet, War and Faërie have a certain resemblance to one another. Both are set beyond the reach of ordinary human experience. Both are equally indifferent to the needs of ordinary humanity. Both can change those who return so that they become "pinned in a kind of ghostly deathlessness," not just unable to say where they have been but unable to communicate to those who have not been there what they have seen and experienced. Perhaps worst of all, both war and Faërie can change out of all recognition the wanderer's perception of the world to which he returns, so that never again can it be what it once was.

And so Frodo—or Looney, if you want to take it back to its beginning—speaks out of more than his own experience. He speaks for Geoffrey Bache Smith and Rob Gilson, bereft of their lives and their future; he speaks for Remarque's young hero Paul Bäumer, robbed of his youth and of his world; he speaks for John Ronald Reuel Tolkien, who felt intensely the loss of a precious fellowship. Whoever the voice in "The Sea-bell" is intended to be (and it is certainly Tolkien, whoever else it is), the words of the poem, the suffering of the speaker, describe an experience all too recognizable to anyone who lived through it, of alienation from the reference points of familiar experience, of a world gone past the point of no return, longing for something it once had and ought to have been able to keep.

This wholly private and uncommunicable experience was shared in isolation by a whole generation of writers who wrote it again and again, each in his own particular way, trying over and over to speak the unspeakable, to exorcise the dream. "History is a nightmare from which I am struggling to awake," declared Nietzsche, for whom recurrence, while inevitable, was not always and not altogether beneficent. Tolkien would have agreed. Dream and nightmare are two sides of the same coin, and whether the dream is beneficent or hideous, whether the dreamer is Frodo, or Looney, or the unnamed voyager, the waking brings its own kind of desolation. Like Paul Bäumer, like the speaker in "The House of Eld," the dreamer may awake into another kind of nightmare, weary, broken, rootless, without hope in a world he does not recognize that will not recognize him. Unable to find his way anymore, fixed in his own despair, he knows only his own isolation. "To myself I talk / for still they speak not, men that I meet."

"The Sea-bell," then, can be read and comprehended in several mutually reinforcing contexts. Generically it can be ranged alongside Coleridge's "The Ancient Mariner," Browning's "Childe Roland to the Dark Tower Came," Eliot's *The Waste Land* as one of a number of romantic and modern poems of desperation and loss, as a statement of despair. Artistically it is a powerful expression of the dark side of Tolkien's work, standing both as his corrective to Barrie and as the bleak, alternative fate that might have haunted Frodo's dreams. On a personal level it can be read as a statement about his own bereavement at the loss of Faërie. And in larger context, one both personal and historical, it can be understood as an echo and a reminder of all the loss that war and peace and change and living in the world can bring.

Pitfalls *in* Faërie 11

Faërie is a perilous land, and in it are pitfalls for the unwary
and dungeons for the overbold.

—"On Fairy-Stories"

But for all its dark power and its echoes of a past too deep to forget,
"The Sea-bell" expressed only one mood, showed only one side of
a many-mooded, many-sided, variable man. Toward the end of January 1965, less than three years after he had revised "The Sea-bell,"
Tolkien's creative imagination turned toward a different Smith,
one who lived to fulfill his gift and to pass it on. This was the
unassuming craftsman-hero of his last story, *Smith of Wootton
Major*. The thematic connections that link "The Sea-bell" and
Smith are tempting to build on, but the differences are just as important. In looking at either work, critics have tended to focus on
the one outstanding feature that is common to both, the prohibition against the return to Faërie. Based largely on this prohibition,
they have concluded that Tolkien's vision of himself was as "a
mortal deserted by the immortals and barred from their company"
(Shippey 211). This is accurate, but it must be read differently in
the context of each work. For while the prohibition seems clear in
both, the mood is different in each, as is the spirit in which the
prohibition is received. Moreover, the timing of each is different
as well. "The Sea-bell" was conceived early in Tolkien's creative

life, *Smith* very near its end. One is a negation, the other an affirmation; one is a cry of longing for lost beauty, the other an autumnal acceptance of things as they are.

The differences in mood and attitude that distinguish these two short works also set the boundaries of Tolkien's perspective on Faërie and on what in "On Fairy-Stories" he called "the *aventures* of men in the Perilous Realm." As clearly as anything he wrote, these two works embody his own desires and disappointments and contrast his unfulfilled yearnings and his reconciliation to the limits of mortal time. Like "The Sea-bell," *Smith* is an account of the journey into Faërie. Or rather, into Faery, for in this story Tolkien used a different spelling. He tried out variants—Fayery and Fayerey—then settled down to a middle form, Faery. The change was clearly intentional and seems to have been coincident with some alterations to the concept of the Otherworld and its accessibility. No other motive for this change is readily apparent, though Tolkien may simply have wanted a plainer, perhaps more English (rather than French) spelling. Or he may have meant the new form to associate itself more readily with the central artifact of the tale, the star, described as "fay." In any case, his use of the simpler form is consistent throughout the story.

But Faërie or Faery, Tolkien is looking at that Otherworld in a different mood—with one notable exception—from that of "The Sea-bell." It is as if in reworking "Looney" into "The Sea-bell," in darkening the picture of the voyage into Faërie, Tolkien had worked through his own deepest feelings and memories and regrets. It is more than possible that the effort he put into revising "The Sea-bell" released his imagination to find a different voice and to envision and explore a more benign aspect of the relationship between the world and Faërie. The result was that in this new story the loss of enchantment, though still a grief, weighs less heavily. This grief is balanced, too, by consolation, by appreciation of the value of the ordinary human community.

The story is deceptively simple. At a village festival a boy named Smith receives in a piece of cake a magic star. Though he does not know it, the agent of the star's placement in the cake is the King of Faery, operating incognito as the chief cook's apprentice. As his name predicts, Smith grows up to be a craftsman, a creator, and with the star as his passport he makes many journeys into Faery.

These journeys are the heart of the story, though nothing happens in them to advance or change the course of the plot. At last, with advancing age, he is made to realize that he must pass his gift on so that it may be baked into another cake and received by another child.

If "The Sea-bell" can be read as—on one level, at least—Tolkien's corrective to *Mary Rose*, then *Smith of Wootton Major* might well be seen as a kind of corrective to "The Sea-bell," sweetening the bitterness of the pain and gently balancing the loss with renewed appreciation for the things of this world. *Smith of Wootton Major* is the bright counterpart of the dark "Sea-bell," retaining the poignance but transcending the grief. Like "The Sea-bell"— and *The Hobbit* and *The Lord of the Rings* (and, though less explicitly, *The Lost Road* and *The Notion Club Papers*)—it is a story of the journey There and Back Again. It is about the uncommunicable experience of Faërie, about what it is like to find it and what it is like to give it up and go on. The visions in each work are equally beautiful and terrible, but in *Smith*, as in *The Hobbit*, the longing is assuaged, the torment is stilled, and the traveler returns to peace with himself and with his world. Like Frodo, Smith must finally leave Faery and not return; but unlike Frodo, he finds consolation in family and friends, in the things of this world. Like the voyager in "The Sea-bell," the traveler in *Smith of Wootton Major* is given to know that this Otherworld is not for him; but unlike the voyager, he is not summarily and arbitrarily banished from the enchantment (though it must be acknowledged that on one occasion he is sternly warned away). Rather, he comes finally to give it up of free will—albeit reluctantly—and returns to ordinary life and love, not isolated but enriched by where he has been and what he has seen.

The genesis of *Smith* was a preface that Tolkien had been asked to write for a new edition of George MacDonald's *The Golden Key*. Although Tolkien's disapproval of allegory was a matter of record— "I cordially dislike allegory in all its manifestations," he wrote in the Foreword to *The Lord of the Rings*—this notwithstanding, and although he particularly disliked the kind of allegorical didacticism that was a MacDonald trademark, he chose to begin his preface to MacDonald's book with an allegory of his own (one of the few he ever wrote or liked) devised to explain to children the meaning of the term *fairy:*

Fairy is very powerful. Even the bad author cannot escape it. He probably makes up his tale out of bits of older tales, or things he half remembers ["old, half-remembered things" was what he had called *The Adventures of Tom Bombadil*], and they may be too strong for him to spoil or disenchant. Someone may meet them for the first time in his silly tale, and catch a glimpse of Fairy, and go on to better things. This could be put into a short story like this. There was once a cook, and he thought of making a cake for a children's party. His chief notion was that it must be very sweet . . . . (Carpenter 242)

The preface was never finished, but the story he had begun to tell continued to fire Tolkien's imagination. He came to realize that it had developed an independent life and wanted completion.[1] Using his original concept of a Cook and a Cake, he gave it the working title "The Great Cake." But as the story developed it grew beyond that. Though the title was not formally changed until the story was finished (a complete late typescript still bears the title "The Great Cake"), the boy soon displaced the cake as the focus of the story, and Smith—the craftsman, the maker, the creator—became as important a figure as the Cook. The point of the story grew to be less about the true nature of Faery (though that is still important) and more about Smith's acceptance of the fact that at the end he must give up the star, and with it his entrée to Faery, so that the torch may pass.

Though *Smith* has not come in for as much critical attention as some of the other short works, it has still received more scrutiny than its dark brother "The Sea-bell," perhaps precisely because it is a story and not a poem and perhaps also because it appeared as a single publication and not as part of a collection. Or perhaps because the mood it communicates is less unrelievedly bleak than that of the poem, more hopeful, although less direct and explicit. The appeal of *Smith* lies finally in what appears to be its effortless blend of simplicity and complexity, for the story's seemingly transparent surface covers unexpected depths of suggested meaning. The operative word here is "suggested," for the tale defies and defeats any one-to-one correlation or arbitrary signification, and the too-easy interpretations that its apparent simplicity encourages roll over it without denting the surface. It is undeniable, however, that Tolkien's original allegorical impulse left its ghost in the narrative, a ghost that has haunted the tale ever since, tempting readers to see in it a variety of specific correlations from its author's views on art or religion or scholarship to half-hidden references to the choices of his own life.

The result has been that nearly every critic who has paid serious attention to *Smith* has tended to allegorize it or at least to extract some sort of specific meaning from it beyond the pattern of the story. Most have found the tale worth the reading and given it credit for conveying a meaning beyond its apparent simplicity. Jane Chance Nitzsche found hidden Christianity and saw in it "the reward of grace for humility and suffering" (67). Others have succumbed to the temptation to see still more specific correlations to the author's life and work. This is equally easy, for the story of the blacksmith with a passport into Faery who realizes that with the passing of time he must give it up has obvious parallels with its author's creative life. Clyde Kilby saw it as a story of "the creative process and the special problems of a fantasy writer like Tolkien" (37). T. A. Shippey saw in it an allegory of Tolkien wrestling with his own duality, the scholar-fantasist torn between philology and fiction, the sober student of "lang." whose runaway imagination takes him straight into "lit." Shippey sees in the Master Cook a "philologist-figure," in the lazy baker Nokes—the bad guy, if the story can be said to have one—a "critic-figure," and in the hero, Smith, a craftsman who never becomes a Cook or bakes a Great Cake: a "Tolkien-figure" (204).

Humphrey Carpenter saw *Smith* not quite as explicit autobiography but as a manifestation of, or creative vent for, what he called Tolkien's "anxiety over the future and his growing grief at the approach of old age" (242). Carpenter was taking his cue from Tolkien, who himself called it "An old man's book, already weighted with the presage of 'bereavement'" (*Letters* 389), and said of it that it was "written with deep emotion, partly drawn from the experience of the bereavement of 'retirement' and of advancing age." In the face of the story's enigmatic simplicity it is tempting to have it represent aspects of its author's life or work, rather than to allow it to present on its own terms the vision of Faery that Tolkien was striving to create. There is some validity in both the autobiographical and the allegorical elements that are genuinely to be found for those who seek them; nevertheless, neither accounts for the story's gossamer appeal.

It must be conceded, however, that to some extent it invites reading as allegory and that Tolkien is in part responsible. Dislike it though he might, having started with an allegorical conception he found it hard to shake off, and as a consequence it is all too easy to play at the same game: at its simplest, to see in the sweetness of the cake the mistaken notion that many people have and try to communicate to children about the prettiness of Faërie; to make the star the hidden light of imagination; and so on. In a long unpublished essay,[2] Tolkien paralleled the story with his own ruminations on its content—theme, action, characters, and surrounding history. Among the many concerns worked at in the essay, if not altogether worked out, is this vexing question of allegory. Tolkien conducted a running argument with himself on the question of whether the story is or is not an allegory, at times rejecting and at times developing the allegorical possibilities of the tale. Sample paragraphs show the range of the pendulum's swing. He began by declaring unequivocally that "This short tale is not 'allegory,' though it is capable of course of allegorical interpretation at certain points. It is a 'Fairy Story,' of the kind in which beings that may be called 'fairies' or 'elves' play a part and are associated in action with human people, and are regarded as having a 'real' existence, that is one in their own right and independent of human imagination and invention" (fol. 21r.). He continued to protest in this vein, later in the same essay assuring his reader (and reassuring himself) that "There is no need to hunt for allegory. Such teaching as this slender story contains is implicit, and would be no less present if it were a plain narrative of historical events." Yet almost immediately he conceded that, although overt religion has been consciously kept out of the tale, still

> The Great Hall is evidently in a way an "allegory" of the village church; the Master Cook with his house adjacent, and his office that is not hereditary, provides for its own instruction and succession but is not one of the "secular" or profitable crafts, and yet is supported by the village, is plainly the Parson and the priesthood. "Cooking" is a domestic affair practiced by men and women: personal religion and prayer. The Master Cook presides over and provides for all the religious festivals of the year, and also for all the religious occasions that are not universal: births, marriages, and deaths. (fol. 25v.)

It is clear from this, Tolkien's own protests to the contrary, that the initial allegorical impulse as manifest in his original preface was never wholly abandoned. The critics who see allegory, with whatever varied interpretations, are responding to real signals. The very simplicity of the story's events and characters is an invitation for any who wish to try their own hands at interpretation. However, this tends to work against the "Fairy Story" effect that Tolkien said he was striving for, and the application of too much specific meaning both burdens and crystallizes a story whose greatest charm lies in its unpretentious air, its effortless ability to imply without stating.

Of the critics who pay serious attention to *Smith*, Paul Kocher comes nearest to taking the story on its own terms. Kocher's reading also carefully skirts the hidden trap of autobiography, for although he found in *Smith* Tolkien's farewell to his art, calling it his "Prospero speech," he also conceded that the hero of the story might just as well be "any practitioner of the White Art who travels far 'from Daybreak to Evening' and in his old age comes home, tired, to hand his passport on to his successors" (204). A farewell to art is there, but also the reassurance that the art itself remains, to be taken up by the aftercomers. Kocher reads the story for what it says rather than for whatever meaning can be teased out from between the lines. The story is its own meaning, and while Kocher acknowledges "the elegiac tone of the ending, with its falling leaves and sunset," he also recognizes "its attempt to find in homely things comfort for a youthful intensity of life never to be reached again" (204).

Probably one of the best comments on the story was made by Roger Lancelyn Green. Reviewing the story when it was published in October 1967, Green observed that the effect of the story transcends any explicit reference and warned against looking too hard for a specific message. He wrote of it that "To seek for the meaning is to cut open the ball in search of its bounce" (*Letters* 388). This may prove to be the best summation of the story's appeal. The bounce is clearly there, but to search for it is to defeat its effect; to allegorize it is to deaden the bounce completely.

Not every reader has liked the story, or found it to have any bounce at all. One completely negative view was that offered by one Christopher Williams in a review published in *New Society* on December 7, 1967. "Among a faery elite" took exception to just about every aspect of the story. It curtly dismissed Tolkien's vision of Faery as nothing more than a "medievalist's vision of a Cellophane flowerbed"; it diminished the importance of the star and its finding by asserting—against the evidence supplied by the text—that the way one gets from Wootton to Faery is "by predestination"; and finally it dismissed Tolkien's whole effort by declaring that

> In good fantasy stories the real and the imaginary are knotted together, each depending on, and illuminating, the other. Tolkien makes the blighting error of preserving a hierarchical distinction between the two. Imagination thus becomes a formal gift, remote-controlled by pallid parent-figures, and not the right and possible prerogative of every child, as modern children expect it to be. They will probably reject the instinctive elitism of *Smith of Wootton Major*, its condescending attitude towards reality, and the singularly wet vision of the imaginary it proposes. I think they'll be right. (fol. 162r.)

Williams seems to have been exactly the sort of reader Tolkien had in mind when he wrote of *The Lord of the Rings* that "Some who have read the book, or at any rate have reviewed it [a nice distinction], have found it boring, absurd, or contemptible; and I have no cause to complain, since I have similar opinions of their works, or of the kind of writing that they evidently prefer" (*Fellowship* 6).

Williams's prose leaves no doubt that he found *Smith of Wootton Major* to be boring, absurd, and contemptible. By "pallid parent-figures" he presumably meant the King of Faery, and perhaps also the first Cook, who left the star that Alf the prentice put in the cake. Just how pallid they are, and just how parental, is of course up to the judgment of every reader. Williams's characterization of them as such, as well as his assumption that "modern children" (apparently a different and better sort than all their predecessors) expect imagination as a right and not a gift, may say more about his own attitude toward parent-figures and his own instinctive elitism, different perhaps, but surely no better, than that he found in *Smith of Wootton Major*. Williams's acerbic commentary, which undoubtedly speaks to and for the taste that Tolkien was describing, is characteristic of an antiromantic reaction, a militant and narrowly defined modernity that arose after World War I. It reflects the very kind of nouvelle approach to art that Tolkien and Lewis had reacted against and, in reply, to which they had agreed, back in 1936, to write for themselves the kind of stories they liked.

But Tolkien was doing more than just writing for himself the kind of story he liked to read. He was also reaching for some definite and long-sought goals, goals at once artistic, theoretical, and technical. He was trying once again to find some way of reconciling the simultaneous occurrence of Faërie time and human time. He was trying to work out a vision that would recognize the independent existence of the two worlds yet show their interdependence. And he was trying as well to create a true fairy-tale quality without the use of a traditional fairy-tale plot.

The last of these goals was also in many ways the easiest to reach, and comments from readers sympathetic to both his use of and departure from tradition in the story show that (for some, at least) he succeeded. Eileen Elgar, to whom Tolkien sent a copy, wrote him of her delight in finding it to be "*an original* tale— nothing in it about the third son of a woodcutter setting off in quest of adventures, and marrying a princess!" and called it "a most beautiful story" (fol. 150r.). Another early enthusiast, John Gand, of the *Oxford Mail* and the *Oxford Times*, wrote Tolkien that *Smith* "takes its place quite seamlessly in the great tradition of fairy tales," and he then went on to give his own special definition of that tradition and to single out the least traditional aspect of the story—that is, the sense of longing it conveys: "Everyone has their own personal sense of the tradition. For me 'Smith' belongs to it because of the unflawed simplicity of the narrative—it is most exquisitely written—and because of the true pang of yearning which comes from the relationship between Smith and Faery— sad in that it has a time-limit, beautiful in that it confers a grace on human life which is handed on" (fol. 154r.). Gand's focus on the "true pang of yearning" and on the time-limit factor in Smith's relationship with Faery is perceptive, for this is the last boundary of Faery, not an imaginative or geographic boundary but a temporal one, though no less impassable for being so.

It was above all in this aspect of the story that Tolkien worked through his own final relationship to that uncrossable boundary whose limit is that of mortal time. The clearest evidence for this lies in the story's key line, the message given by the Queen of Faery to Smith to pass on to the King—a message meant for Smith himself, though he does not know it: "The time has come; let him choose." The "time" is the time for Smith to give up the star; the "choice" is his choice of his successor. Tolkien's drafts of the story show that he tried out other phrases before settling on the final form of the message, and especially on the key words, "time" and "choose." The first message was simply "You are awaited." In its use of the second person it seems to be addressed only to the King, although it could be taken to mean Smith, whose return to the human world is awaited. In any case, it was very soon changed to "The time has come," and this, without the final clause, is how it remained through several drafts. Only in the later stages of the story did the message take its final form, the more distant third-person reference replacing the second-person address. It is tempting to guess that, as it did, the message came to be as much for the author of the story as for its hero.

It was in the writing of *Smith* that Tolkien came to confront and accept the limits of his own ventures into Faërie, his own travel through time, and it was in that story that he came finally to acknowledge in the way he knew best his growing sense that his time was running out. Reflecting on his story, he wrote that "a time comes for writers and artists, when invention and vision cease and they can only reflect on what they have seen and learned." But he was also at pains to point out that "that is not the whole point of the tale. Which includes sacrifice, and the handing on, with trust and without keeping a hand on things, of power and vision to the next generation" (fol. 36r.).

Yet for all its sunset glow, its voluntary if painful farewell to Faërie, the atmosphere of peace and acceptance that *Smith* conveys was hard come-by, as its predecessor "The Sea-bell" bears witness. It was distilled out of Tolkien's deepest memories of his own adventures in the perilous realm. At the heart of the story is the figure that Tolkien returned to again and again in his fiction—the wanderer, the restless, unquiet human traveler between the worlds. Much of what he wrote suggests that Tolkien felt himself to be such a one, and it can be no surprise that the wanderer and his journey figure so largely in so much of what he wrote. The real connection between two disparate systems of time and space is the human figure who moves between them. Bilbo may return to take up his old life at the end of *The Hobbit*, but he is off again trending into Faërie at the beginning of *The Lord of the Rings*.

Frodo, who follows him, grows beyond the Shire and must seek his consolation and his healing over the sea. Edwin Lowdham leaves his young son to take to the sea once more in his endless quest for "seas a great deal further off," and that son, now grown to manhood, is about to follow after him as *The Notion Club Papers* sputters inconclusively out.

This unrest, this "wandering-madness," has been a characteristic motif of Tolkien's work at least since "Looney," and probably since the early story of Eriol. But it was not until he wrote *Smith of Wootton Major* that he was able fully to make his peace with it. What most distinguishes the figure of Smith—especially from that of both Looney and the voyager of "The Sea-bell"—is that Smith is enriched by his experience, whereas Looney and the voyager are baffled and alienated by theirs. Smith is permitted into Faery, allowed to wander there at will, and only much later and after many visits made to understand that at last he must bid it a permanent farewell. And even then he is escorted from that world back into his own by one who has dwelt in both: Prentice who is Alf who is the King of Faery. What Tolkien denied to Looney and the wanderer of "The Sea-bell" he bestowed on his Smith, the blessing of acquaintance with the fairy folk and a real, if limited, understanding of their world and its ways.

It is important to the story and to its bounce that someone else has been there before him. Behind Smith hovers the enigmatic, unexplained figure of the first Cook. This first Cook (first only in appearance in the narrative and not in the succession of Master Cooks, of whom there have been many before the story begins) has an importance to the story in almost directly inverse proportion to the amount of time he is actively in it, for according to Tolkien it is he who "seems to have set going the events that occupy this tale." He is the major human motive force behind the action. It is the first Cook who brings back to Wootton Major Alf the apprentice, who is much later revealed to be the King of Faery. It is the first Cook who at his final departure leaves the star that will be baked into the cake and found by Smith. Although he is the first character introduced in the story, we are told very little about him, only that he is the reigning Master Cook, that he went away suddenly one day, and when he came back brought with him Alf, who became his apprentice. In very short order he goes away again, just as suddenly and without explanation, leaving the field and the rest of the story to Smith. He is given a last mention (and some much-needed background) at nearly the end of the story, when the King of Faery tells Smith that the departed Cook was Smith's own grandfather, that his name was Rider, that he was a great traveler, and that it was he who left the star. He seems like a kind of latter-day Bilbo Baggins, disappearing suddenly, then returning just as suddenly with a magic token, passing it on to a successor, and then going away again.

But the story itself barely hints at his real significance. As with the equally mysterious and even less accessible Edwin Lowdham of *The Notion Club Papers*, readers are left with tantalizing, unanswered questions about the first Cook. Just what is the importance of this traveler between the worlds? Where does he travel and why? What is his real connection with Alf and with the star? Where does he go after his final departure? We have a sense, again as in *The Notion Club Papers*, of some unseen power at work. But though Tolkien took care to keep this aspect of the story out of the narrative proper, to leave it implicit, barely hinted at, he nevertheless needed to know the answers for himself. In the essay he wrote for *Smith*, far more complete and comprehensive than his notes for the *Papers*, Tolkien went to some lengths to develop what he called an "exterior" history of the story and of the first Cook in particular, a history and chronology that begin with his birth and bring events up to the time when the story takes over, when the first Cook returns from a journey bringing with him Alf, the apprentice.

It seems clear from this background as well as from his activities within the narrative itself that this figure is, in fact, intended to be one of Tolkien's far-traveled characters. This line of wanderers is one that reaches all the way from this last story back to the very first and includes Alboin Errol, Edwin Lowdham, Frodo Baggins, Bilbo Baggins, Eärendil, and Ælfwine-Eriol, and of course Tolkien himself—all the Elf-friends. In some tales, most notably in *The Hobbit* and the story of Eärendil, this figure is the main character, and his wanderings are the stuff of the story. In others, such as *The Notion Club Papers* and *Smith of Wootton Major*, he is on the edge of the action, shadowy, more than a little mysterious, and perhaps all the more effective for that reason.

The single exclusion from this group is the voyager of "The Sea-bell." Whoever this figure is, whether Tolkien calls him Looney or hints at a relationship to Frodo, he is utterly, one might say brutally, shut out from this or any fellowship. This exclusion both from Faërie and from human contact is the whole point of "The Sea-bell" and of its hinted connection to *The Lord of the Rings*. Whereas the whole point of *Smith*, while it is not the direct opposite of "The Sea-bell," not exactly a welcome into Faery, is to imply that there is at the least a necessary interaction with that world. In *Smith of Wootton Major* the two worlds most explicitly touch and interact. The point of fusion between Faery and the outside world is, as in all of Tolkien's fiction, but most successfully in *Smith*, that wandering figure, be he Cook, seafarer, or hobbit, in whom and by whom Faery and human time and space are made to touch. *Smith* thus represents the culmination of a major shift over the years in Tolkien's concept of that world and suggests that he had come to a newer view of Faery as being—at least to some extent—on a two-way street. This is most clearly embodied in the character of Smith himself and his journeys into Faery but has already been introduced in the person of the first Cook, for the story manages to suggest, without stating, the direction of his journeys and to suggest also that his return with Alf was in accordance with some plan, though the fact that this plan actually originates in Faery is intentionally kept out of the narrative.

What the story only implies (and necessarily keeps implicit, if it is to maintain its bounce) is made explicit in the unpublished essay that Tolkien wrote in conjunction with the story. Here he makes it clear that in point of fact the story is as much about Faery's relationship to Wootton as it is about Wootton's relationship to Faery. Where the elven dwellers in the faërie world of "The Sea-bell" ignored the overtures of the solitary voyager and were indifferent to his desires, the elven folk of this latest Faery are actively concerned with and perhaps even dependent on the spiritual life of Wootton Major and therefore (it would seem) are careful for the welfare of its inhabitants. It is their unsolicited effort to bring Wootton back from its increasing vulgar materiality that forms the even deeper background to the "external" history that lies behind the story.

This background, at once the most important and the most hidden aspect of the story, rests on a concept of the necessary interaction of Faery and the human world, a concept that Tolkien presented as de facto and needing no explanation in the narrative but that he gave considerable time and attention to working out in his unpublished *Smith* essay. Both these writings are deeply involved in Tolkien's effort to attain the other two of what I have suggested were his unstated goals in the writing of *Smith*, the reconciliation of Faery time and human time and the independent yet interdependent nature of the two worlds. These were less susceptible of easy solution than was his goal of creating the fairy-tale atmosphere, which, though taxing, is after all a technical rather than a theoretical problem. In the story itself, and even more in the essay that Tolkien wrote as a supplement to and explication of his narrative, he returned again to the problem of validating his concept of the cotemporous existence of separate yet permeable worlds.

It is a concept distilled out of both the thought processes of "On Fairy-Stories" and the emotion of "The Sea-bell." Yet the concept goes beyond either of these earlier efforts to find a deeper, richer value in the complexities, the seeming contradictions, the beauty and danger of that other world. In *Smith* Faery is still perilous, still potentially threatening to the visitor, but now in its own way also an element whose presence is as necessary to the spiritual health of humankind as are food and water to its material well-being. Evidence for the beauty and the threat are to be found both within and without the narrative. The story itself shows both faces of Faery and gives equal space to enchantment and danger. The essay is more one-sided, concentrating primarily on the beneficent aspects of this Otherworld and on its necessary relationship to the human one. Within the story the star functions as Smith's permission and protection, warning away the Lesser Evils and guarding him against the Greater Evils, though he can be variously terrified or enchanted by what he sees. His adventures range from dancing with maidens to witnessing the grim march of warrior-seamen toward an unknown destination.

On one journey he is given the gift of an undying flower by a maiden (the one he dances with) who turns out to be the Queen of Faery. This flower has a curious role in the story. Smith takes it home and keeps it in a casket, where it remains unwithered. Unlike the star, it seems to convey no power or magic, yet it also seems meant in some way to balance the star (also stored away in a box between appearances) that must be relinquished, as a gift that can be kept, a token and a memento. As such it suggests a further parallel between Smith and *The Lord of the Rings*. Like

Arwen's gift to Frodo of a jewel to replace the lost Ring, the Queen of Faery's gift to Smith of the flower will be his last and most enduring memento, a comfort when the star is gone. In a very real sense these two gifts bracket Smith's adventures in Faery—the one representing his entry into that world, the other an enduring reminder and a farewell. One is celestial, the other earthly. One is an image of something high and remote, an unreachable goal. The other is there for the plucking, an earthbound beauty springing from the ground under his feet, a reminder both of where he has wandered and where he must come to rest.

But between these two images Tolkien has interposed an enigmatic third, one that seems to stand in direct opposition to the other two and appears to call into question the interdependence of the two worlds, or at least to make the point that the two-way street is no well-traveled thoroughfare, nor is it a road easy and pleasant to traverse. This is the birch tree whose branches are stripped bare when it shelters Smith from the furious wind that tries to hunt him down. Smith's encounter with the wind and the birch tree stands as perhaps his most powerful experience in Faery and is far and away the most compelling, most daunting scene in the story. It is at once the most direct and the most forbidding of his adventures in Faery, for while the star provides entry, and the Queen welcomes Smith and invites him to dance, the wind pursues him and the birch tree tells him vehemently to get out and stay out. Here is no firm but gentle invitation to relinquish his right of entry and yield place to another, such as Smith later gets from the King, but a summary dismissal, a notice to quit.

The scene is one of the most vivid in the whole story and marks a noticeable shift in tone. In his wanderings, Smith has come upon a lake whose depths contain "strange shapes of flame" and "fiery creatures" going to and fro. So far, so good. We are in the perilous realm and must expect some danger, or the adventure would not be worth the having. The atmosphere here is not unlike some of the more ominous scenes Smith has already observed, the waves on the Sea of Windless Storm, the ships, the elven mariners. Stepping onto the lake's surface, he finds that it is not water but "harder than stone and sleeker than glass." But just here there is a change. He falls on the hard, unyielding surface, and with the fall suddenly shifts from being an observer of the scene to being a participant, perhaps even an agent in it. With his entry into the action, the tone and the mood change dramatically. With his fall a "ringing boom" runs across the lake, awaking the Wind, which harries and drives him back from the lake, "whirling and falling like a dead leaf." It is then that he finds the birch.

> He put his arms about the stem of a young birch and clung to it, and the Wind wrestled fiercely with them, trying to tear him away; but the birch was bent down to the ground by the blast and enclosed him in its branches. When at last the Wind passed on he rose and saw that the birch was naked. It was stripped of every leaf, and it wept, and tears fell from its branches like rain. He set his hand upon its white bark, saying: "Blessed be the birch! What can I do to make amends or give thanks?" He felt the answer of the tree pass up from his hand: "Nothing," it said. "Go away! The Wind is hunting you. You do not belong here. Go away and never return!"
>
> As he climbed back out of that dale he felt the tears of the birch trickle down his face and they were bitter on his lips. (*Smith* 32)

What are we to make of this episode, of its violence and its near-total disregard for human interaction? In a conventional fairy tale we would anticipate that the beneficent birch was to be Smith's friend, the nature-spirit that helps him on his way, a benign and feminine presence there to whisper a spell or give a word of guidance. And so it does, but not in the terms we expect.

The reply to Smith's "Blessed be the birch" and to his offer to repay is the stark, uncompromising "You do not belong here!" The tree has paid dearly for sheltering Smith, and its only response to his thanks is to reject them and him, and tell him to get out. The hardness of the lake is replicated in the hardness of the birch tree's judgment. The fury of the Wind, the bitterness of the tree's tears all speak of a world beyond Smith's mortal experience or mortal ability to understand and mark him clearly as an intruder in the enchanted land, unwanted, unwelcomed, and punished for his presence. The vehemence of the episode cuts sharply across the mood of the story and leaves the reader puzzling how to fit it in. It is enigmatic at the very least, at once provocative and problematic to those probing the story for more meaning than may be readily apparent.

Though it is by far the most powerful, this was not Tolkien's first treatment of the birch tree. Two of his poems in *Songs for the Philologists* deal with the birch. One is in Anglo-Saxon, *"Éadig Béo Þu,"* "Good Luck to You." The other is in Gothic—the only Gothic poem in the lot. In fact, as Shippey points out, although it is by a modern hand, it is the only poem extant in that dead and buried language by any hand. It is called *"Bagme Bloma,"* "Flower of the Trees." Both poems praise the birch. *"Bagme Bloma,"* an unusually beautiful lyric, far lovelier in the Gothic than in English translation, hails the birch as *"bagme bloma, blauandei | fagraf-ahsa, liþulinþi,"* "the flower of the trees in bloom, fair-haired and supple-limbed" and includes a line strongly reminiscent of the scene in *Smith: "Andanahti milhmam neipiþ, | liuhteiþ liuhmam lauh-muni; | laubos liubai fliugand lausai, | tulgus, triggwa, standan-dei | Bairka baza beidiþ blaika/ fraujinondei fairguni,"* "Evening grows dark with clouds, the lightening flashes, the fine leaves fly free, but firm and faithful the white birch stands bare and waits, ruling the mountain." Unlike *Smith*, however, here the tree is free of any human contact. *"Éadig Béo Þu"* takes a different approach, *"herian Beorc and byrcen cynn, | láre' and láreow, leornung-mann—"* praising "the Birch and the birch's race, the teacher, the student, and the subject" (Shippey 228–29).

Shippey's discussion of these "birch poems" connects them with Scottish folklore, specifically with the Scottish ballad of "The Wife of Usher's Well," wherein the Wife's drowned sons, called back from the dead, wear hats of birch, the tree that grows "at the gates o' Paradise." He also cites a tale reported by Sir Walter Scott of an apparition who wore the birch so that "the wind of the world" might not have power over him (Shippey 206–7). Moving forward from the poems to the birch tree episode in *Smith*, Shippey suggests that

> Smith's Wind, then, could be the world; the birch is its tradi-tional opponent, scholarly study; but that study, like the birch hats of the drowned sons, also acts as a passport, into and out of Middle-earth. It is a kind of Golden Bough; not between Earth and Hell, like Aeneas's bough, but between Earth and Paradise.

All this has a bearing on Tolkien's fable, and on his state of mind. The birch protects Smith, but is left naked and weeping. Did Tolkien feel he had *exploited* philology for his fiction? It also tells Smith to "go away and never return," a command he cannot obey. Why should he have included this embargo, from within Faërie, against revisiting it? Did he feel, perhaps, that in writing his fiction he was trespassing in a "perilous country" against some unstated law? (207)

While it is prudent to frame ideas as questions—Did Tolkien feel he had exploited philology? Did he feel that in writing fiction he was trespassing?—rather than to present them as opinion, we may still grant Shippey the rather narrow plausibility of his interpretation. But it adds little to the story. To describe the birch, as Shippey does, as a representation of "learning, severe learning, even discipline," to make the Wind into "the world" and the birch into "its traditional opponent, scholarly study," to turn the tree into "a kind of Golden Bough between Earth and Paradise," these translations do little to account for the effect of the episode *within the story itself*. Indeed, they work to diminish it. It is appropriate to look for correlations between an author's life and his work; nevertheless, these speculations, though they are legitimately derived from the available evidence, would place a heavy burden on a story whose effect depends not a little on the lightness of its touch.

Moreover, such speculations cannot approach the emotional power of the episode, which connects more with the lightening flashes of *"Bagme Bloma"* than with the scholarly emphasis of *"Éadig Béo Þu,"* or the hat-wearing apparitions of the Scottish ballad and Scott's anecdote. Nor do they add materially to an understanding of the story. Smith already has his passport into the Otherworld— the star. He doesn't need another one. There is no need, moreover, to see the episode as representing Tolkien's sense of transgression for venturing into Faery (fiction) "against some unstated law," since Smith does, as Shippey himself points out, return again to Faery.

As with other comparisons in this study of early and late versions of the same material, comparison with other drafts of the story is informative but not decisive. The episode with the birch does not appear at all in the early (and much shorter) drafts, and it's worth noting that when it did appear it exhibited some notable differences from the published text. The lake, the birch, the leaves, the tears are all there, but with a slightly different flavor. To begin with, the lake is not hard, nor does Smith venture onto (or into) it. There is no fall, no "ringing boom," which in the published story seems to be what wakes the Wind. Instead, Smith tastes the water from which it gets its name, Lake of Tears, and finds it bitter. He walks on the hillside among many trees, "young and fair and in full leaf," and when the Wind comes "roaring like a wild beast," it tears up "all that had no roots" and drives before it "all that could not withstand it." Only one of these is Smith, who then is not the sole victim but part of a general storm. All the trees are stripped of their leaves, leaving them naked, and the leaves "whirl like clouds in the sky." All the trees weep, not just the birch, and their tears "flowed from their branches and twigs like a grey rain, and some gathered into rivulets that ran down into the lake," thus giving the lake its name and (presumably) its flavor.

The birch tree is still Smith's shelter from the Wind, and its reply to his offer of thanks is nonverbal. Smith feels it "pass up his arm." The answer is similar but not so emphatic as in the final version. "Go away from here!" the birch tells Smith. "The Wild Wind is hunting you." This is considerably less sweeping than the "You do not belong here!" of the final version. Here nothing at all is said about Smith not belonging in Faery. Moreover, the birch gives Smith a message for the King. "If you see the King tell him. Only he can still the Wind once it is aroused." The anger of the Wind seems in this draft to have more a general than a specific target, for though it is hunting Smith, it is also attacking all the trees, not just the birch under which he shelters. The Wind has clearly done this sort of thing before, as the Lake of Tears bears witness.

There is no doubt that Tolkien's final version is more intense, more sharply focused, and considerably more ominous. And certainly as the passage intensified, Tolkien's sense of trespass could have intensified as well, leading to the reading suggested by Shippey. But the fact that the episode developed out of this earlier version speaks equally in favor of a more general but no less powerful reading of the passage for its meaning in the context not of Tolkien's life but of the story itself. The scene both invites and defeats attempts to interpret it, for no interpretation can match the power of the scene itself. It demands attention but it defies exegesis. Or rather, exegesis, explanation, allegorization can contribute little or nothing to the value of the scene, whose impact is all the more powerful for being inexplicable. It is as if Smith had suddenly changed places with Looney. And perhaps, after all, this is exactly what has happened. The perceiving sensibility has flashed back, for a moment, to an earlier, harsher vision, a vision of Faërie rather than Faery. A door has opened, and a wind from an earlier world has blown through the newly dark and empty spaces. Perhaps it is as simple as that.

This passage is unique, however. Nowhere else within the story does Tolkien draw so stern a picture of Faery's attitude toward humanity. The moment stands on its own as Tolkien's clearest picture of the "otherness," the utter (to the human experience) strangeness of this world. Sometimes the human figure cannot bridge the gap. Yet Smith, like Tolkien, does venture in again. The birch tree's warning keeps him away for a while, but finally he does go back. And when he does, no similar ominous episode occurs. Any "sense of transgression" Tolkien might have felt was clearly impermanent, if present at all, for Smith's further adventures seem all beneficent. Although like Looney he cannot "clearly remember nor report to his friends" what he sees in Faery, he remains "a learner and explorer," not, as in "The Sea-bell," an intruder with gladdon-sword and reed-mace who might deserve to be driven out.

And yet the episode is evidence that even now, and if only for a moment, Tolkien was clearly of two minds about the nature of humanity's relationship with Faery. He was not the only writer to experience such ambivalence. That other venturer into Faërie, James M. Barrie, forced to switch hands due to writer's cramp, was heard to remark that he "thought more darkly down his left arm" (Birkin 284). Certainly Tolkien's creative, imaginative self thought more darkly, more down the left arm, than did his rational self. Turning from the story to the essay on *Smith* and writing (as we may imagine) more down the right arm, he develops a very different picture of the relationship with Faery. In the essay, Tolkien concentrates almost entirely on the beauty of the Otherworld, on its spiritual value, and on its beneficent and necessary influence on the human world. It is in this essay that he provides what may have been his clearest, latest word on a personal definition of this enchanted Otherworld. He wrote that:

> Faery represents at its weakest a breaking out (at least in mind) from the iron ring of the familiar, still more from the adamantine ring of belief that it is known, possessed, controlled, and so

(ultimately) all that is worth being considered—a constant awareness of the world beyond these rings. More strongly it represents love: that is, a love and respect for all things, "Inanimate" and "animate," an unpossessive love of them as "other." This "love" will produce both *ruth* and *delight*. Things seen in its light will be respected, and they will also appear delightful, beautiful, wonderful even glorious. Faery might be said indeed to represent Imagination (without definition because taking in all the definitions of this word): esthetic, exploratory and receptive; and artistic; inventive, dynamic, (sub)creative. This compound—of awareness of a limitless world outside our domestic parish; a love (in ruth and admiration) for the things in it; and a desire for wonder, marvels, both perceived and conceived—this "Faery" is as necessary for the health and complete functioning of the Human as is sunlight for physical life. . . . (fol. 26r.)

This is as revealing as it is beautiful in its evocation of a personal, private world, its recognition of awareness and desire as concomitant elements in the imaginative life. It is hard to imagine that the man who wrote these words would have felt deeply or permanently that he was a transgressor, however much he may have been aware of the inhuman aspects of the perilous realm. For no great leap of imagination is needed in order to see in this long definition the poet's description of and prescription for his own needs or to conclude from it that he was speaking from experience and that Faery was as necessary for his own spiritual health and complete functioning as sunlight for his physical life.

Another, more practical purpose of the essay was to enable Tolkien to fill in to his own satisfaction those details the story left out but that he felt were essential for its full effect. In defense of these details and of their omission from the story, he maintained that

. . . the beginning and end of a story is to it like the edges of the canvas or an added frame to a picture, say a landscape. It concentrates the tellers [*sic*] attention, and yours on one small part of the country. But there are of course no real limits: under the earth, and in the sky above, and in the remote and faintly glimpsed distances, and in the unrevealed regions on either side, there are things that influence the very shape and colour of the part that is pictured. Without them it would be quite different, and they are really necessary to understanding what is seen.[3] (fol. 12r.)

Here is some of the "bounce" that the critics were looking for, though in this case we need not cut open the ball in order to find it. It worked to keep the story aloft without ever superseding it, for this private explication of history and theory, the filling in of the unnarrated background, freed him to write the story in front of it, so to speak, and thus to preserve the fairy-tale quality that he said he was after. For Tolkien was in his own way also searching for the bounce. It was plainly easier for him to arrive at what Faërie is and what it is good for than to clarify with any certitude how it does it.

As the essay progressed it developed into one more attempt on Tolkien's part to evolve and codify a working theory of space-time, a theory that should possess, like his Secondary World itself, the "inner consistency of reality." That he was unable, finally, to develop such a theory and make it consistent is less a comment on his invented world than on his real one, which has so far defeated similar efforts by many more rationally inclined, scientifically oriented twentieth-century minds than Tolkien's. He did not want finally and forever to reconcile space-time but simply to find some premise that would give him a sound enough theoretical base on which his Faery and the ordinary world could believably stand together and coexist. Nonetheless, his attempt, though largely unsuccessful, did not fail completely and is worth attention both for itself and for the light it throws on this and other, related efforts. His discussion for *Smith* began with a consideration of the spatial and temporal relationship of Wootton and Faery.

> The geographical relations of Wootton and Faery are inevitably, but also intentionally left vague. In such stories there must be some way or ways of access from and to Faery, available at least to Elves as to favoured mortals. But it is also necessary that Faery and the world (of Men), though in contact, should occupy a different time and space, or occupy them in different modes. Thus though it appears that Smith can enter Faery more or less at will (being specially favoured), it is evident that it is a land or, world of unknown limits, containing seas and mountains; also

it is plain that even during a brief visit (such as one on an evening walk) he can spend a great deal longer in Faery than his absnce [*sic*] counts in the World; on his long journeys an absence from home of, say, a week is sufficient for exploration and experiences in Faery equivalent to months or even years. (fol. 21r.)

As it usually does, space proved simpler to deal with than time. It lent itself more easily to travel, and such travel, being more traditional, was easier to account for.

As for place. Entry into the "geographical" bounds of Faery also involves entry into Faery Time. How does a mortal "enter" the geographical realm of Faery? Evidently not in dream or illusion. . . .

It is common in Fairy tales for the entrance to the fairy world to be presented as a journey underground, into a hill or mountain or the like. . . .

My symbol is not the underground . . . but the Forest[4]: the regions still immune from human activities, not yet dominated by them (dominated! not conquered!). If Faery Time is at points contiguous with ours, the contiguity will occur in related points in space—or that is the theory for the purpose of the story. At certain points at or just within the Forest borders a human person may come across these contiguous points and there enter F. time and space—if fitted to do so or permitted to do so. (fol. 21v.)

Recall that Pwyll Prince of Dyfed, hero of the First Branch of the *The Mabinogion,* entered the Otherworld by way of a wood. The similarities among actual Welsh myth, Tolkien's theory, and the physics and metaphysics of the Lórien episode in *The Lord of the Rings* are notable. For the forward action of *The Lord of the Rings* there must be within Middle-earth a point or points at which Faërie (Lórien) time and space are contiguous with that of mortals. It is not merely romance of setting that led Tolkien to make Lórien a wood, for in his personal geosymbology this provided that at certain points within its borders a human person (or persons—in this case the Fellowship) would be permitted "to enter F[aërie] time and space." His preference for a wood over the more usual fairy-story topos of the underground (usually in the form of a fairy mound or hill) as the place of entry is surely connected not just to *The*

Mabinogion but also to the association of Middle English *wode,* *wood* with both "wood" and "mad," that is, outside the realm of ordinary experience.[5]

The convention of the wood as the predictable setting for unhuman, extraordinary experience is a standard of medieval and Renaissance narrative. Tolkien knew this, as Shakespeare knew it, as Dante knew it. Moreover, the acceptability of this poetic convention offered a way around the unsolvable temporal mechanics of the situation. It allowed him to move out of time and into space and to conceive a geography both magical and mappable. In the case of *Smith* Tolkien used both terrain and direction to seat his latest otherworld comfortably in a tradition of myth and legend. Like the Irish Otherworlds, like his own Númenor, this Faery "is situated (or its entrances are) westward." And one gets there by walking, not (as Williams's waspish review assumes) by predestination. The forest lies on the western edge of Wootton Major, whose one inn bears over its door a stone with a worn and faded carving of three trees and the inscription *"Welcō to þe Wode."*

The nearby but smaller village of Wootton Minor is closer to the forest, being described as "a village in a clearing," and the even smaller village of Walton (cited in the prehistory but not in the story proper) is "a distant village beyond Wootton Minor." The key to the significance of these place names is in their etymology. Both *Wootton* and *Walton* derive from words that mean "town in or near a wood." *Wootton* comes from Old English *wudu-tun,* "TŪN [town] in or by a wood," and *Walton* has its source in Old English *W(e)ald-tun,* "TŪN in a wood or on a wold." Thus all three villages are by name and deliberate design in close proximity to the wood of Faery. "The western villages of the country, among them the Woottons and Walton, were originally main points of contact between Faery and this country of Men; they had been at an earlier period actually within the Forest borders, as their names signify" (fol. 23v.). Walton, even deeper in the forest than Wootton Minor, is evidently still the point of entry into Faery for those humans who venture there. So much is background leading up to the part of his history that comes into the story proper. But behind this background is a deeper background, the "interior" history, more specific to Faery and to its relationship with the human realm. As Tolkien imagines it, this relationship is "one of love: the Elven Folk, the chief and ruling inhabitants of Faery, have an ultimate kinship with Men and have a permanent love for them in general. Though they are not bound by any moral obligation to assist Men, and do not need their help (except in human affairs), they do from time to time try to assist them, avert evil from them and have relations with them, especially through certain men and women whom they find suitable" (fol. 23v.–24r.).

Within the story proper, the chief person found suitable to gain entry to Faery is, of course, Smith. His home after his father's death was the "Old Smithy House," described in the essay as being "on the West Road, the last house in the village on that side," that is to say, on the westward edge of Wootton Major and therefore on the edge of the forest. The practical reason for this proximity to the forest is presumably for easy access to fuel, but the more profound reason is surely for easy access to Faery. Geographically, at least, Smith is halfway there even when he is in the ordinary world. Where he is temporally is quite another matter. Tolkien had worked out a scheme that would establish the physical relationship of Faery and the world and their proximity to one another. But he had also felt it necessary to try to resolve the deeper, more metaphysical consideration of their temporal relationship. Here he found himself almost at once in deep water and struggling to keep his head up:

In many Fairy Tales use is made of the idea that time passes quickly in Faery, so that a man who finds his way there may come out after what seems a brief episode to find that years, even centuries have passed. Except as a mere device to bring a man out of the past into contact with a (to him) future time— that is in a tale of which this is the real point, and Faery as such is not seriously considered—I have always felt this to be a mistake: a mistake in credibility, if Faery of any kind is taken seriously. (fol. 21r.)

This discussion has a direct bearing on Tolkien's treatment of time in other, similar instances, most specifically in the Lórien chapters in *The Lord of the Rings*, and such instances are based on the same, still unresolved, theoretical premise. He could not make it work on a practical level, but he could not forego the beauty and the (for him) utility of the concept. This forced him, finally, to adopt an untenable rhetorical position, for while on the one hand he rejected the faërien time warp as a "mere device," and a "mistake in credibility," on the other hand he declared that "The Faery of this tale is a particular one. If one accepts it while 'within' the tale, then clearly the Rulers of Faery . . . must be able to arrange that the experiences in Faery of favoured human persons may be enjoyed without dislocation of their normal human life. The time of their Faery must be different, even though it may be at points contiguous. For them human time is or may be also longer than that of Faery" (fol. 21v.).

This will not do. He cannot have it both ways. To declare so positively that the time warp is a mistake in credibility and at the same time to maintain the principle that a sojourn in the Faery world should bring about "no dislocation of normal human life" is to try to have your cake and eat it. It is to reach for a next-to-impossible accommodation between logic and imagination, like trying to balance allegory and no-allegory, a balance that even the Rulers of Faery would not be able to arrange. Tolkien must surely have been aware at some level of the inconsistency of such a position, or he would not have kept on trying over and over to find a way to make it work.

It is just as surely more important both for his imagining mind and for the work it produced that he at least made the effort. For finally, of course, he was a poet, not a logician or a physicist. And though he did not altogether succeed in reaching that balance, neither did he altogether fail, for the situations he created in pursuing the reconciliation are among his most provocative and the characters through whom he sought to bridge the worlds are those whom we ourselves would like to follow to those "shores a great deal further off." If he wavered between Faery time and human time, between the beauties and dangers of the perilous realm and the world of everyday, if he sought ways to reconcile them while sensing deeply that they were unreconcilable, his search led him to create works of great beauty and power, works whose possibilities for expanding the mind and imagination led him and have led his readers ever on and on.

For his search after an answer to the question of relative time—unsuccessful though that search may have been—showed him how J. W. Dunne and others had handled the problem, led him to try his hand at realms of speculation and mystery far beyond those of most of his contemporaries, led him to *The Lost Road* and *The*

Notion Club Papers and *The Lord of the Rings*. And *Smith of Wootton Major*. None of these fully succeeds in achieving a sound theoretical footing for its treatment of the time-space problem. None manages to be solidly based on laws logically derived from a set of postulates. But that is merely to say that in none of these stories is the time-space connection mathematically demonstrable. It is worth remembering, however, that neither is mathematics fully demonstrable at its highest levels. It was the mathematician Gödel who demonstrated that any set of postulates whose elements all support one another with no variables becomes a closed system and thus is self-defeating, leaving no room for further invention. As the physicist Roger Jones explains Gödel's proposition, "any branch of mathematics sufficiently complex to be of interest to mathematicians . . . . will be either inconsistent or incomplete." Based on Gödel, Jones carries it further, to say that "if you try to derive the laws of arithmetic in a logical fashion from any set of postulates, simpler than arithmetic itself, either you will arrive at contradictory results (inconsistency) or there will be results that you know to be true, but which you cannot derive from the postulates (incompleteness)" (Jones 158).

To say that Tolkien's vision was not perfect does not limit his work; rather, it sets it free. It is not a closed system. It is both inconsistent and incomplete, and it certainly arrived at results which, though he knew in his heart to be true, he could not logically derive from the postulates. His world is too vital, too dynamic to be harnessed to a diagram. It is too intensely human, in every sense in which that word can be understood. For that reason it matched his time, and for that reason it will transcend it. His vision is not perfect; it is just unforgettable. It tugs insistently at our imaginations; it completely engages our sensibilities. It is profoundly moving. Above all, it leaves us knowing deeply that there is more to be found in his fiction than meets the eye, that something wonderful and mysterious and deeply significant lies just beyond our rational perception, and that if we were to be given only a little more time, we would be able to see it.

Epilogue:
His Gift of Glee

> I would draw some of the great tales in fullness, and
> leave many only placed in the scheme, and sketched.
> The cycles should be linked to a majestic whole,
> and yet leave scope for other minds and hands . . .
> —J. R. R. Tolkien

Smith of Wootton Major should make a fitting conclusion to this
study on Tolkien's treatment of time and Faërie, for while it leaves
some questions unanswered, it is yet a poetically satisfying treatment of the subject. But the picture is more complicated, and perhaps there can be no final conclusion, no resolution of the contradictory elements of Tolkien's imagination. Material written in the
years just before the composition of *Smith,* but not published until nearly thirty years later, shows Tolkien still wrestling with problems of logical consistency and metaphysical coherence concerning the interconnection of the lives, worldviews, and probable
futures of his two races of Elves and Men.[1] The outcome of his
wrestling was a more systematized account that replaced poetry
with theory and substituted for his intuitive sense of his world an
intellectual rationale. But this is a predictable sequence and, indeed, not unlike what often happens to primary myths. Experience of and emotional participation in the vigor of the tales give
way, as the stories harden, to more theoretical constructs. Theology inevitably begins to supersede mythology. One has only to

contrast the Gospels with Aquinas's *Summa Theologica* to see the process at work.

Circumstances of protracted composition and recomposition and the delayed publication of the great body of mythic material that is the Silmarillion have resulted in a curious resemblance between Tolkien's invented mythos and the mythologies of the primary world. The whole picture is less like a painting than a restored mosaic, a composition pieced together out of recovered fragments long after its original life and use. Tolkien's habit of starting, stopping, and circling back to retell in multiple ways in verse and prose the stories of his legendarium meant that there was for most of it hardly ever a final text, only variant and competing versions. To be sure, *The Lord of the Rings* was begun, worked through (albeit with many halts and revisions), and brought to a conclusive and final form in which it was published. There is thus for this work at least (allowing for discrepancies between the first and second editions and the predictable number of printing errors) a more or less fixed and final text. But Christopher Tolkien's serial publication of the multivolume *History of Middle-Earth* shows that this was the exception rather than the rule. The uncompleted state of much of the material, plus the fact that the great body of it was not published until after his death, has given Tolkien's mythology some of the puzzling aspects of recovered text that scholars are more used to finding in the scattered stories and references of Celtic or Greek or Icelandic mythology.

So powerful a body of work as Tolkien's mythology has inevitably the effect of inviting his readers to want to find—or at least to look for—the kind of coherence and consistency we are used to finding in novels and to show understandable signs of distress when such consistency is not present, when various early and late versions seem to contradict one another. At the same time, the presence of so much material from so many stages of development leaves readers confused about the status of the "canon," or even whether there is one. Such concern is a natural concomitant of the persuasive reality that Tolkien's imagination has given the world but is finally irrelevant to the power of his work. His own words, put in the mouth of the protagonist of his short story "Leaf by Niggle," are a better commentary on his created world than any amount of critical speculation. "'It's a gift!' he [Niggle] said. He was referring to his art, and also to the result; but he was using the word quite literally" (104). Tolkien's gift, his art, was a natural talent, but the result was in large measure the inadvertent gift of his situation in and feelings about his time. An important impetus for his subcreation was his uneasiness with the twentieth century, his desire to escape it, and his knowledge that such escape was only partly (and then only imaginatively) possible. What, finally, does this say about his work? About the man himself? About his time?

He drew from and built on the imaginations of his peers and predecessors, from Du Maurier to Dunne, but what he took he remade, using it to underpin and ground his structure. Because of his concern with time in all its aspects, his work, both internally and externally, makes a bridge between time present and time past. His fiction has and will continue to recapture for an audience raised on realism and thinly nourished by the modern novel the excitement and wonder of time-traveling into Faërie, into the older modes of literature of epic and romance and fairy tale. His stories remind us how timely these forms are, and in so doing they reconnect our sensibilities to the truths these kinds of narrative can express so vividly. When we read his work we—like Ramer—fall "wide asleep" into a dream more real than ordinary waking experience. We come out of it with a new perception of the present, waking world.

As to the man himself, what Tolkien wrote came out of his deepest sense and continuing exploration of who he was. His was a journey of discovery as perilous, as poignant, as poised between wonder and terror as that of Frodo or Looney or Edwin Lowdham. He was his own bridge, his own Janus-figure looking forward in looking backward, dividing yet connecting past and future in one present awareness. No one reading his work with care and sympathy can fail to see in him the oldest and newest of the Elf-friends, the ultimate avatar of Eriol-Ælfwine, the thread linking imagination with myth and myth with history and history with the modern age. Taking his whole body of work as the manifestation of one hopeful, deeply troubled, and percipient vision, it requires little imagination to see Tolkien as his century's Observer 2, the observer at infinity, encompassing all the others, including that of the reader.

His relation to his century is reluctant, critical, deeply concerned. The same double vision that enabled him to see through his own time to the past that made it also allowed him to see in that mirror of the past the clouded reflection of the present. He was an exile speaking to exiles, some who knew that they were, and many more who didn't but who felt a longing to which he gave a voice, a longing for Faërie, for the Fortunate Isles, for those shores a good deal further off that ceaselessly beckon the voyager. In January 1944, with the second war apparently at its darkest, he quoted some lines of Anglo-Saxon in a letter to his son Christopher:

> Longað þonne þy læs þe him con léoþa worn,
> oþþe mið hondum con hearpan grétan;
> hafaþ him his glíwes giefe, þe him God sealde.

From the Exeter Book. Less doth yearning trouble him who knoweth many songs, or with his hands can touch the harp: his possession is his gift of "glee" (=music and/or verse) which God gave him.

And then he wrote what he most truly felt and believed and experienced in his heart and in his mind, a statement of belief and profession of faith out of which he fashioned his Secondary world:

> How these old words smite one out of the dark antiquity! "Longað"! All down the ages men (of our kind most awarely) have felt it: not necessarily caused by sorrow, or the hard world, but sharpened by it. (*Letters* 66)

No truer comment on the spirit of his own work could be made. Surely, none is needed.

Notes

1. Tolkien's generation of scholars called it Anglo-Saxon. While currently the preferred designation is "Old English," Tolkien consistently uses the older "Anglo-Saxon," as does Christopher Tolkien in writing of his father's work. The two terms are interchangeable in the present text.

2. Christopher Ricks, "Prophet," *New York Review of Books*, Jan. 24, 1974, 44–46.

I. BETWEEN WORLDS AND TIMES

1. Tolkien's concern with the accurate accounting of time is manifest in his wartime letters to Christopher, wherein he worries about errors in "synchronization, v. important at this stage, of movements of Frodo and the others" and the problems of "struggling with the dislocated chronology of the Ring" (*Letters* 97).

2. "Past" is a shortened form of "passed," the past participle of "to pass, to take place, to happen"; "present" comes from the present participle of *pareses*, "to be before [one], to be present"; "future" is the suffixed form *bhu-tu* in Latin *futurus* of Indo-European *bheu-*, "to be, to exist, to grow." These forms have long since lost almost all trace of their verbal power. See Watkins's "Appendix on Indo-European Roots."

1. *New Yorker,* July 31, 1989, 19.

2. Tolkien's contemporary, E. R. Eddison, particularly deserves greater mention than the focus of the present study permits. He cites Du Maurier as an influence in an unpublished letter in the collection of the Bodleian Library, Oxford. Eddison's use of time certainly owes something to Du Maurier, as does his treatment of at least two of the women in his Zimiamvian trilogy. The Duchess of Memison derives from the Duchess of Towers, and Mary Lessingham, the heroine of Eddison's *A Fish Dinner in Memison,* has much of her quality as well. The love of Mary and Edward Lessingham has some of the time-and-space-transcending aspects of Peter and the Duchess. In addition, Mary's death many years before that of Edward and his subsequent lifetime of waiting for her recall the similar fates of Peter and the Duchess.

3. The similarity of these seekers and their searches to the gurus, disciples, spiritual communes, and transcendental meditators of the 1960s and 1970s is not without significance. In times of rapid social change, inquiring souls tend to turn inward for answers to the questions that outward circumstances raise. Both may derive from the same continuing impulse.

4. For a deeper view of Barrie's connection with the Du Mauriers, see Andrew Birkin's *J. M. Barrie & The Lost Boys,* a remarkable history of childhood and obsession.

5. Ms. 6, fol. 21r., Tolkien Collection, Bodleian Library, Oxford.

6. Letter to the author from Priscilla Tolkien, Aug. 15, 1991.

3. STRANGE POWERS OF THE MIND

1. See Christopher Tolkien's extended commentary on this in "The History of Eriol or Ælfwine," in *The Book of Lost Tales,* Part Two.

2. In this connection see Tolkien's two pencil sketches entitled "Before" and "Afterwards" in Hammond and Scull, *J. R. R. Tolkien, Artist & Illustrator* 34–35 (shown as figs. 30 and 31), which show Tolkien's fascination with the meanings embedded in these words and his interest in conjoined time and space. "Before" shows a long perspective framed by flaming torches, perhaps a hallway, or dark corridor, receding into the center distance and ending in a lighted doorway. The viewer is in the position of one about to enter the corridor. Thus the title "Before" conveys the dual notions of "standing in front of" and "awaiting, or anticipating." The sketch is remarkable for its mood, which conveys both foreboding (the dark corridor) and hope (the lighted doorway). "Afterwards" shows a figure emerging from a lighted doorway on the left. The figure's head is bent, resting in one hand, while the other hand stretches out. Ahead and to the right a pathway (again flanked by lighted torches or flambeaux) recedes into the middle distance. This picture is less ambiguous than "Before," for the suffix *-wards* effectively confines the meaning to past time, with no implicit allusion to space. Something has happened, and the picture shows the consequence.

3. The resemblance, and others like it, have led to lively debate on the subject conducted in *Vinyar Tengwar,* a newsletter of Tolkien linguistics. See especially *Vinyar Tengwar* 19 (Sept. 1991): 8–23. Whether Tolkien consciously intended his

invented languages to be a part of the Indo-European complex is a question that must remain moot until more of his work in that area is available for study.

4. Ryan has published several commentaries on correspondences between Tolkien's languages and actual historical ones, ranging from the fairly obvious Anglo-Saxon of Rohan to Celtic, Sumerian, and Akkadian.

4. OVER A BRIDGE OF TIME

1. Note that the word has two meanings: one is nominal, meaning "directional flow," especially of a river or body of water; the other is adjectival, meaning "present," "at the moment," "up to date." In a metaphorical sense, of course, the two are related and suggest related perceptions of time.

2. Christopher Tolkien notes this passage as "the first suggestion of the idea that Lórien existed in a mode of Time distinct from that of the world beyond its borders, unless it is present in Keleborn's [earlier] words" (*Treason* 283–84). Keleborn's earlier words to the Company refer to their dwelling "here in exile while outside in the world many years run by" (*Treason* 249).

3. The unpublished drafts found in the Marquette Archive Tolkien Collection, Marquette University Library, Milwaukee, Wisconsin.

4. For more on this, see Christopher Tolkien's comments in *The Treason of Isengard* 285–86: "I can only interpret this to mean that within Lórien the Company existed in a different Time—with its mornings and evenings and passing days—while in the world outside Lórien no time passed. They had left that 'external' Time, and would return to it at the same moment as they left it." Compare also Tolkien's "Audoin just closing the door" note to *The Lost Road*.

5. WHERE THE DREAM-FISH GO

1. Christopher Tolkien discusses this in *The War of the Ring* 234–35, 270–72.

2. One obvious and undoubtedly intentional reference, clearly autobiographical and clearly tongue-in-cheek, is to a very minor character, not even a walk-on, a mere mention, though of some importance to the unfolding of the mystery at the heart of the story. It is "old Professor Rashbold at Pembroke," described as a "grumpy old bear" whose one contribution to the story is the translation of a crucial piece of Anglo-Saxon prose. Citing *Letters* 218, 446n, Christopher Tolkien notes that *Rashbold* is a translation of *Tolkien, Toll-kühn* (*Sauron* 151). The last-listed member of the Club is John Jethro Rashbold, an undergraduate of Magdalen College and presumably a younger relative of "old" Rashbold, who almost certainly corresponds to Christopher Tolkien. Young Rashbold attends meetings, for his initials appear at the bottom of the entries together with the other participants, but he does not speak.

3. For more on this see Tolkien's illustration *Xanadu* in Hammond and Scull.

4. "At the hill's foot Frodo found Aragorn, standing still and silent as a tree; but in his hand was a small golden bloom of *elanor*, and a light was in his eyes. He was wrapped in some fair memory: and as Frodo looked at him he knew that he beheld things as they once had been in this same place" (*Fellowship* 366).

5. There is no evidence that Tolkien had read David Lindsay's *Devil's Tor* (though

he had read, and in *The Notion Club Papers* refers to, Lindsay's *A Voyage to Arcturus*). Nevertheless, his use here of a meteorite as a vehicle for extrasensory experience strikingly recalls the meteorite in *Devil's Tor* that is the focus of the supernatural events in that fantasy.

6. TRAVELERS BETWEEN THE WORLDS

1. Although Tolkien normally spelled *Adûnaic* with a circumflex over the *u*, the text of *The Notion Club Papers* consistently omits the circumflex.

2. Tolkien had worked with E. V. Gordon on a projected edition of *The Seafarer* and *The Wanderer*. When Gordon died in 1938, he left an uncompleted draft, which his widow reworked and brought out as her own edition in 1960.

3. My information comes from John Pope's commentary on *The Seafarer* in his edition of *Seven Old English Poems* 84–91. For further commentary Pope cites G. V. Smithers, "The Meaning of *The Seafarer* and *The Wanderer*," *Medium Ævum* 26 (1957): 147–51.

4. These are apparently the Adûnaic equivalents of "Elf-friend" and "Steadfast, Faithful" *(Tréowine)*.

9. FALLING ASLEEP AGAIN

1. From Quenya *lot(h)*, "flower"; *lór*, "dream"; plus *-ien*, "land."

10. A DREAM OF LIGHT AND DARK

1. That the merry Bombadil and the half-mad speaker in "Looney" are coeval is evidence, if more is needed, of the marked contrasts and shifts in mood of which Tolkien was capable and which the light-dark dichotomy in his work so strongly suggests.

2. Letter to author, January 25, 1991.

11. PITFALLS IN *FAËRIE*

1. Ms. 9, Tolkien Collection, Bodleian Library, Oxford.

2. Subsequent citations from this essay, found in Ms. 9, will be cited by folio numbers.

3. The similarity of this to the concept of Niggle's picture in the much earlier "Leaf by Niggle" is clear, as is Tolkien's tacit confession that his imagination tended to lead him outside the edges of the canvas. He found it difficult to resist straying into those remote and faintly glimpsed distances and exploring the unrevealed regions on either side. His awareness of the lure is shown in a letter to Christopher Tolkien, in which he wrote that "A story must be told or there'll be no story, yet it is the untold stories that are the most moving. I think you are moved by *Celebrimbor* because it conveys a sudden sense of endless *untold* stories: mountains seen far

away, never to be climbed, distant trees (like Niggle's) never to be approached" (*Letters* 110–11).

4. See also the "fairy world" of Lórien.

5. While it has no direct, demonstrable bearing on the subject under discussion, it is worthy of note that *wode* is the base of the Anglo-Saxon name for the chief of the Northern gods, Woden, whose Norse counterpart, Oðinn (base *oð*, "madness, frenzy") is a god of poetry as well as of madness. Notable also is one of Oðinn's stock names, or epithets, *Gangleri*, "the Wanderer."

EPILOGUE: HIS GIFT OF GLEE

1. See especially *Athrabeth Finrod Ah Andreth,* "The Debate of Finrod and Andreth," and "Myths Transformed," in *Morgoth's Ring.*

Bibliography

Auden, W. H. Introduction. *The Visionary Novels of George MacDonald.* Ed. Anne Freemantle. New York: Noonday Press, 1954.

Balderstone, John L., and J. C. Squire. *Berkeley Square.* London: Longmans, Green, 1929.

Barfield, Owen. *Poetic Diction.* 3d ed. Middletown, CT: Wesleyan University Press, 1973.

Barrie, James M. *Dear Brutus.* In *The Admirable Crichton and Other Plays.* New York: Charles Scribner's Sons, 1926.

———. *Mary Rose.* In *The Admirable Crichton and Other Plays.*

Bauschatz, Paul. *The Well and the Tree: World and Time in Early German Culture.* Amherst: University of Massachusetts Press, 1982.

Birkin, Andrew. *J. M. Barrie & the Lost Boys.* New York: Clarkson N. Potter, 1979.

Briggs, Katherine. *An Encyclopedia of Fairies.* New York: Pantheon, 1976.

Carpenter, Humphrey. *Tolkien: A Biography.* Boston: Houghton Mifflin, 1977.

Du Maurier, Daphne. *Gerald: A Portrait.* Garden City, NY: Doubleday, Doran, 1935.

Du Maurier, George. *Novels of George Du Maurier.* London: Pilot Press, 1947.

Dunne, J. W. *An Experiment with Time.* London: A. and C. Black, 1927.

————. *An Experiment with Time.* 3d ed. London: Faber and Faber, 1934.

Edel, Leon. *Henry James: A Life.* New York: Harper and Row, 1985.

Eksteins, Modris. *Rites of Spring: The Great War and the Birth of the Modern Age.* Boston: Houghton Mifflin, 1989.

Ekwall, Eilert. *The Concise Oxford Dictionary of Place-Names.* Oxford: Clarendon Press, 1964.

Ellis, Peter Berresford. *Celt and Saxon: The Struggle for Britain AD 410–937.* London: Constable, 1993.

Ellman, Richard. *James Joyce.* Rev. ed. New York: Oxford University Press, 1982.

Fiedler, Leslie A. *Olaf Stapledon: A Man Divided.* Oxford: Oxford University Press, 1983.

Fussell, Paul. *The Great War and Modern Memory.* New York: Oxford University Press, 1975.

Hieatt, Constance. "The Text of *The Hobbit.*" *English Studies in Canada* 7 (Summer 1981): 212–24.

Hammond, Wayne G. *J. R. R. Tolkien: A Descriptive Bibliography.* Winchester, England: Oak Knoll Books, 1993.

Hammond, Wayne G., and Christina Scull. *J. R. R. Tolkien, Artist & Illustrator.* Boston: Houghton Mifflin, 1995.

J. R. R. Tolkien: Life and Legend. Catalogue of the Exhibition to Commemorate the Centenary of the Birth of J. R. R. Tolkien (1892–1973). Oxford: Bodleian Library, 1992.

Jones, Roger S. *Physics as Metaphor.* Minneapolis: University of Minnesota Press, 1982.

Kilby, Clyde. *Tolkien and The Silmarillion.* Wheaton, IL: Harold Shaw, 1976.

Kocher, Paul. *Master of Middle-earth: The Fiction of J. R. R. Tolkien.* Boston: Houghton Mifflin, 1972.

Lewis, C. S. *The Dark Tower and Other Stories.* Ed. Walter Hooper. New York: Harcourt Brace Jovanovich, 1977.

Lewis, Warren. *Brothers and Friends: The Diaries of Major Warren Hamilton Lewis.* Ed. Clyde S. Kilby and Marjorie Lamp Mead. San Francisco: Harper and Row, 1982.

Lindsay, David. *A Voyage to Arcturus.* New York: Macmillan, 1963.

The Mabinogion. Trans. Lady Charlotte Guest. 1906. Trans. Gwyn Jones and Thomas Jones. London: J. M. Dent, 1949.

Moberly, C. A. E., and E. F. Jourdain. *An Adventure.* Ed. Joan Evans. New York: Coward McCann, 1955.

————. *The Ghosts of the Trianon: The Complete* An Adventure. Ed. Michael H. Coleman. Northamptonshire: Aquarian Press, 1988.

Nitzsche, Jane Chance. *Tolkien's Art.* London: Macmillan, 1979.

Ormond, Leonée. *George Du Maurier.* London: Routledge and Kegan Paul, 1969.

Pokorny, Julius. *Indogermanisches etymologisches Wörterbuch.* 2 vols. Bern: Franke Verlag, 1959–69.

Pope, John C., ed. *Seven Old English Poems.* New York: Bobbs-Merrill, 1966.

Priestley, J. B. *Man & Time.* New York: Crescent Books, 1989.

Remarque, Erich Maria. *All Quiet on the Western Front.* Trans. A. W. Wheen. New York: Grosset and Dunlap, 1929.

Ryan, J. S. "Cultural Name Association: A Tolkien Example from *Gilgamesh.*" *Mallorn* 22 (April 1985).

———. "Indo-European Race-memories and Race-fears from the Ancient City of Uruk." *Angerthas* 22 (March 1988).

Sale, Roger. *Modern Heroism: Essays on D. H. Lawrence, William Empson and J. R. R. Tolkien.* Berkeley: University of California Press, 1973.

Shippey, T. A. *The Road to Middle-Earth.* London: George Allen and Unwin, 1982.

Smith, Geoffrey Bache. *A Spring Harvest.* Ed. J. R. R. Tolkien. London: Erskine MacDonald, 1918.

Songs for the Philologists. By J. R. R. Tolkien, V. Gordon, et al. London: English Department, University College, 1936.

Stapledon, W. Olaf. *Last and First Men and Star Maker.* New York: Dover, 1968.

———. *Last Men in London.* New York: Jonathan Cape and Harrison Smith, 1931.

Ten Old English Poems. Trans. Kemp Malone. Baltimore: Johns Hopkins University Press, 1941.

Tintner, Adeline. *The Pop World of Henry James.* Ann Arbor: UMI Research Press, 1990.

Tolkien, J. R. R. "The Adventures of Tom Bombadil." *Oxford Magazine* 52, no. 13 (Feb. 15, 1934): 464–65.

———. *The Adventures of Tom Bombadil.* London: George Allen and Unwin, 1962.

———. "Bagme Bloma." In *Songs for the Philologists* 12.

———. "Beowulf: The Monsters and the Critics." In *Tolkien: The Monsters and the Critics and Other Essays.* Ed. Christopher Tolkien. London: George Allen and Unwin, 1983.

———. *The Book of Lost Tales, Part I.* The History of Middle-Earth, vol. 1. Ed. Christopher Tolkien. Boston: Houghton Mifflin, 1984.

———. *The Book of Lost Tales, Part II.* The History of Middle-Earth, vol. 2. Ed. Christopher Tolkien. Boston: Houghton Mifflin, 1984.

———. "Éadig Béo Þu." In *Songs for the Philologists* 13.

———. *The Fellowship of the Ring.* Vol. 1 of *The Lord of the Rings.* 2d ed. Boston: Houghton Mifflin, 1967.

———. *The Hobbit.* Boston: Houghton Mifflin, 1966.

———. "Ides Ælfscýne." In *Songs for the Philologists* 10–11.

———. "The Lay of Aotrou and Itroun." *Welsh Review* 4 (December 1945): 254–66.

———. "Leaf by Niggle." *Tree and Leaf*. Boston: Houghton Mifflin, 1965.

———. *The Letters of J. R. R. Tolkien*. Ed. Humphrey Carpenter. Boston: Houghton Mifflin, 1981.

———. "Looney." *The Oxford Magazine* 52, no. 9 (January 18, 1934).

———. *The Lost Road and Other Writings*. The History of Middle-Earth, vol. 5. Ed. Christopher Tolkien. Boston: Houghton Mifflin, 1987.

———. *Morgoth's Ring*. The History of Middle-Earth, vol. 10. Ed. Christopher Tolkien. Boston: Houghton Mifflin, 1993.

———. "On Fairy-Stories." *Essays Presented to Charles Williams*. London: Oxford University Press, 1947. Reprinted in *Tolkien: The Monsters and the Critics and Other Essays*. Ed. Christopher Tolkien. London: George Allen and Unwin, 1983.

———. *The Return of the King*. Vol. 3 of *The Lord of the Rings*. 2d ed. Boston: Houghton Mifflin, 1967.

———. *The Return of the Shadow*. The History of Middle-Earth, vol. 6. Ed. Christopher Tolkien. Boston: Houghton Mifflin, 1988.

———. *Sauron Defeated: The End of the Third Age*. The History of Middle-Earth, vol. 9. Ed. Christopher Tolkien. Boston: Houghton Mifflin, 1992.

———. *The Silmarillion*. Ed. Christopher Tolkien. Boston: Houghton Mifflin, 1977.

———. *Smith of Wootton Major*. Boston: Houghton Mifflin, 1978.

———. *The Treason of Isengard*. The History of Middle-Earth, vol. 7. Ed. Christopher Tolkien. Boston: Houghton Mifflin, 1989.

———. *The Two Towers*. Vol. 2 of *The Lord of the Rings*. 2d ed. Boston: Houghton Mifflin, 1967.

———. *Unfinished Tales*. Ed. Christopher Tolkien. Boston: Houghton Mifflin, 1980.

———. *The War of the Ring*. Ed. Christopher Tolkien. Boston: Houghton Mifflin, 1990.

Vinyar Tengwar 19 (September 1991).

Watkins, Calvert. "Appendix on Indo-European Roots." *The American Heritage Dictionary of the English Language*. Ed. William Morris. Boston: American Heritage, 1970.

Watney, John. *Mervyn Peake*. New York: St. Martin's Press, 1976.

Wells, H. G. *Nineteenth Century* (January 1939): 14–15.

Williams, Christopher. "Among a Faery Elite." *New Society*, December 7, 1967.

Wilson, A. N. *C. S. Lewis: A Biography*. New York: W. W. Norton, 1990.

Wilson, Edmund. "Oo, Those Awful Orcs!" *Nation*, April 14, 1956, 182.

Yates, Jessica. "The Source of 'The Lay of Aotrou and Itroun.'" *Leaves From the Tree: J. R. R. Tolkien's Shorter Fiction*. London: The Tolkien Society, 1991.

Index

Adunaic (language), 76, 143, 144, 169, 262n

An Adventure (Jourdain and Moberly), 37. *See also* Trianon

Ælfwine: in *The Lost Road*, 82; in *The Notion Club Papers*, 159, 160, 161, 163; as "The Seafarer," 145–46, 149–50, 162; as a serial identity, 63–68, 71–73, 75, 82, 87, 110, 122. *See also* Eriol; Far-traveled

Akallabeth (Tolkien), 76

Alboin, as "thread," 63–68

Alboin Errol, 64–66, 68, 71–73, 76, 80–85; as serial identity, 110, 121–23; and time-travel concept, 151, 163–64, 197; as Tolkien, 73

Alf, 234, 238, 239. *See also* King of Faery

Alice: *In Wonderland*, 80; *Through the Looking-Glass*, 193. *See also* Carroll, Lewis

Allegory, 7, 231–33

Allen & Unwin, 62, 82, 87, 88

Alternative reality, 36

Amandil, 63, 68

Ancestral consciousness, 159–60, 167–68. *See also* Collective unconscious; Serial identity

Ancrene Wisse, 1

Animus, 44

"Aotrou and Itroun" (Tolkien), 154

Aragorn, 21, 22, 89, 92, 100, 102–3, 137, 195, 202; as Trotter, 102–4, 182. *See also* Lórien

Arthurian myth, 26, 152, 155, 156, 172

Artistic credo of J. R. R. Tolkien. *See* "On Fairy Stories"

Arwen, 241

Atalantie (Tolkien), 76, 151, 169

Athrabeth (Tolkien), 263

Atlantis, 64; dream-haunting, 4, 75–77, 156, 173, 196

"Atlantis-story," 121–23, 130, 168–69. *See also* "Eriol-saga"; Númenor

Atomic bomb, 7, 129, 171–72

Auden, W. H., 4, 7, 74, 78–79, 208–9

A Question of Time
was designed & composed by Will Underwood
in 9½-point Trump Mediæval
on a Gateway 486 PC using PageMaker 5.0
at The Kent State University Press;
imaged to film from application files,
printed by sheet-fed offset lithography
on 50-pound Glatfelter Natural stock,
notch bound and glued into paper covers
printed in three colors on 12-point stock
finished with matte film lamination
by Sheridan Books, Inc.;
and published by
The Kent State University Press
KENT, OHIO 44242